PRAISE FOR *FOREVER AND EVER, AMEN*

"Randy Travis writes his story with humor and candor. As a fellow stroke survivor, I know firsthand that his road to recovery has not been easy, and I applaud his courage in sharing the triumphs and the heartache."

—KIRK DOUGLAS

"Randy Travis saved country music. I wouldn't have had a career if it weren't for him and his music. This is his amazing story."

—GARTH BROOKS

"I have long admired Randy Travis. I admire him for washing dishes and whatever else he had to do to help sustain his dream in the early days. I admire him for sticking to his guns, when the powers that be in Music City told him he was 'too country' to sell records and concert tickets. I admire him for remaining humble after he had proved them all wrong, going platinum, and selling out huge arenas. But I admire Randy Travis most of all for how he has knocked out of the park the curve balls life has thrown him. The physical challenges he has faced would have destroyed every vestige of hope and will to carry on for a lesser man, but this unique and brave individual smiles his way through it all, sense of humor intact, wearing his humility on his sleeve. *Forever and Ever, Amen* tells all about Randy's journey, the slips and falls, the massive triumphs, his bouts with his demons, his Christian conversion, and his indomitable will to survive and live life to its fullest, and he takes us along for the ride. And what a ride it is."

—CHARLIE DANIELS

"Randy and I have been friends for a long time. The first time I heard him sing, I said, 'He's got it!' Randy is one of the greatest singers in the world. I love you, Randy, and people are going to love your book!"

—LORETTA LYNN

"At twelve years old I worked overtime hours on a hog farm and mowed extra lawns to get the money it took to buy a ticket to see my very first country music concert in Amarillo, Texas. My favorite singer, Randy Travis, was coming to town and there was no way I was going to miss it! My Dad dropped me off at the Civic Center and I walked in alone with my Solo paper ticket. I was in the nosebleed section, but I sang along as loud as I could to every word as Randy rattled off hit after hit. I remember thinking, 'I wish I could do that someday!' Randy Travis is a genuine inspiration and one of the true great country voices of all time."

—JOHN RICH OF BIG AND RICH

"I have worked with artists for years and when it comes to authenticity, I always look for one thing—the heart. At the core of Randy Travis is a heart for God. I have observed Randy's faith firsthand, expressed unobtrusively by his kindness, humility, and the way he treats other people. Randy's honesty in dealing with both his triumphs and his failures reveals the truth about God's grace in a way to which we can all relate."

—BILL GAITHER

"Randy Travis, as many of you know, has always been a hero to me. I grew up loving his music and his persona. When I first met him, he was exactly who I expected him to be. Since then, he and I have become close friends; that's something I treasure. I know firsthand how difficult it is to be a traveling singer and everything that comes with it. So, when you read this book, understand that Randy has gone from being someone I just admire for his music and persona to someone I admire for his strength, determination, endurance, conviction, and passion. He's a stylistic singer, a writer, an actor, an artist, a warrior, a patriot, and a great Christian man. I'm proud to not only call him a hero, but a true friend."

—JOSH TURNER

"I remember the first time I heard Randy. Country music, in some sense, had forgotten its roots and changed direction. Then came Randy Travis. The authenticity in his voice was undeniable. He reminded an entire industry of who they are and where they came from. Randy helped shape country music. He's the real deal."

—MICHAEL W. SMITH

"My husband, George Jones, came in the house and said, 'I just heard some kid named Randy Travis on the radio, and he was singing real country music! We have to go buy his album.' We did and before long we became friends with Randy and remained so for the rest of George's life. Every time I see Randy, I can still see George telling me about him and smiling. He still is."

—NANCY JONES

"Randy was on several episodes of *Touched by an Angel* with us and we loved having him on set. He was so kind and gracious and lovely to be around, and his voice was so recognizable. Even his speaking voice, so deep and resonant. I have only the fondest memories of working with him."

—ROMA DOWNEY

"Randy Travis is not a typical fellow. His life has not been a typical life. His story is not your average story. There is sadness, tears, laughter, joy, struggle, failure, victory, and hope in his sojourn. Everyone will 'amen' at some point. I'm honored to know him."

—TOMMY NELSON,
Pastor, Denton Bible Church

"Randy Travis changed the landscape of country music when he arrived on the scene. We are incredibly proud that Warner Bros. Records has been his home since the beginning of his career."

—JOHN ESPOSITO,
Chairman / CEO Warner
Music Group Nashville

FOREVER AND EVER, AMEN

A MEMOIR OF MUSIC, FAITH, AND BRAVING THE STORMS OF LIFE

RANDY TRAVIS

WITH
KEN ABRAHAM

NELSON
BOOKS

An Imprint of Thomas Nelson

Published in Nashville, Tennessee, by Nelson Books, an imprint of Thomas Nelson. Nelson Books and Thomas Nelson are registered trademarks of HarperCollins Christian Publishing, Inc.

Thomas Nelson titles may be purchased in bulk for educational, business, fund-raising, or sales promotional use. For information, please e-mail SpecialMarkets@ThomasNelson.com.

Any Internet addresses, phone numbers, or company or product information printed in this book are offered as a resource and are not intended in any way to be or to imply an endorsement by Thomas Nelson, nor does Thomas Nelson vouch for the existence, content, or services of these sites, phone numbers, companies, or products beyond the life of this book.

Scripture quotation marked KJV is from the King James Version, public domain.

Permissions for use of song lyrics:

"On the Other Hand": Writers: Paul Overstreet / Don Schlitz. Publishers: Scarlet Moon Music, Inc., Screen Gems-EMI Music Inc., Universal MCA Music Publishing, Don Schlitz Music.

"Forever and Ever, Amen": Writers: Paul Overstreet / Don Schlitz. Publishers: Scarlet Moon Music, Inc., Screen Gems-EMI Music Inc., Universal MCA Music Publishing, Don Schlitz Music.

"Heroes and Friends": Writers: Randy Travis / Don Schlitz. Publishers: Sometimes You Win Music Co., Screen Gems-EMI Music Inc., Universal MCA Music Publishing, Don Schlitz Music.

ISBN 978-1-4002-0799-2 (eBook)

Library of Congress Cataloging-in-Publication Data
Names: Travis, Randy, author. | Abraham, Ken.
Title: Forever and ever, amen : a memoir of music, faith, and braving the storms of life / Randy Travis with Ken Abraham.
Description: Nashville, Tennessee : Nelson Books, [2019] | Includes bibliographical references. |
Identifiers: LCCN 2018046406 (print) | LCCN 2018046878 (ebook) | ISBN 9781400207992 (e-book) | ISBN 9781400207985 (hardcover)
Subjects: LCSH: Travis, Randy. | Country musicians--United States--Biography.
Classification: LCC ML420.T76 (ebook) | LCC ML420.T76 A3 2019 (print) | DDC 782.421642092 [B] --dc23
LC record available at https://lccn.loc.gov/2018046406

Printed in United States of America

19 20 21 22 23 LSC 10 9 8 7 6 5 4 3 2 1

AUTHOR'S NOTE

Because of certain circumstances I have experienced, I have relied on a number of individuals to help describe and fill in some details of this story. I have drawn upon the recollections of doctors, lawyers, music executives, fellow artists and writers, longtime band members and crew, friends, and family members to present this story as accurately as possible.

CONTENTS

1. Pull the Plug   1
2. A Troubled Youth   3
3. An Unexpected Rescue   13
4. Too Country   19
5. From Catfish Cook to Recording Artist   25
6. On the Other Hand   33
7. Renewed Hope   45
8. Hitting the Road   51
9. Living the Dream   57
10. Always & Forever   65
11. The Show   83
12. Deeper than the Holler   91
13. Heroes and Friends   97
14. All-American Heroes   105
15. Consider the Source   113
16. Stirrings Within   119
17. Transition Time—This Is Me   125
18. Fans, Flowers, and Food   135
19. Closed Doors, Open Doors   141
20. Born-Again Music   149
21. I Told You So   163
22. The Irish Gig   167

23. Are We in Trouble Now?   173
24. Happy Anniversary   181
25. A Dark and Lonely Road   193
26. Ambushed   201
27. The Man I Am   205
28. Feelin' Mighty Fine   213
29. Flatline   225
30. The Tear That Changed Everything   239
31. Home at Last!   247
32. Bittersweet Reunions   263
33. Old Friends and New   271
34. Mutual Love and Gratitude   277
35. Free Indeed!   283

Acknowledgments   289
About the Author   293

1 —————— PULL THE PLUG

It was a sound I had become much too familiar with—the constant whirr of the machine that was keeping my collapsed lungs breathing, the incessant beep, beep, beep sound of the heart monitor. This was the soundtrack to the constant swirl of pensive doctors and nurses flitting in and out of my hospital room, poking one of my arms and then the other, taking more blood, running another test.

You should always be careful what you say in a hospital room when a patient is unconscious or in a coma. Don't ever utter a negative statement about his or her condition because the person in the coma might well be able to hear you.

I know that is true. Because when I was in that state someone said the unthinkable:

"He's not going to make it."

"Maybe it's time to discontinue life support."

"He can't survive this."

"It's time to pull the plug."

This wasn't the first time my fiancée, Mary Davis, had heard such dire predictions. The doctors had given me less than a 1 percent chance of survival since I'd first entered the hospital in Texas more than six weeks earlier, unable to breathe, with a virus in my heart that had led to a massive stroke and emergency surgery in which a large portion of my skull was removed to relieve the pressure in my brain. That portion of my skull was now secured in a pouch made of my own skin and sewn into my abdomen so the skull tissue could be kept alive until it was safe to reposition it on my head.

The stroke had taken away my ability to speak clearly, and it had paralyzed my right side, so I could barely move. After three weeks in the hospital in Texas, we had transferred to a rehabilitation center in Nashville, where my lungs had collapsed, I had contracted a staph infection, and my body was now septic. At times, I was semiconscious at best and breathing with the help of a machine. I had spent more than six weeks in and out of a coma. A tracheotomy tube stabbed through my throat, and my head was covered with what looked like a 1920s football helmet.

By this point, the doctors had basically given up any hope of my survival, and they probably thought they were being compassionate by encouraging Mary to pull the plug.

Mary leaned in close to me at my bedside, where she had spent every day for the past two months. She pressed her hand into mine. "Honey, you have to let me know if you want to keep fighting," Mary said.

I wanted to shout as loudly as I had ever bellowed, yet no words formed, no sound came out of my mouth. But a single tear trickled from my eye and down my face as I mustered every ounce of energy I had. I squeezed Mary's hand.

She knew.

Mary stood straight up, turned, and faced the doctors. "It's not our choice . . ." She stopped short, the words caught in her throat. She couldn't bring herself to say, ". . . to decide whether Randy Travis lives or dies," but everyone in the room understood. She squared her shoulders and looked straight at the doctors. "I suggest that everybody get on board, and let's do everything we can to save him."

We both knew that my life was in God's hands. Like me, Mary believed that God had plans for my life and that our faith would get us through. We just weren't quite sure how.

But I had braved numerous storms in my life and had frequently faced overwhelming odds, times when others had advised me to give up.

I hadn't quit then—and I wasn't about to quit now.

2 ———————— A TROUBLED YOUTH

"Get on up on this horse, Randy," Daddy urged me. An unusually skillful horse trainer, my dad had taught the horse to kneel down on its front knees so I could climb into the saddle. I scrambled to place my foot into one of the stirrups and threw my leg over the beautiful animal as Daddy took a photograph. With a slight nudge from Daddy, the horse rose majestically to his full height. I was three years old and I felt as though I were on top of the world.

I've always wanted to be a cowboy. From the time I was born as Randy Bruce Traywick—on May 4, 1959, in Marshville, North Carolina, a small town with a population of approximately three thousand people, located about a half hour's drive southeast of Charlotte—I had felt comfortable atop a horse. Thanks to Daddy's profession, all my family members were as at home riding a horse as we were riding in a car.

I was one of six kids in the Traywick household. My mama, Bobbie Traywick, was a quiet, brown-eyed, dark-haired beauty with an angel's heart. Mama worked in a textile mill that made potholders. She was a salt-of-the-earth sort of woman who felt it was her mission to have children, so she and Daddy had six of us within ten years. My brother Ricky is the oldest, thirteen months older than me. I'm second in line, followed by Rose in 1961; David in '62; Sue in '64; and our youngest brother, Dennis, in '68.

Our dad, Harold Traywick, was a tall, lean man who worked in construction but also raised beef cows on our property and trained horses. At one point we had as many as twenty or thirty horses, so I grew up working with them and the other animals. Part of my chores every morning involved pitching hay for the horses and cleaning out the stalls with my brothers. That could be a bit of an adventure sometimes.

In our teen years, my younger brother David grew a marijuana plant right outside the stables. He nurtured that plant, watered it, and watched it grow to nearly four feet high. No doubt he was planning to enjoy a number of home-grown highs. What he didn't realize, though, was that his marijuana plant had grown high enough that one of our horses could stick his neck out the back stable window and nibble on it. Once he started, the horse chomped down that entire plant!

When we went to clean out his stable the next morning, that poor horse's front legs were crossed, and he was leaning over precariously to one side. He slumped over in a stupor, stoned out of his mind, and stayed that way for three days before he finally sobered up and could walk straight. I should have learned a lesson from that horse about the effects of marijuana, but I didn't—not then, anyway.

I loved riding horses, even in the snow. When it snowed—which was always a big deal for kids in the Carolinas—my three brothers and two sisters and I, along with any cousins that might show up, would tie a sled behind one of the horses and use the horse to pull us up the hill. Dragging a sled behind a horse could be dangerous, which for a kid made it all the more fun.

When I was growing up, one of my favorite people in the world was my grandmother, Etta Davis Traywick. We all called her Ga-Ga. One of our older cousins couldn't quite say the word *Grandma*, and every time she tried, what came out of her mouth sounded like *Ga-Ga*, so the name stuck. We had a Lady Gaga long before anyone else!

Ga-Ga lived right next door to us, and she was a pistol, with a great sense of humor. She was a fabulous cook, too, and every year our entire family gathered at Ga-Ga's house for Christmas dinner, complete with turkey and mashed potatoes and gravy, green beans, corn, and plenty of desserts. At other times Ga-Ga prepared steaks or a big roast, and the whole family showed up to eat.

As sweet as Ga-Ga was, Daddy was just the opposite. Our dad was a man of contradictions. He could be tough as nails or soft as mush, depending on when you talked with him and how much he'd had to drink. The trouble was that Daddy liked to drink—a lot—and when he did he turned violent, threatening people, fighting with others, breaking furniture, and shooting at anything that got in his way. Fortunately, he never actually shot any people, but he came close!

For most of my early life, my siblings and I were afraid of Daddy, and I'm pretty sure Mama was too. None of us could understand why he was so mean to Mama or to us. He especially seemed to take out his anger on Ricky and me—knocking us around, beating us with leather horse reins, and screaming obscenities at us for the smallest thing we did or didn't do, anything that didn't meet his expectations.

When he wasn't drinking, Daddy was a smart, hardworking man. During my childhood he supported our family well by building high-priced homes in and around Charlotte. When he had money, Daddy bought us almost anything we wanted—all six of us kids had our own horses by the time we were five years old, as well as go-carts and, later, Honda motorcycles. But when the booze took over, Daddy's behavior turned loud, obnoxious, and even dangerous. Not only did he bang Mama and us kids around, Daddy had a rap sheet with the local police that stretched back over more than twenty years. Most of his arrests were alcohol related—everything from driving while intoxicated to public drunkenness, assaulting a law-enforcement officer, discharging a weapon in a restricted area, and threats and personal assault. Our dad was well known in our community as a rowdy rebel, ready to fight.

The one thing Daddy and I could agree on was our taste in music. We both loved traditional country music. Daddy knew every song by Hank Williams Sr. and was sort of a frustrated musician himself. He played guitar and wrote a few songs and even recorded two of them. With enough alcohol in his veins, he'd sometimes get up in a bar or club and sing.

I loved country music, too, but I didn't really want to play guitar, and the truth is, I didn't care much for singing at that time in my life. But Dad insisted. "Both you boys will be guitar players, and one of you will be a singer," he told Ricky and me. "Which will it be?"

Ricky chose not to sing, so by default the singing fell to me. Singing seemed to come naturally to me, and folks who heard me said I had a talent for it. Some told me that my low baritone voice—even as a boy—was distinctive.

I learned to play guitar, too, although Ricky was always a far better guitarist than I was. To motivate my learning, Daddy bought me a used Gibson acoustic guitar. When I was nine years old, he paid for guitar lessons for Ricky and me from a local teacher, Kate Mangum, who lived about five miles from us. We loved Miss Kate, as we called her, and she taught us basic chords so that we could actually play songs. One of the songs I wanted Miss Kate to teach me was "I Saw the Light," by Hank Williams. She strummed around a bit and found what she thought was a good key for my voice, then taught me how to play the song on guitar.

"Will you sing it for me?" she asked kindly. "Your brother Ricky won't sing. He just wants to play guitar."

"Okay," I said rather bashfully. Miss Kate strummed along with me as I sang the lyrics. When we finished, she seemed pleased.

"You sing that song as well as Hank Williams," she told me.

I wasn't accustomed to getting compliments from Daddy, so I ate up Miss Kate's encouraging words. "Do you really think so?" I asked.

"I sure do," she said. "If you work real hard, someday you might be a singer like Hank Williams."

She was a teacher encouraging a naïve student, but I embraced Miss Kate's words and took them to heart.

Miss Kate taught us every week for nearly three years. Meanwhile, the other four kids began taking lessons, too, and soon we were playing all sorts of instruments. Dennis and Ricky played electric guitar, and Ricky occasionally played drums. Our sister Rose played piano. Our brother David played bass, and our sister Sue played mandolin, banjo, and dobro. I played acoustic guitar and sang most of the lead vocals.

It didn't take long for lessons and practice to turn into performances. We played stone-solid traditional country music at venues such as the Moose Lodge in Monroe, North Carolina, and the local VFW in Marshville, as well as at fiddlers' conventions around the Carolinas—popular festivals showcasing much more than squeaky violin playing. The fiddlers' conventions featured musicians playing banjos, mandolins, dulcimers, and guitars, as well as fiddles and were part competitions, part music workshops, and partly just good old-time jam sessions.

But we didn't have to go to a convention to have a jam session. As our family grew, Daddy built additions onto our original house. When we started taking music lessons, he built an eight-hundred-square-foot music room onto the back of our house—complete with a dance-floor, a fully stocked bar, a kitchen, and a bathroom. The room boasted a stage on one end and two jukeboxes, one on each end of the dance floor. Daddy decked out the music room with wagon-wheel lights and wallpaper portraying cowboy images, complete with horses, hats, and spurs. On weekends, he'd invite forty to fifty friends to bring some food and an instrument and join him to sing, pick, and dance, and of course the kids always participated too. Those gatherings were informal, fun, often rowdy, and the music was definitely country.

At home or in the car, our radio was usually tuned to WSOC-FM, a country-music station out of Charlotte. If music was playing around the Traywick home, it was never anything but old-time country music. And I loved it! The more I learned about music, the more I appreciated the intricate inflections and phrasing of singers such as George Jones, Merle Haggard, and Lefty Frizzell. I listened to their music so much it became a part of me. Although I never took any formal singing lessons, I think I subconsciously learned from George, Merle, and Lefty and patterned my style after theirs, subtly applying their techniques to my voice. So when someone said, "Hey, Randy, you sound a lot like George Jones," I took that as a great compliment.

Eventually the other kids in our family fell away from performing music, but my older brother, Ricky, and I continued with it. By the time I was nine, Ricky and I had already played our first gig as a duo, the Traywick Brothers, at a fiddlers' convention held at Marshville Elementary School. The Traywick Brothers sometimes included a couple of our cousins, but mostly it was just the two of us. Ricky and I soon became regular performers at talent shows, school events, benefits, and even local honky-tonks and bars. We also played in clubs, although our young ages meant Mama or Daddy always had to accompany us. Daddy bought us matching outfits—white pants with a red shirt and a red neckerchief. We played at a bunch

of VFW (Veterans of Foreign Wars) clubs, Kiwanis events, just about anywhere someone would let us play.

When I was ten years old, my dad bought me a new guitar for Christmas.
He bought Ricky a set of drums, and the racket we produced together was
enough to wake up the ghosts from Christmases past!

Daddy entered Ricky and me in every fiddlers' contest we could get to,
and before long we were winning first prize in our age group. At each event
Daddy picked out the songs he wanted us to perform—usually something by
Hank Williams, George Jones, Lefty Frizzell, Merle Haggard, or some other
traditional country artist. And Daddy expected us to win. When we didn't, he
let the judges know about it. He was tough on us, too, yelling at us if we hit a
wrong note. If I didn't sing a song just right, Daddy often made me start over
from the beginning. I really didn't want to sing in public, but Daddy seemed
obsessed with me being a performer, so who was I to argue with my dad?

Daddy was old school. "If I told you once, you better listen," he'd say.
And he meant it. He expected immediate obedience, especially from Ricky
and me, and by the same token, we knew if Daddy said it, if he told us he
was going to do something, that's what he was going to do, whether anyone
liked it or not. His word was the law around our house.

Mama was a saint, and she was the one who smoothed out some of
Daddy's rough spots. Even though we were not regular church attenders—
she occasionally went to Hamilton Crossroads Baptist Church and later to
Fountain United Methodist Church—she tried her best to instill biblical
values in all of us kids, values such as kindness, truthfulness, honesty,
humility, and integrity. She read the Bible to us, and she tried to show grace
and mercy. With Daddy, she had plenty of opportunity to practice both.

I loved Mama dearly and wanted to defend her. On one occasion, when
I was around ten years old, Daddy got drunk and started beating on Mama,
so I took up for her, jumped on him, and pulled him off her. Daddy was
a big man, and I was slight and skinny, so I didn't hang around long after
Daddy rolled away from Mama. I scampered out the door with Daddy
chasing behind me with his gun aimed in my direction. Daddy was bigger,
but I was faster. I ran into a cornfield and hid there for two days trembling
with trepidation—with no food or water—until Daddy sobered up and
calmed down.

My sanctuary—where I could escape the craziness of Daddy's drinking and his abusive, constant overcorrecting—was not really a place. It was my horse, Buckshot. One of my first horses had been Nugget, a palomino, and later, in my teens, I would have a wide-chested sorrel quarter horse I named Cody. But Buckshot was my favorite. Riding horses was a family affair for the Traywicks, and some of my best memories of my childhood are those times when our whole clan saddled up and rode together through the woods, fields, and trails around our home. At times I'd ride for miles with my friend, Tim Griffin. And when I had something on my mind, I'd ride for hours all by myself—just Buckshot and me.

We had about fifty acres on our property, and there were plenty of back-country roads, so we rode our horses everywhere. Sometimes we'd ride our horses to Mr. Pruitt Phifer's country store about a mile away from our house. We'd tie off the horses out back and go inside to get sandwiches and drinks or some snacks. One of the favorite hangouts in Marshville—about five miles away from our house—was a place called the Wagon Wheel, and we'd often ride our horses right up to the drive-through window to get some burgers and milkshakes.

I was just starting to get the hang of the guitar when, in a fit of rage, angry about something Ricky had done, Daddy grabbed my guitar and— *bam!*—smashed it to pieces. I was angry when I came in and saw it, but I didn't dare confront Daddy about it. Daddy was a big guy—and I wasn't. For a while, I borrowed guitars from other family members. Later, when I was about fourteen years old, Daddy saw that I had taken more interest in music, so he bought me a new Gibson Dove guitar. Actually, he bought six of them, one for each of his kids. The Gibson Dove soon became my favorite guitar, and I play it to this day. I wouldn't use it onstage, but when I reach for a guitar around the house, I pick up the Dove.

My first car was a *truck*—a '65 Chevy. I was a pretty good driver, but I tended to drive too fast and too recklessly. I rolled that truck on three separate occasions. I shudder when I recall the first time I turned the truck over while it was still moving. Of course I wasn't wearing a seatbelt back then, so as I tumbled through the air, I thought, *This is odd. I'm on the ceiling . . . now I'm on the floor. . . .* Still rolling, I thought, *I'm back in the seat . . . I'm back on the ceiling . . . I'm on the floor again.*

Had I died in that wreck, those would have been my last thoughts. Real profound, wasn't I? It's a good thing God was watching out for me, long before I really knew Him.

The wreck didn't slow me down, though. I still loved to drive fast, so fast that my younger brother Dennis was afraid to ride with me. When Dennis was in elementary school, sometimes Mama asked me to pick him up from school. I pulled up in my blue pickup, and Dennis reluctantly climbed inside. He held on for dear life during the entire five-minute trip home.

Ricky and I were troublemakers from early on. We got into a lot of fights with some of the local ruffians and in some serious trouble too. Most people in Marshville just figured we were following in Daddy's footsteps. Maybe we were.

When I wasn't causing trouble with Ricky, I was doing so with my friends. I gave in to peer pressure early on, and I started running with the wrong crowd, mostly a bunch of guys a few years older than I was. I was smoking cigarettes and drinking alcohol by the time I was ten years old. Not long after that I was using marijuana regularly—and not for medicinal purposes.

I was skipping school too—a lot. Many mornings I'd go in the front door of the school building and out the back without attending classes. I'd goof off all day with my buddies, then go home around the time I thought Mama might be expecting me. The principal realized what I was doing and tried to give me a break. He allowed me to go outside and pick up cigarette butts in the parking lot rather than tell Daddy I'd been skipping classes. But that wasn't enough to persuade me to actually go to school. I finally quit after completing only the eighth grade. I wasn't stupid; I was bored. I was getting horrible grades anyhow, so dropping out of school seemed inevitable. Mom and Dad didn't emphasize education. Consequently, not all of us kids graduated high school, and none of us went to college.

While our teachers didn't have a great influence in our lives, our local police did; they knew us well. We were more than rambunctious kids doing dumb things—we were actual juvenile delinquents. For instance, Ricky and I once broke into the Nicey Grove Baptist Church and held a beer party there. We were charged with breaking and entering. In separate incidents I was arrested for public drunkenness, for driving while intoxicated, and for attempting to elude an officer of the law. On too many occasions to remember, our local police hauled Ricky and me into jail. I was arrested so many times that I knew the officers at the Monroe County Courthouse and jail by name—and they knew me on a first-name basis.

Daddy always came down hard on us when he had to bail us out sometime during the night, but he wouldn't go to court with us. That was Mama's job, he figured. No doubt that was a blessing, because the judge knew Mama to be an upright woman and probably had mercy on Ricky and me largely because of Mama's character.

I was every parent's nightmare during my teen years. I possessed a fiery temper that I kept under control most of the time, but when it erupted I could do some serious damage. I did bad things just for the sheer evil of doing them. For instance, I once threw a brick through the front window of Pruitt Phifer's country store so Ricky and I could steal some pocketknives and Timex watches—and Mr. Phifer was a family friend! Thankfully he didn't press charges.

A lot of the trouble I got into as a teenager revolved around alcohol and vehicles. I totaled two cars, a couple of pickup trucks, and a horse and buggy. The horse survived okay, but the buggy didn't fare as well. I even "borrowed" Ricky's car one day and wrecked it trying to get away from the police. At one point, I was running the throttle wide open, and the police clocked me at more than 135 miles per hour when I lost control and spun around backward several times, crashing through a cornfield at more than 70 miles per hour before finally coming to a stop. I was okay, but Ricky nearly killed me when he saw the damage to his car!

Although the Marshville police extended a lot of grace to Ricky and me, they couldn't cover their eyes and ears when we got caught red-handed trying to rip off a van. I was already on probation because I had recently been arrested several times—once for a DUI, again, driving on a revoked license, and once for disorderly conduct. So when we were arrested for trying to steal a van, there was little doubt that we'd be heading to prison.

Despite our rowdy behavior, Ricky and I were still playing music all around the area. About that time, in 1975, we entered a music talent contest at Country City USA, a club owned and operated by Frank and Elizabeth Hatcher. That talent contest turned out to be a pivotal point in my life.

3 ——— AN UNEXPECTED RESCUE

I was only sixteen years old and not legally allowed to be in Country City USA on my own, so Mom and Dad went along with us to the contest. Mrs. Hatcher—"Lib," as she preferred to be called—was working on some papers at a table near the front of the club the first time she heard me singing. Apparently she was so struck by my voice, she literally stopped what she was doing and dropped the papers. Later I heard that it wasn't a stack of papers that she dropped, but a book, and eventually the story morphed into her dropping a stack of plates. I don't know what she dropped, if anything. All I know is that I felt Lib took an interest in me.

More than a hundred hopeful acts had entered the contest at Country City, so the process of elimination took several weeks. Ricky and I won the contest that first night we competed and were invited back to the club to continue on in the competition, our next performance scheduled a few weeks later. But unfortunately Ricky's court appearance took place about that same time. Mine was scheduled for a month or two after Ricky's. The judge sentenced my brother to serve one year in a minimum-security facility, so he went to prison and that ended our music career together. I felt sorry for Ricky and was mad at the judge for bustin' up our duo, but an appeal of Ricky's sentence seemed useless.

I was in a quandary. What should I do? I hadn't performed by myself prior to Ricky's departure. He and I usually worked together, with him playing lead guitar and me singing and playing rhythm. But it would be a long time before Ricky was released from prison. I didn't want to miss out on the opportunity, so I decided to perform on my own during the finals of the Country City USA competition. And I won!

The prize included a small amount of cash, a dinner at Staley's Charcoal Steak House, and a few hours in a local recording studio. The best reward, however, was that Lib offered me a part-time job at Country City—as a dishwasher and a part-time cook in the kitchen. "Of course, you'll be able to sing a song or two once in a while at the club," she said.

That's all I needed to hear. I took the job, even though it was sparse pay and a forty-five-minute drive from home.

I was real shy back then. I didn't talk much onstage and not a great deal more when I was offstage. But although she was eighteen years my senior, I found Lib easy to talk with, and she seemed to think I was something special. A short (barely five feet tall), platinum-blond woman with gentle eyes, who spoke with a trace of a lisp, she combined a genuine concern and compassion with a hard-driving business sense. She seemed sincerely interested in my future and impressed by my voice and told me so often. I wasn't accustomed to someone being so kind and supportive, and I soon came to trust her.

One night after we closed and were cleaning up the club, I confessed to Lib that the likelihood of me being able to continue working for her was slim.

"Why, Randy?" she wanted to know. "Don't you like working here?"

"No, I like it just fine, but I might have to go away for a while," I hedged, not really wanting to tell her about my larcenous past.

"What are you talking about?" she pressed.

I broke down and told her about my miscreant behavior and my upcoming court case.

Contrary to being put off by my confession as I had feared, Lib seemed sympathetic and motivated. "I believe in you, Randy," she told me. "And we're going to do all we can to keep you out of prison."

When it came time for my hearing before the judge, Lib went along with me to the courtroom. She also brought John Harper, a popular radio personality at WSOC-FM who frequently freelanced as our emcee at Country City. Together, they convinced the judge that I should be given one more chance. After all, I was working at Country City in Charlotte now and no longer running with the hooligans I'd been hanging out with in Marshville. Lib promised that she would help me stay on the straight and narrow path, and John vouched for me that I was doing a good job at Country City.

The judge glared at me skeptically. "Son, I'm going to let you go one more time," he told me. "But if I see you back in my courtroom again, you'd better bring your toothbrush." I knew he wasn't kidding, and the prospect of prison if I messed up again was almost certain. In the end he granted me five years' probation instead of sending me to prison. He allowed Lib and Frank to take custody of me, and he set up the probation so I could live in Charlotte with the Hatchers. I was still underage, so Mom and Dad signed documents permitting Frank and Lib to be my legal guardians. I moved in with them and began working at Country City USA full time.

Daddy was on board with the whole situation because he had hopes that I might do more music at Country City. Mama was reluctant but went along with it. To her I was still one of her babies, and although I'd be only a forty-five-minute drive away, Charlotte was a different world from Marshville.

Lib Hatcher turned out to be a great influence on me, though. She seemed so at peace with herself—equally comfortable in a pretty dress or frumpy sweatpants. More important, she modeled for me a different way of life. In her I saw a person who was willing to pour herself into helping other people. She seemed especially willing to help me, and I responded. At her urging, I separated myself from some of my rowdy friends and my dangerous behavior. I stopped drinking and doing drugs, and I quit fighting. I did a complete turnaround. Still, she kept a close watch on me, and I probably needed the supervision. Had it not been for her, I might easily have continued a life of petty crime and ended up wallowing in obscurity.

Of course, at that time, I was too young and naïve to see Lib's more controlling and manipulative characteristics. All I knew was that Lib had saved me. I felt strongly that she believed in me. I was grateful for all that she was doing for me and would have done anything she asked me to do—and did.

I actually enjoyed working with Frank and Lib at Country City. In addition to serving up burgers, steaks, and catfish in the kitchen, I cleaned the club, mowed the lawn, and did other basic maintenance. I especially looked forward to those nights when someone in the band called out, "Hey, Randy, come on up and sing something." I'd quickly take off my white cooking jacket, throw on a dress shirt, and bound onto the stage, sometimes with cooking grease still on my hands. I'd sing a classic country song along with the house band—I was singing a lot of Merle Haggard in those days—and the patrons at the club would cheer like I was playing in a huge arena. I guess they thought it was a hoot that the cook would come out and sing.

Occasionally I'd also pick up my guitar and sing a song I had written myself. I had dabbled in songwriting since I first learned to play guitar as a kid, attempting to emulate the songs I'd heard on the radio. But I'd tossed almost everything I'd written over the years into the garbage can—literally. I didn't think my songs were good enough.

Eventually, though, I stopped trying to write like other people and started putting my own thoughts into lyrics and chords. I didn't know much about music theory or formal notation. (I still don't.) I just knew what I liked, what I thought sounded good and felt good. Ironically, although I was still a young man, many of the songs I wrote expressed "older" themes. At Country City I heard a lot of stories about broken relationships and about people struggling to make ends meet or otherwise going through tough times. I related to those stories, possibly because of the rough life I'd lived. So I wrote songs such as "Reasons I Cheat" and "Send My Body (Home on a Freight Train)." Gradually I became more confident in my writing. And whenever I slipped in one of my own songs at Country City and the crowd responded positively, their support boosted my confidence to write more.

Business at Country City was booming by then, and we remodeled the club. We even bought a mechanical bull that had been in Gilley's, the famous country nightclub in Texas where *Urban Cowboy* was filmed. That "bull" brought even more people into our club. Almost every night there was a line out the door of people waiting to get inside. A lot of them wanted to eat, drink, hear the music, and dance, but just as many wanted to get onto that mechanical bull. Part of my responsibilities at the club included operating the wild bull. Of course, I'd also sing onstage any time I had the opportunity. So I would sing and do a short set, then we'd take a twenty-minute break and I'd hurry offstage and back to running the mechanical bull. I think that bull was the biggest money maker we had at the club.

I was singing as often as six nights a week, cleaning the facility and maintaining the property during the daytime, and I was content. Lib became convinced, however, that I could do more—that I could actually make it in country music and maybe even become a country music star. Although Lib had no previous experience managing a country music artist, she became my manager in addition to being my boss at the club. I dreamed that maybe I could make a living by singing and writing music. But even though I knew Lib was a hard worker, I could not even imagine how much effort she would put into achieving those dreams—both hers and mine.

About that time we bumped into two major obstacles—Lib's husband, Frank, and my dad.

In addition to being part owner of the club, Frank worked as a pipeline contractor, a job that required him to travel a great deal. He was often away from home for days at a time. Not surprisingly, he grew increasingly suspicious that Lib was interested in more than my singing ability. To be fair, he wasn't wrong. We did spend a great deal of time together, and it didn't just involve music. I had no strong moral compass as a teenager, and I had few qualms about sex before marriage as a seventeen-year-old. So often as soon as Frank took off on another business trip, we hopped into bed.

But then Frank issued Lib an ultimatum: either him or me. Apparently he expressed to her in no uncertain terms that he wanted to sell the club and send me packing, or else he was leaving.

I couldn't say whether their marriage was in trouble before I showed up at Country City USA. But I do know what the result of that ultimatum was. When Frank laid out her options in such black-and-white terms, Lib wasted no time. "Come on, Randy," she said. "I'm leaving, and I'm taking everything." She cleaned out the house, taking the curtains and curtain rods and even the outlet and wall-switch covers. She took me and everything else she could grab and moved into a mobile home. By March 1980, she and Frank had divorced.

Maybe my dad saw the Hatchers' potential marriage problems looming when he came to hear me at Country City, or maybe he was just being his belligerent self, but he began to cause problems almost every time he showed up. Not surprisingly, he drank too much, and on more than one occasion he'd get in arguments with other customers or with Lib when she tried to calm him down or with me. Especially with me. He sometimes smashed beer bottles or turned over tables in the club, threatening people and brandishing his .38 caliber pistol.

I just couldn't understand my dad, no matter how hard I tried. We butted heads often, mostly over what he considered Lib's control in my life. He couldn't see the good in her that I did and sometimes I was convinced that his heart was made of rock. When my dad and I got into an argument one night out in the parking lot, Dad got so angry that he jumped into his car and literally rammed it into the side wall of the club, causing severe damage to the wall, not to mention his car. After that Lib banned Daddy from the club and refused to allow him on the property.

The tension between Lib and my dad put me in a tough spot. Although I had a difficult relationship with Daddy, he was still my father. I respected him and wanted to please him. On the other hand, Lib was one of the best things that had ever happened to me in my young life, and I felt a strong allegiance to her. So although Daddy urged me to come back home, I decided to stay in Charlotte.

4 ——————————— TOO COUNTRY

Country City USA had established a reputation as one of the hot spots to play in the Carolinas. Especially for artists who ordinarily did not draw the more than ten thousand fans needed to fill the Charlotte Coliseum, Country City provided a popular alternative. When established country artist Joe Stampley came to perform he heard me sing a few songs. He and Lib discussed producing a record on me.

We drove over to Nashville, and Lib paid Joe to produce two singles, "Dreamin'" and "She's My Woman," which she then pitched to every major music label in Nashville, trying to get a recording deal. They all turned us down. "It's too country," said most of the ones who responded at all. *Too country?* How can country music be *too* country? I didn't understand the music business at all.

Eventually we managed to get the record picked up by Paula Records, a small label out of Shreveport, Louisiana, that Joe had recorded for early in his career. I was eighteen years of age by then, and my debut single, "She's My Woman," released under my own name, Randy Traywick.

Lib and I had watched the Loretta Lynn movie, *Coal Miner's Daughter*, and we took a lesson from the way Loretta and her husband had traveled from one radio station to the next, attempting to persuade them to play her music. We mailed out records to a number of radio stations, then got in the car and hit the road, traveling up and down the East Coast promoting the single to radio-station program managers and deejays anywhere we could.

The deejays and station managers were always nice to us, but not all of them played the record. Enough did, however, that "She's My Woman" briefly landed on the *Billboard* charts for two or three weeks at #94 (of 100 songs listed). After all that effort, I'd hit the bottom of the charts with a resounding thud. The second single, "Dreamin'," didn't catch on, either.

I wasn't disappointed, though. After all, I had made a record. And some people had bought it and some radio deejays had played it. I felt sure that with enough time and effort I might be able to make a living playing and writing some music.

During our earlier years together, Lib and I had to scrimp and save to make ends meet. We had no money for extravagances. Even though I worked full time for the nightclub, there was little real money exchanging hands. My pay was having a place to lay my head.

Knowing how I enjoyed keeping my body in shape, one Christmas Lib surprised me with a special present: an inexpensive set of barbells and a weight-lifting bench. "You didn't need to do that," I said. I knew that she really couldn't afford to spend the money, so I appreciated the gift all the more.

Then I got to thinking, *I need to give her a gift in return.* But if the boss was nearly broke, my financial situation as her employee was even worse. I emptied every pocket and scraped together every penny I could find so I could go buy her a small gift. I borrowed Lib's car—I didn't have one at the time—and drove to the nearby drugstore. I dumped all my change on the counter and bought her a couple of small Revlon Cinnamon Bronze lipstick applicators, an item I'd once heard her say she liked. I took those lipsticks home, wrapped them up, and gave them to her for Christmas.

It was a tiny gift, but she seemed to appreciate my effort and said so. She was even more impressed that I had noticed what sort of lipstick she used. I realized that it wasn't the size or cost of the gift that mattered; it was the thought and love behind the gift.

Lib and I kept trying our best to get something going musically in Nashville while still living in the Charlotte area. We traveled back and forth from Charlotte to Music City again and again. We spent a few days in Nashville during each trip, knocking on doors and trying to get connected. But it was like throwing little pebbles into a big pond. Most of our efforts sank to the bottom and disappeared.

We did have one success, though. Through her persistent networking, Lib got me booked on Ralph Emery's early-morning television show on the local NBC affiliate. Ralph Emery was an icon in country-music broadcasting. He had hosted the late-night, coast-to-coast radio show on WSM-AM for more than fifteen years and was a frequent host on the Grand Ole Opry as well as a familiar face on TV. His morning Ralph Emery Show had been launched in 1972. In 1983 he pioneered an evening show known as *Nashville Now* on the fledgling Nashville Network while continuing to host the morning show.

When I walked into the studio around five in the morning, I was in awe of Mr. Emery. He came up to me but he didn't say hello. He looked at me and asked with sort of a grunt, "Are you any good?"

His question took me off guard. I managed to say, "Some good."

Later, after I performed on the show, Ralph stopped to talk with me, something he rarely did with new artists. With a twinkle in his eye, Ralph said, "Randy, the answer to my question, 'Are you any good?' is, 'You're darn right I'm good!'"

I felt that was a great compliment.

Ralph Emery may have liked me, but few others in Nashville seemed to want to hear my music. Of course, there is always enormous competition in the music business, but part of the problem Lib and I encountered had to do with timing.

Ever since the 1980s hit movie *Urban Cowboy* featured the soft-pop sounds of Johnny Lee's "Looking for Love (in All the Wrong Places)," pop-rock-sounding "country" artists were being signed all over Nashville. But nobody was signing traditional country acts. When I came along and we were trying to attract attention, traditional country was not being sought after by record labels. It wasn't pitched by producers or welcomed by music executives. Everybody wanted "new country"—pop-contemporary sounds that to me sounded more like rock-and-roll over a lush orchestral bed.

Artists such as Kenny Rogers, who had made the transition from the New Christy Minstrels to country to *new* country, were soaring on the pop charts—and that was great for Kenny. Many people who heard him on the pop radio stations were not even aware of his previous country successes. Lee Greenwood and T. G. Sheppard were having big hits, too, with their Vegas big-band style of country. Same goes for Ronnie Milsap, who had incredible pop success with "It Was Almost Like a Song" and other great recordings. On the female side, Anne Murray and Olivia Newton-John also enjoyed tremendous popularity.

So at the time I came along, record labels were looking for country artists who had the potential to "cross over"—to have success on country radio, reaching a younger crowd of listeners, but be able to land on the pop charts as well. In their minds, my voice and my songs represented a complete throwback to a time they considered long since past.

I continued cooking, cleaning up, and cranking out country-music standards at Country City USA for nearly six years, but Lib and I knew that if we were going to experience any real success in country music, we'd have to move to Nashville. To me, Nashville was a big, scary place. Nevertheless, in August 1981, we took a leap of faith and made the move.

We bought a dilapidated, two-story, gabled, yellow-brick house at 1610 Sixteenth Avenue South. The house needed a lot of repairs, but it was located at the far end of Nashville's famous Music Row, the area of the city where many of the top studios and music companies were located at the time. Elvis had recorded down the street at RCA's Studio B, and tour buses cruised by in front of Bobby Goldsboro's House of Gold Music, across the street from our renovation project. Lib frequently groused, "Someday they'll be pulling up in front of our house."

I had done some construction work as a kid, so I got busy cleaning up the place, making repairs and remodeling. Meanwhile, Lib landed a job managing a local music venue known as the Nashville Palace, located out of town near the Opryland Hotel and within walking distance of the Grand Ole Opry House, where the famous WSM live radio show took place, featuring the superstars of country music.

The Nashville Palace showcased a lot of up-and-coming acts, some current stars, and a few who had been around so long they were no longer working the circuit but could still stir up a crowd. Once Lib established herself, she hired me at the Nashville Palace, too—again, as a busboy, cook, and dishwasher. Sometimes I worked in jeans and a white T-shirt, and at other times I put on a white cook's jacket. Occasionally, when things got slow, the guys in the house band (appropriately named Nashville) called me up from the kitchen, and I'd sing a couple of songs with them, always country music standards.

The house band members worked for seventy-five dollars a night at the

Nashville Palace, so nobody was getting rich, but they sure loved to pick. And I loved singing on the Palace stage, even though the audiences were often quite small, especially on weeknights. Sometimes I was still in the kitchen when the band kicked off the introduction to a song I was supposed to sing, and my apron went flying. After singing I'd go back to the kitchen, where I fried more catfish.

Drew Sexton, the band leader and piano player, introduced me to a guitar player, Rick Wayne Money, who had just come off the road from touring with popular country star Johnny Rodriguez. Everyone called Rick "L.D.," a nickname that Tom T. Hall had dubbed him with when L.D., fresh out of high school, went on the road with Tom and his band. Before long L.D. became a mainstay with the Nashville Palace house band, and we became good friends.

In March 1983 I auditioned to be a contestant on the TNN television program *You Can Be a Star*. The show was a precursor to television talent shows such as *American Idol*, *The Voice*, *America's Got Talent*, and others. Unfortunately, I didn't make the audition cut. I guess the show's producers felt that I didn't have what it took to be a star.

But Lib wouldn't give up. An ambitious workaholic, she knocked on every door of opportunity and tried to push her way inside. She loved the work and was always looking for the next project—and of course, I was her main project. When it came to my music and me, she refused to take no for a final answer. Her aggressive personality was almost like a bulldozer knocking down a sapling.

Friends told Lib, "You're nuts. You're investing so much of your time and money, and you have such a small chance of hitting it big with Randy."

To be honest, I wasn't really thinking of "hitting it big" back then. I suppose I had some dreams of country music stardom, but mostly I felt that I would be happy if I could make a living by writing and performing music.

I didn't really know it, but Lib had set her sights much higher.

♫ ♪

One of the regular customers at the Nashville Palace was country music icon James Cecil "Little Jimmy" Dickens. Jimmy had come to the Palace when the club was doing a special promotion called Opry Night, which featured stars from the Grand Ole Opry once a week during the summer. The club was always crowded for those special events.

Jimmy often ate dinner at the restaurant before going down the street to perform on the Grand Ole Opry. He was in the audience one night when I sang at the Nashville Palace, and of course I made a point to say hello to him when I saw him sitting at one of the tables. "I'm so honored to meet you, Mr. Dickens," I said.

"Just call me Jimmy," the superstar said. "Everyone does." Little Jimmy Dickens and I got to be friends. We talked often about music and life, and one night after he ate dinner he shocked me. "Randy, why don't you come on over to the Opry with me and sing a song?"

"You want me to sing with you on the Opry?"

"No," Jimmy said with a laugh. "I want you to sing on the Opry during my portion of the program."

I cleaned up the kitchen and finished my chores a little early and then washed up. I put on some dress clothes and went along with Little Jimmy Dickens to the Grand Ole Opry House. He took me through the backstage "artists' entrance," and I was in awe. I was even more awed when Jimmy stopped in the middle of his set and told the crowd, "I want you to hear somebody really special." Jimmy introduced me to the crowd, and I walked out onto the famous Grand Ole Opry stage. I was an unknown artist without a record deal. Shucks, I didn't really even have a record. But Little Jimmy Dickens gave me a chance.

I had planned to sing the Hank Williams classic, "I'm So Lonesome I Could Cry," backed up musically by some of Jimmy's band members and the Opry's staff band. As I began to sing, I felt my voice quiver. I was scared to death, so nervous I could hardly hold on to the microphone. It was a feeling unlike anything I had ever before experienced.

It didn't help that throughout my song, Jimmy stood about three feet away from me, watching and listening to me sing. I thought, *Jimmy, why don't you go stand someplace else?* But he didn't. He stayed right there with both eyes on me. I had never in my life been that excited and that nervous to perform.

The crowd responded kindly but not enthusiastically. After all, as far as they were concerned, I was taking time from Jimmy. But Jimmy was encouraging, and I looked forward to a day when I could perform on that famous stage as a bona fide country artist.

5 ——— FROM CATFISH COOK TO RECORDING ARTIST

I made the rounds in Nashville, attempting to meet recording company executives, songwriters, publishers—anybody who might be able to help me move my career out of the kitchen and onto the stage. I heard about the Acuff-Rose Invitational Golf Tournament taking place at Henry Horton State Park near Chapel Hill, Tennessee, about an hour's drive south of Nashville. Acuff-Rose was one of the premier music publishers in Nashville, founded by country music icons Roy Acuff and Fred Rose. Over the years the publisher's catalog had included songs by writers such as Roy Orbison, Don Gibson, Lefty Frizzell, and the Everly Brothers. The annual golf tournament often brought out country music stars such as Chet Atkins, Del Reeves, Archie Campbell, and a host of others.

"I think we should go," Lib said.

"Lib, I don't even play golf," I said, wincing at the thought.

"You don't need to play," she said. "We'll just go. There will be a lot of music industry people there. We might meet somebody important."

I didn't argue.

"And bring your guitar," Lib added. "Maybe you can sing a song or two."

I dutifully put my guitar in the car, and we made the drive from downtown Nashville to the park, where we were delighted to discover that, in addition to a beautiful golf course, Henry Horton boasted a lovely country-style inn and conference center. Since that's where many of the tournament's social activities were taking place, that's where I hung out, with Lib aggressively making "cold calls," introducing me to anyone she thought might be remotely connected to the music business.

Near the end of the day, as the players completed their rounds and were relaxing at the inn prior to dinner, Lib struck up a conversation with Elroy Kahanek, an independent record promoter (who later was hired to do radio promotions for Atlantic Records) and told him all about me. After a few minutes of conversation, Elroy turned to me. "Hey, come on over to the room. There are a couple of guys you should meet. And bring your guitar."

When Lib and I walked in, several golfers were sitting on the beds and chairs, and a few other guys were milling around. I recognized Gary Morris, whose recording of "The Wind Beneath My Wings" was a huge hit and would later win Song of the Year from both the Academy of Country Music and the Country Music Association. Elroy introduced me to Charlie Monk, head of CBS Songs, a major music publisher in Nashville, and Keith Stegall, an accomplished songwriter who had moved from Louisiana at the suggestion of Kris Kristofferson and was now a country artist on Epic Records. Keith had written hit songs such as "We're in This Love Together" for Al Jarreau and "Sexy Eyes" for the band Dr. Hook.

Elroy told the guys in the room about me—that I had been working at the Nashville Palace. He probably didn't know that I was the cook. "Randy has written some great songs," Elroy said. "Sing something for the guys, Randy."

I opened my guitar case, lifted out my instrument, and tuned it just a bit. I sat down on the side of the bed and sang two songs I had written: "Reasons I Cheat," and "Send My Body (Home on a Freight Train)." I could see Keith and Gary exchanging looks of surprise as I sang.

When I finished, Keith said, "Holy cow, what a voice!"

"Thank you, Keith," I said shyly.

"I'd love to hear more of your material," Charlie Monk said. "Bring some songs by the office sometime."

A few weeks later, Lib and I met with Charlie at the publishing offices of CBS Songs, where Keith was already signed as a writer and working on some new material. Charlie was managing Keith and planning to open his own company, and they had a partnership in place, but Keith was still with CBS Songs.

Charlie was intrigued that many of the songs I had written at a relatively young age possessed a worldly street sense and sounded as though they had been written by someone much older. "I guess I've just lived a lot of life in a relatively short time," I told him. Nevertheless, Charlie didn't push to sign me to CBS Songs, since he was planning to leave the company. He did, however, hint that he might be interested in creating a partnership when his new company, Charlie Monk Music, was up and running. We left encouraged but with nothing tangible to show for it.

Afterward, as we were leaving, we were chitchatting with Keith in the front office, and he mentioned that he was looking for his own office space.

"We have a big house up on Sixteenth," Lib said. "Come on up and look at the rooms and see if something will work for you."

Keith visited us at the house and decided to rent a room from us for a hundred dollars per month to use as an office. After that he was at the house every day for more than a year. We also rented out office space downstairs to *Radio and Records* (*R & R*), a music-industry trade magazine. Better yet, *R & R* paid me thirty dollars a week to clean their offices. Every penny counted in those days, and I was grateful for the extra income. I did that for several years and still have my last check from *R & R* framed and preserved under glass.

Upstairs, Lib and I had a bedroom, a dining table, and a den with a television and a couch. We shared our kitchen and bathroom with whoever worked in our "office," also on the second floor. Carol Harper, one of our first assistants, worked at a desk out on the screened-in porch.

The toughest job in the office was that of Lib's personal assistant. Over the years, literally dozens of women worked in that capacity, some for only a few hours. She often made her assistants cry, and many of them quit. A couple went out for lunch and never came back.

If I happened to talk to one of the cute girls, I noticed that she was soon gone. Another reason some assistants left was that Lib refused to close the office over the holidays, not even on Christmas Eve. We received a number of packages every day, delivered by United Parcel Service and Federal Express as well as the US Postal Service. She didn't want to miss any of the mail coming in, so she insisted on keeping the office open, even when every other music business in Nashville closed. Music Row would be dark, but our lights would still be on.

Every few weeks, Lib cooked up a special meal and invited several friends to join us—including Keith Stegall, Charlie Monk, our friend Ann Tant, and Grand Ole Opry star Johnny Russell, whose song, "Act Naturally," had been recorded by Buck Owens and later the Beatles. A large man, who weighed about three hundred pounds and ate blackberry cobbler on a platter at the Nashville Palace, Johnny had a great sense of humor and sometimes substituted as a host on the television show *Nashville Now*. We had met him at the Palace and had invited him over for a Southern-style dinner complete with chicken-fried steak, green beans, delicious homemade soup, and cornbread. Lib was a fabulous cook, and Johnny loved to eat, so we all became good friends.

Partly because I enjoyed Lib's cooking so much, I always worked out to stay in shape. Each morning I jogged the length of Sixteenth Avenue South, from our house all the way to the opposite end of Sixteenth, at the head of Music Row, where the Country Music Hall of Fame was located at that time. As I made the turn, I looked up at the Hall of Fame and wondered what it would be like to have my name and image on a plaque in that building with so many of country music's most illustrious performers—music icons such as Roy Acuff, Johnny Cash, Patsy Cline, Marty Robbins, and Gene Autry. *Someday*, I'd dream, *someday*, as I wiped the perspiration off my face and headed back up Music Row.

In addition to my daily run, I spent as much time as possible in the basement pumping iron. I bought a set of weights and barbells and set up a chin-up bar in the basement of our house. In time I was doing squats with 245 pounds resting on my shoulders. I saved up some money and eventually bought a few exercise machines as well.

When Keith Stegall came by, I tried to convince him to join me, but in those days musicians weren't nearly as into fitness as many are today. "Come on down to the basement," I said to Keith. "I've set up a gym down here." He followed me down the old spiral staircase and nodded his head at my makeshift gym.

"I admire your determination," Keith said, "but I'm not interested in working out with you. I couldn't keep up with you anyhow!"

On more than one occasion, Lib called down to Keith's office and said, "Randy's playin' tonight. Come on out to the Palace." She and I met him in the restaurant and asked, "Have you eaten anything yet?"

"No, not yet," Keith said.

With barely a blink, Lib looked at me and ordered, "Randy, go back there and fry some catfish for Keith."

I dutifully reported to the kitchen, prepared a delicious catfish dinner, and brought the plate out to our friend. "Here ya go," I said, placing the dinner on the table. Then I changed my clothes and got ready to sing several sets with the house band.

Keith was best known for his songwriting, but he also knew a lot about making records. His dad was a well-known steel guitar player who had backed up Johnny Horton, whose song, "The Battle of New Orleans," had won a Grammy Award in 1960. Keith had grown up in a recording studio. As a young man he had written songs and produced albums for a Christian folk group, the Cheerful Givers, touring the US and a few foreign countries with them. He'd made four or five albums with the group and had even done a solo album on himself. He regularly engineered his own song demos at CBS Songs.

Lib saw an opportunity.

To promote my performances at the club and to have a product to sell after the shows, Lib and I thought I should record a live album. We talked to our Nashville Palace boss, John A. Hobbs, and he seemed open to the idea.

John A., as he was known to many Grand Ole Opry stars and to the locals who frequented his establishments, had been good to me. In addition to several restaurants and bars, John A. also owned a country-western clothing shop, from which he sometimes picked out show clothes that he gave to me for free to wear onstage. A big, barrel-chested man with a gravel-throated voice and dark tinted glasses on his round face, John seemed to take a fatherly interest in my success.

"John A. is willing to pay for us to do a live album on Randy," Lib told Keith Stegall. "Would you be willing to produce it?"

"I think I could do that. Sure," he said.

Lib didn't mention paying Keith, and Keith didn't ask for anything. So Lib "hired" him to produce a live album on me under the name of Randy

Ray, the name I used for appearances at the Palace. After the single on Paula Records fizzled, we had realized that my last name was difficult for many people to remember, so Lib had come up with the stage name.

Keith called Johnny Rosen, who owned Fanta Sound's remote recording truck—a full twenty-four-track studio console in the back of a trailer—and set up the recording. Meanwhile, the guys in the house band worked hard to prepare, rehearsing with me during the afternoons before their regular gigs at night. L.D. arranged a great intro to the song "Good Intentions" and added the signature guitar lick in the middle of "I Told You So." Both of these were songs that I had written ("Good Intentions" I cowrote with Marvin Coe) and would show up later on other albums.

Lib and I went to work promoting the project, announcing at every show that we were going to record the album at the Palace. We wanted to make sure we had a large, lively audience for the event.

On a Friday night in November 1983, the Nashville Palace was packed, with more than four hundred people in the audience. It was a magical evening. We recorded "Send My Body (Home on a Freight Train)," "Promises," "You Ain't Seen Nothing," and a number of other songs I had written or cowritten. Charlie Monk advanced us some money for my songs, and we copublished them with Charlie's new company. I didn't really know the details of the deal. Lib put the last page of the agreement in front of me and said, "Sign this," so I did. I was unconcerned about the specifics. I was just glad that somebody wanted my songs.

Little Jimmy Dickens handwrote the back liner notes for the album on Grand Ole Opry stationery, and he said some of the nicest things I've ever read in print about me. He ended by saying, "I think Randy Ray is by far one of the most talented writers and performers that I have ever heard. Give any song in this album a chance and it could be a hit. Sit back and listen to one of tomorrow's stars."

Little Jimmy's words were almost prophetic, at least in light of what happened eventually with many of those songs. I still treasure those kind words by one of the Grand Ole Opry's greatest icons.

We called the album *Live at the Nashville Palace*. It was basically a "custom" album, a recording not financed or promoted by a major label—or even a minor label, for that matter. Just as he had promised, John A. Hobbs provided the money to pay for the recording. Because the Palace was located on Music Valley Drive, we decided to release the album on our own quickly made-up label: Music Valley Records.

When the album was finished, complete with a few guitar overdubs and minimal background vocals, Keith copied several of the songs and played them around town for various record executives, hoping that some might catch a vision for our music. None did. Everybody turned us down flat, some more emphatically than others. When Keith played a few songs for Bob Montgomery, a highly accomplished music publisher and producer in Nashville, Bob sardonically said to Keith, "If this crap hits, it's gonna set the town back twenty years!"

Ironically, nobody for whom Keith played the songs said that the music wasn't good. They just all thought I was "too country."

6 —————— ON THE OTHER HAND

When I wasn't busy working at the Nashville Palace, I recorded more demos of my own music, including some songs I'd been writing. I also sang demos for other artists, doing a lot with Keith Stegall.

Lib kept trying to pitch me to most of the record companies in Nashville. Every one of them said no. Most of the major labels turned us down twice and some three times. Over and over we heard, "You're too country. That sound will never sell—not albums, not tickets."

I was disappointed but not discouraged. After all, I'd been hearing that remark again and again for nearly ten years.

That Christmas Lib and I bought Keith a small gold-nugget pendant as a present and a token of our appreciation for all his hard work on my live album. We enclosed a note that said, "Hopefully next year we'll be able to afford the chain for a necklace."

In January 1984, I appeared on the Nashville Network's *Nashville Now* television show to promote my album. It was my first time to perform on a nationally broadcast television program. Superstar Barbara Mandrell was also a guest on the show that night, and she told the audience that I performed regularly at the Nashville Palace and that I had recorded the live album there. She didn't say whether she'd heard it, but even a mention by Barbara Mandrell was significant.

Wearing black pants and a gray, country-style sports jacket, I sang my song, "Send My Body (Home on a Freight Train)." I was as nervous as a cat at a dog show. Ralph Emery, who hosted the show, must have noticed my uneasiness, because after my song he walked over to me and quipped, "Why is that microphone shaking?"

I didn't have a good answer, but I laughed and said, "That's a good question."

Ralph was kind. "Randy, don't be nervous," he said. "You're among friends."

I calmed down a bit and felt more at home. At the end of the show, I sang "I'll Fly Away" along with Ralph, the Brower Brothers, and Barbara Mandrell. I was so excited I honestly thought I might fly all the way to heaven.

Later that year, on July 16, I appeared on *Nashville Now* again and sang another one of my own songs, "I Told You So." I had recorded it on the live album, too, so it made good sense to push it. I love to sing Merle Haggard songs and had thought about doing one on the show, but Charlie Monk cautioned me against that. "Randy, do not sing anything on television by George Jones or Merle Haggard or Lefty Frizzell," he said emphatically, "because everyone will think you are copying them. Do your *own* songs."

So I did. And I have done so ever since, but I still love to sing George, Merle, or Lefty songs.

Ralph Emery seemed intrigued by the idea that I was still working as a dishwasher and a cook at the Nashville Palace. He always asked questions about my cooking. So the next time I was a guest on his show, I took him a full-course steak, shrimp, and lobster dinner and presented it to him while on the air. That was one of the few times I ever saw Ralph close to speechless.

During the time that Keith was trying to help us secure a recording deal, he was also working on his own music career and had been making good progress as an artist. He had bought a tour bus from Lee Greenwood and was traveling extensively, playing shows around the country while writing and recording songs for his own album, which was being produced by Kyle Lehning for Epic Records. He was juggling all those responsibilities and also using his own money trying to help launch my career.

In November 1984 we were all delighted when Martha Sharp, an artists and repertoire (A&R) director for Warner Bros. Records, came out to the Nashville Palace at Charlie Monk's invitation to hear me. Martha was also a songwriter with a successful run of pop songs under her belt. But along with her friend and colleague at Warner Bros., Judy Harris, she had developed a taste for traditional country music, the sort that nobody was recording but George Jones, Merle Haggard, and a few others and that few major country radio stations were playing. Martha was also business-smart, and she saw a niche that nobody was filling.

Martha sat at a table with Charlie, Keith Stegall, Lib, and me. I had been washing dishes prior to her arrival, and I was so shy I barely spoke to her that night. After a while I got up and went back to the kitchen, where I changed into a shirt and came out to sing. Martha later told me that she had been quite favorably impressed with my singing ability and stage presence, even though she knew that my classic kind of country was not where the industry was heading at the time.

At one point during the evening, Martha turned to Keith and asked, "If I can make a record happen, would you be interested in producing it?"

"I'm on the road so much as an artist," Keith told her, "I wouldn't feel comfortable in trying to produce anything of Randy's by myself. But I have a wonderful friend, Kyle Lehning, who is producing my next album. Perhaps he and I can do something together."

Martha had not met Kyle Lehning, but she knew of his reputation. Kyle had achieved enormous success with a pop duo, England Dan & John Ford Coley. Prior to that he'd had a solid track record as an engineer at Glaser Sound Studios in Nashville, working on hits with artists such as Willie Nelson and Kenny Rogers. Ironically, many of the artists who had been produced by Kyle or had him play on their albums were considered "new country," so Martha wasn't certain he'd be willing to do something with a more traditional sound. Besides, Kyle was busy working on Keith's solo album.

"Let me talk with Kyle," Keith suggested, "to see if he might be interested."

Martha left that night without making any sort of commitment, not even a "Don't call us; we'll call you." I felt certain we'd just heard another no. I wasn't even disappointed; I was getting real used to hearing no.

Although I wouldn't know it till years later, Martha hadn't really said no. She went back to her office excited about how much she wanted to sign me, but worried about how she could pull it off.

True to his word, Keith told Kyle about me. One day in the studio, while the two of them were working together on Keith's album, Keith said to Kyle, "Man, I want you to hear something and tell me what you think." He put on a cassette recording of my live album and punched PLAY.

Kyle listened to only about thirty seconds of the music before saying, "Who is this guy?"

"His name is Randy Ray," Keith said, "and he's the catfish cook out at the Nashville Palace."

"He's great!" Kyle said. "His voice kills me."

Keith agreed. "Yeah, that's the way he sounds."

"What's going on with him?" Kyle asked.

"Well, I've been pitching his stuff all around town, but we can't get anyone to take him seriously."

"Really?" Kyle was intrigued. "Count me in," he said. "Anything I can do to help, let me know."

One night soon after that, Kyle stopped in at the Nashville Palace to hear me. He and I had never met at that point, and prior to Keith's taking the cassette tape to him, Kyle had never heard of me. I knew that Kyle had produced England Dan & John Ford Coley and was working with Dan Seals as a solo artist. After I sang a few songs, Kyle and I met briefly that night, and he told me that he was impressed that I sounded exactly as I had on the live album, without any artificial embellishments.

Charlie Monk was managing Keith Stegall at the time, and he heard that Kyle had visited the Palace and listened to me sing. Charlie called Kyle and told him, "Martha Sharp from Warner Bros. has been kind of interested in Randy Ray. Maybe if you called her, it might help."

Kyle knew Martha by reputation only, and Martha was aware of Kyle's great success as a producer, but they had never worked together. She took his call. "I heard this kid, Randy Ray, on a tape that Keith Stegall gave me," Kyle told her, "and Charlie Monk encouraged me to call you. He said that you might be interested in him."

"Yes . . ." Martha responded tentatively.

"Well, I'd love to work with him. If you ever decide to move forward on a project with him, let me know."

That was just the added incentive Martha needed. She plunged into the turbulent waters.

Martha knew it was going to be a tumultuous struggle to sign me—a traditional country singer—to the Warner Bros. label. It might even get her fired. Her former boss, Jimmy Bowen, had turned me down three times. So she proceeded carefully, without even consulting her current boss, Jim Ed Norman, head of the Nashville division. She later said, "I had never really signed an artist on my own before, so I wasn't sure of all the details." But she called the Warner Bros. contracts department at the company's California headquarters and got all her paperwork done for the deal. She boldly initialed the agreement exactly as Jim Ed might before she even told Jim Ed. She later explained to her boss, "I just knew in my heart it was all there— the voice, the personality, the look, the youthful sexiness. This will work."

The deal proposed by Martha was that Warner would pay for four "sides"—four recorded songs—including the studio time, musicians, and other production costs. If they liked the results, they would advance money for us to do an entire album. If they didn't like them, we'd part ways. That wasn't exactly a major commitment on Warner's part, but it was a better offer than anyone else had given us. It was the *only* offer anyone had given us!

I recorded four songs for Warner Bros. at Emerald Sound Studio, now the site of Benchmark Sound, with Keith Stegall and Kyle Lehning coproducing. Warner Bros. eventually pitched one of the songs, "Prairie Rose," as part of the soundtrack for the movie *Rustler's Rhapsody*, a Western spoof. The soundtrack included songs from a variety of artists such as Gary Morris, The Nitty Gritty Dirt Band, Pam Tillis, and one of my childhood heroes, cowboy star Roy Rogers.

We also cut a Merle Haggard song, "Carryin' Fire"; my song, "Reasons I Cheat"; and "On the Other Hand," written by Paul Overstreet and Don Schlitz. Don had already achieved enormous success with his first cut, the #1 hit song, "The Gambler," recorded by Kenny Rogers, and Paul had established his down-to-earth phrasing on songs such as "Same Ole Me," a big hit for George Jones.

As Don and Paul later told me the story, the creation of "On the Other

Hand" was one of those serendipitous experiences that sometimes happen to highly creative people. They had been working on an entirely different song when they came to an impasse. When Paul suggested a possible line, Don countered with, "On the other hand. . . ."

". . . there's a golden band," Paul suggested as the line popped into his head.

Don jumped in with, ". . . to remind me of someone who would not understand."

They continued bouncing ideas back and forth that way, finishing the entire song in less than half an hour.

The song literally came to Kyle in a manila envelope through the mail, sent by Pat Higdon of MCA publishing. How rare is that? People in the music business know that hardly *ever* happens—that a song will show up in the mail, actually reach the right producer, and get recorded.

I loved that song the first time I heard it; it had such a natural feel to me. I took ownership of the song and made it my own, although Paul and Don were a bit reluctant to have a newcomer record it. Like most of us, the writers had a gut feeling that the song would be a hit, so they had hoped that a more established, higher-profile artist such as Merle Haggard or George Jones might cut it. But a cut was a cut, and if it worked out well, the song would be on Warner Bros., a well-known label, so the writers acquiesced. I guess the recording turned out pretty well for Paul and Don. I know it did for me. When we finished the four sides, we played them for Martha. She loved what she heard and was willing to take a chance on signing me to do a full album.

On February 14, 1985, I officially signed a contract with Warner Bros. Records to record a full album if one of the first four songs "caught." Warner reserved the option to record a second album if the first one sold well. I could not have been more elated. But I still had to go back to work that night cooking catfish at the Nashville Palace. There were about a hundred people in the Palace showroom the night they announced that I had gotten a record deal. The emcee called me out of the kitchen and onto the stage as he made the announcement.

"This is the greatest day of my life!" I said. Then I went back into the kitchen to wash dishes.

Somewhere between the process of signing the contract and recording the music, Martha Sharp decided we should change my name—again. I had recorded my first record under the name of Randy Traywick—my real name—and that had not worked. People mangled the name and mispronounced it in all sorts of weird ways. One emcee had even introduced me for a show with "Here he is, Randy Tire-Wick!" Someone else had referred to me as Randy Trailways. So I had not balked when Lib had suggested that we use the name Randy Ray for the live album. But that name change hadn't seemed to help much. It certainly hadn't helped me get a record deal.

Martha discussed the dilemma with Nick Hunter, head of promotions at Warner Bros. He, too, agreed that I needed a different name. Martha ruminated on it, and the answer came to her in the middle of the night: *Randy Travis*. She suggested it to me, and I said, "Okay, I can live with that." Plus, I knew and liked the music of a former country artist Merle Travis.

After I started playing under the name of Randy Travis, in fact, some people thought that I might be Merle's son or related to him in some other way. Nope, we had no family association, only a mutual love for country music. But the confusion continued for a while. A sweet woman approached me one night and said, "I was a big fan of your daddy."

"You *were?*" I asked, forgetting about Merle for a minute. I couldn't imagine that she even knew Harold Traywick!

On July 17, 1985, Warner Bros. released "On the Other Hand" as a single to radio stations nationwide. We all had high hopes for the song, but despite our best efforts it fizzled and died on the *Billboard* charts at #67. We were devastated. It felt as though my recording deal was DOA—dead on arrival.

Our disappointment doubled when Keith Stegall told us that he needed to move ahead with his own career. "I think I'm spreading myself too thin," he told Kyle and me. "I'm trying to write songs, produce Randy, and work as a touring artist. It's awkward at times when I hear a good song that might work for both Randy or me. I'm going to bow out from the production thing and get back to being an artist."

"If it's okay with you," Kyle said, "I'd like to continue working with Randy."

"By all means," Keith said, graciously turning me over to Kyle.

Lib was upset over Keith's departure and felt that he was leaving the project because he lacked faith in me. She tried to talk him into staying on board with us. But Keith was determined. "I feel in my gut that I need to back away. It is not that I don't believe in Randy," Keith said. "I'm just trying to do the right thing."

Kyle and I were sad to lose Keith from our team, but we all felt sure we would work together again.

We wouldn't know it until later, but not everyone thought that "On the Other Hand" was a dud. Joe Talbot, one of Nashville's true traditionalists, had played steel guitar for country-music icon Hank Snow and later represented Rickenbacker guitars. In the 1960s Mr. Talbot had been one of the first people to open record-pressing plants in Nashville. A tall, rugged man with a deep voice, he was often heard chiding music artists, "I don't care what you do; just keep it country." Years later, when Mr. Talbot was on the Country Music Association board of directors along with Don Schlitz, he told Don that he was driving through town the first time he heard "On the Other Hand." He said he'd pulled his car over to the side of the road and listened to the entire song as tears filled his eyes. "I was so happy that I'd finally heard a country song on the radio," Joe Talbot said.

Then, on August 6, 1985, I sang "On the Other Hand" for the first time on *Nashville Now*. It received a tremendous response, the kind of response we had hoped the single might evoke but hadn't. We knew we needed to get another song out—soon—so Martha, Kyle, Lib, and I began searching through songs. We found what we thought was a fantastic demo sung by T. Graham Brown. Kyle and I nearly jumped out of our chairs when we heard it.

"That sounds like a Lefty thing," I said.

Kyle looked back at me blankly. "A lefty thing? What do you mean?"

I knew that Kyle's first musical loves had been jazz and rock and roll and that he had a pop background and wasn't steeped in country music. Nevertheless, I stared back at him. "Lefty."

"Lefty who?" Kyle asked.

"Do you mean you've never heard of Lefty Frizzell?"

"The name sounds familiar, but I don't know his stuff."

I was wearing a sports coat, so I stuck my hand into the inside pocket and pulled out a cassette copy of Lefty Frizzell's greatest hits that I'd been carrying with me. I handed the tape to Kyle. "Here," I said. "I think you better listen to this."

Kyle promised that he would, and I'm sure he did.

The song we discovered that day was titled "1962" and had a fantastic opening hook: "Operator, please connect me . . . to 1962." We loved it and felt it could be a good fit for me. But since I had been only three years old in 1962, Kyle suggested that we record the song and change it to "1982." Martha advanced us some more money, and we went back in the studio and recorded the song "1982." I felt sure it could be a hit. Kyle did too.

On November 20, 1985, Warner released "1982," and it shot up the charts, all the way to #6, turning out to be my first hit song. With this success, Warner advanced us enough money to complete my first full label album. We titled it *Storms of Life* after the song written by Max D. Barnes and Troy Seals, telling the story of a man devastated by emotional turmoil. On that song, as on every cut on the album, I threw myself into the lyrics, living the stories vicariously and singing with as much feeling as I could. Country music is basically about the stories of life. I'd already lived a lot of life and wasn't yet thirty years of age, and I could relate to the emotion in the songs, so I sang them as though they had happened to me—because most of them had! I think that's what made many of our songs so believable to the listeners.

Kyle must have thought so too. When somebody asked him about the secret to our success, he quipped, "I have a great singer. I'm just mixing his vocal up front in the songs."

During this entire time, I continued working at the Nashville Palace. But after my appearance on television and the success of "1982," I started receiving numerous invitations to perform in small clubs in Georgia and Alabama. Lib and I decided we should hit the road. So we did, in a van we borrowed from John A. Hobbs, and for a while it seemed that I was singing anywhere people asked us to come.

When I first started doing shows outside of the Nashville Palace, I couldn't afford to hire a full-time band, so for a while, I performed with the house band wherever we went. Usually we took along Drew Sexton as my piano player, and Drew worked with the house band to get my songs rehearsed and sounding right. When we were really flush with cash or it was an important engagement, we took along L.D. as well.

It was always tricky to work with house musicians. Some were great, but others were something less than top-notch, and even the great ones required making adjustments. So it was a happy day indeed when we started making enough money to hire our own full-time band. That first band included Rocky Thacker on bass, Tommy Rivelli on drums, Drew Sexton on keyboards, L.D. (Rick Wayne Money) on lead guitar, and Gary Carter on steel guitar. As soon as we could afford a fiddle player, we hired David Johnson, a classically trained violinist who had played with the house band at Country City USA in Charlotte.

When David first came to audition for our band at Country City, he told me that he played mostly symphony music. "Do you play country music?" I asked him.

"I don't know. What's country music? I guess I do. Music is music, isn't it?"

We went through the audition, and David played along to every one of my songs. I knew I had found our fiddle player—classically trained or not.

David said, "You know, I think I'm going to like this country stuff."

We couldn't afford a big, fancy tour bus in those days. So we bought an old bread truck from Ronnie Reno, Merle Haggard's good friend and a great musical talent in his own right. Ronnie had converted the bread truck into sort of a camper with five bunks and some storage space. It wasn't fancy. It had air conditioning, but not much else. Nevertheless, I was proud of that old bread truck. "Look at that thing," I gushed. "A bread truck! It carries the band and all the equipment to the shows. It's almost like a bus!"

We traveled that way for quite a while. The musicians rode in the bread truck with most of the equipment, while Lib and I drove a rented car or van loaded with my guitar, some more equipment, and our merchandise. Lib usually drove, and I tried to sleep in the back seat on the way to our next show. I woke up many mornings with my back feeling like an accordion.

Sherwood Cryer, one of the owners of Gilley's in Texas, had an old bus that had been formerly owned by Johnny Lee when he toured extensively after his huge hit, "Looking for Love (in All the Wrong Places)." Sherwood was willing to sell the bus to me inexpensively, but he wanted me to try it out first. "Take it and drive it a while. Make sure it runs well and you really like it," Sherwood said. "I'm in no rush to sell." So we took that bus on several long runs. Eventually, we saved enough money and bought it so we could all travel together in one vehicle.

In early March 1986, we received a surprising phone call from Hal Durham, longtime general manager of the Grand Ole Opry. I heard Hal ask Lib if I was interested in becoming a member. Opry members must be invited, so she knew this was a big deal, but she played coy. "I'll talk to Randy and call you back," she told Hal.

Of course, it didn't take long for me to think about that choice. I've always been a fan of the Opry and the artists who are members. My answer was definitely yes. In fact, I felt as though I needed to pinch myself to make sure I wasn't dreaming. *Interested? Are you kidding? You bet I'm interested!* Every country artist dreams about being invited to join the Grand Ole Opry, and now they were extending that invitation to me! Amazing!

The actual induction would take place later in the year, Hal informed us. At twenty-seven years of age, I was set to be the youngest male artist ever inducted into the Opry at that time.

Not that I had time to sit around and celebrate. We stayed busy touring all year long. I did, however, make time to sing at the Opry on March 7, 1986. Also on the show that night were Opry favorites Grandpa Jones, Connie Smith, Minnie Pearl, Riders in the Sky, and my old friend Little Jimmy Dickens. I wore a burgundy dress shirt, a gray sports jacket, and black jeans with a large belt buckle. To my surprise, Little Jimmy joined me onstage at one point and officially invited me to become a member of the Opry. Nobody in the house had to guess at my answer! The induction would take place around Christmastime, but I felt as though I had already received my gift.

On April 14, 1986, Lib and I attended the Academy of Country Music Awards show at Knott's Berry Farm in California, hosted by Mac Davis, Reba McEntire, and John Schneider and telecast live by NBC-TV. I wore a traditional black tuxedo complete with a black bowtie. It was the first time I'd ever attended an awards show, and I had been nominated for the Top New Male Vocalist award, so I wanted to look good. The ACMs also had a category for Top Male Vocalist, which was a bit confusing, but I was thrilled to be in there anywhere. After all, other than my custom projects, I didn't even have an album that most people could purchase. Although "On the

Other Hand" had cracked the charts the previous summer and "1982" had done well on the radio since it came out in November, my first Warner Bros. album was not even scheduled to be released until June, so I really didn't expect to win anything that night at the awards show.

The Top New Male Vocalist award was presented by Nicolette Larson, Juice Newton, and Steve Wariner. I think everybody in the room—me included—expected the award to go to T. Graham Brown, who had enjoyed a great year. I was actually surprised when Steve said, "The top new male vocalist is . . ." Steve had the envelope upside down, so there was a brief pause before he continued. "The winner is . . . Randy Travis!"

I bounded up onto the stage as though I'd done it a thousand times— and maybe I had in my mind, but this was the real thing! I didn't really have an acceptance speech ready, so I smiled nervously and tried to collect myself. Then, in an awkward ramble, I said, "Oh, I thank the Lord for this, and thanks to Mother and Daddy for always being behind me. I love you so much. And all the folks at Warner Bros. who have been so kind to me, especially Martha Sharp, I appreciate that. And my producer Kyle Lehning, who I think is great. And my manager, Lib Hatcher, who has always been behind me . . ."

My mind was racing, trying to thank everyone in less than thirty seconds, and I'm sure I sounded scattered and scrambled. "And to all you folks who played the record, I appreciate it. And all you folks who voted for me, thank you. I appreciate it." The music started playing, and I nodded good-bye as I headed offstage.

This was the first music award I'd received since I was a teenager in Marshville, and I was especially thrilled that rather than a statue or a piece of glass-looking acetate, the award was a cowboy hat atop a trophy.

I had no sooner walked offstage than Lib snatched the award from me. She was so excited, she wouldn't let go of it. It was almost as if *she* had won the award! After the show, we were mingling with the crowd when somebody walked up to me and said, "This must feel pretty good."

"It sure does!" Lib butted in, hugging the trophy to her breast.

I just smiled. "Yeah, it does," I said bashfully.

7 ———————— RENEWED HOPE

Kyle Lehning and I developed a deep trust in each other as we worked in the studio during those years. We had what could be called a "benefit of the doubt clause" in working together. If I wasn't sure about a certain song that Kyle suggested, I always gave Kyle the benefit of the doubt, and he did the same for me. If Kyle had a song that I thought wasn't good for me, I'd go learn the song anyway and give it my best effort. I never tried to sabotage a song; nor did Kyle.

When I first played "I Told You So" for Kyle, using only an acoustic guitar, Kyle was skeptical. But when we did it in the studio, it was magic. On the other hand, I was reluctant to record "Look Heart, No Hands," but Kyle thought it was a good choice for me. When we got in the studio and the band started playing, the song came alive to me. We all felt that we had a hit.

For both Kyle and me, the reward was the work. We loved working in the studio together, and the collaboration was rarely difficult.

Kyle understood who I was as an artist and helped me choose songs that were a good fit for me. He also gave me some of the best musical advice I'd ever receive: "Don't record 'em if you don't love 'em." Consequently, we didn't waste a lot of time on things that didn't work, trying to force something onto a recording. If we started working on a song and it didn't feel right, we'd trash it and move on to the next. If it didn't live in me somehow, or if it didn't sound believable to Kyle, we'd let it go.

We recorded my album *Storms of Life* over a long period of months, partly because Martha Sharp kept feeding us new songs to try. Martha had access to a treasure trove of great traditional country songs that had been pitched to Warner. Oddly, at that time nobody else wanted to record them. The whole time Kyle and I were working on the project, she kept searching for the best songs in the bunch. We'd record something, then Martha would show up with a new song she thought might be even better, so we'd go back into the studio to work on that one. Eventually, though, we settled on what we thought was a good collection of strong, believable material.

When the album was finally done, Kyle and I sat alone in the control room of his Morningstar studio on the north side of Nashville and listened to the entire album from beginning to end. As the last notes faded away, Kyle turned in his chair and smiled. "That sounds like a pretty good record," he said. I nodded in agreement. "Based on how much money we've spent making this record," Kyle said, "if we sell forty thousand copies, Warner Bros. might let us make another record."

My eyes brightened. "That would be really good," I said. I didn't know enough to have high hopes or low. We had completed the entire album for around sixty thousand dollars. Compared to today's recording budgets, that was a pittance, but it seemed like a fortune to me at the time. And neither Kyle nor I had a clue just how well it would do, especially considering the failure of our first single, "On the Other Hand," the previous year.

We'd had such high hopes for that song when we put it out the previous July. And it *had* made it onto the *Billboard* charts. But when it peaked at #67, a long way from being considered a hit, we'd been terribly disappointed.

Kyle and I were convinced that the song was strong. We believed in it so much, we pressed Warner to give it another chance. Rereleasing a song was rarely done in the music business. If a song or an artist didn't quickly connect with the public, the company normally moved on.

Nevertheless Kyle's friend, the brilliant singer-songwriter, Paul Davis, had done some research and discovered that in certain parts of the country—Mississippi, Louisiana, and some other areas—"On the Other Hand" had indeed done remarkably well. The song had gone to #1 in Meridian, Mississippi, for instance, and Warner Bros. had received an order for ten thousand singles for jukeboxes in Texas. If we could do that on a larger, wider basis, we'd really have something going.

After the success of "1982" as a single, Nick Hunter, the radio promotions guy at Warner, called us and said, "You're gonna get your wish. We're going to put out 'On the Other Hand' again."

We were ecstatic, but we knew it was a risky move. While we weren't the first to ever rerelease a song, it was not common practice for a record company to send out the same record to radio stations, hoping they would play it. Some deejays might say, "Hey, you guys sent this to me before, and I didn't like it. Why would I play it now?"

Martha thought it might help if we rerecorded the song. Kyle's no to that suggestion was kind but emphatic. "Martha, I heard that song on the radio in Nashville, and it sounded killer on the radio. We've already done the best recording of 'On the Other Hand' that we could possibly do. I can't make a better record on Randy of that song. Please give it a chance."

She did. Warner rereleased the original version of "On the Other Hand" on April 2, 1986. On April 26 it debuted on the *Billboard* charts at #64, and it blew up from there.

When the full *Storms of Life* album finally released on June 2 of that year, I was still performing at the Nashville Palace, but at least now I was listed on the weekly program with other artists such as Little Jimmy Dickens, Boxcar Willie, and Jeanne Pruett.

The first week in June 1986—the same week the album hit—I performed as part of the Warner Bros. showcase at Fan Fair (now the CMA Music Fest), the weeklong country music festival held annually at the sweltering Tennessee State Fairgrounds in Nashville. Thousands of people planned their vacations around Fan Fair because it was a unique opportunity to see and hear so many country artists in one location and to meet them at their autograph booths after the shows. Although Fan Fair was always hectic, with fans standing in long lines to get autographs, it was also a performer's dream—a large group of fans who hung on every note and word of the music.

We kicked off my set with a few Merle Haggard songs and a Hank Williams medley. Then, when we began the first chords of "On the Other Hand," the crowd of nearly twenty-five thousand people stood up and cheered. It was incredible!

We closed with "American Trilogy," the medley of songs that Elvis had done in his shows that included "Dixie," the old spiritual "All My Trials," and "The Battle Hymn of the Republic." We received another rousing standing ovation before leaving the stage.

Backstage, Kyle looked at Martha Sharp and said, "Wow, we're in for the ride of our lives."

Martha had been helpful to Kris Kristofferson's career, but this was her first big A&R success. It was thrilling but uncharted territory for all of us. So we decided early on that no matter what happened, we were simply going to stay true to the music. Traditional country music was all I wanted to do—it's all I knew *how* to do. I had no ambitions to be a "crossover" artist, dabbling in pop music. My only goal was to sing the best country songs with as much emotion as I could muster.

Kyle had told me about a famous Mother Teresa comment, "I'm not here to be successful; I'm here to be faithful." I could relate to that because I felt something similar toward country music. I simply wanted to be faithful to the traditional music that had been passed down to me. I was happy to be successful, and I enjoyed knowing that my songs were being played on the radio, but most of all I just wanted to sing great country music.

Then the dream became a reality. On July 26, 1986, "On the Other Hand" became the #1 song in the nation. We were on top of the charts!

Just two weeks later, on August 9, 1986, the full album, *Storms of Life*, hit #1 on the *Billboard* charts. I shook my head in wonder when I saw my name in the magazine listed right along with so many of my heroes. The album produced four big hits: the singles "1982" and "On the Other Hand" plus "No Place Like Home" and "Diggin' Up Bones," a song about a fellow finding reminders and remnants of a devastated marriage relationship. Interestingly, "Diggin' Up Bones" was a hit with young kids as well as adults. They had no idea what the lyrics were talking about, but they loved the catchy chorus about "diggin' up bones." The song would land on top of the charts on November 8, 1986—my second #1 single in a row!

Maybe because of that success, Lib felt emboldened to reach out to a professional publicist. Never hesitant to spend our own money to promote my music, we were unwilling to rely entirely on Warner Bros. to present me to the media or to look for opportunities such as acting to broaden our audiences.

Lib had heard that Evelyn Shriver, a top New York PR person, had taken an interest in country music and was even contemplating a move to Nashville. Evelyn was an ambitious expert in her field who had worked with recording artists such as Diana Ross and actors such as Henry Winkler of

Happy Days and Larry Hagman of the hit show *Dallas*. We scheduled an interview with her, and she blew us away with her ideas for promoting not only my music, but me. Evelyn wanted to land media coverage in major cities all across America. She planned to get me on the cover of country magazines and every other major mainstream magazine as well.

We liked what we were hearing. So we hired Evelyn, brought her onto our staff, and paid her salary as our personal publicist, something that few country artists were doing at that time. Evelyn would be worth every penny.

♪ ♫

In the late summer of 1986, on a rare day when I was home, I received an urgent early-morning phone call from the Country Music Association. Ricky Skaggs had been scheduled to announce the nominations for the 1986 CMA Awards in a televised press conference at Opryland Hotel that morning, but his seven-year-old son, Andrew, had been shot in a senseless road-rage incident. Andrew would eventually recover, but right then Ricky was at the hospital with his son, so the CMA representative asked if I could fill in at the last minute. "It's easy," she said. "All you have to do is read each category and the nominations. We'll have everything ready for you."

"I'll be glad to help," I said and hastily headed for the shower. I threw on my clothes and a country-looking sports coat and raced across town to the hotel.

A large assortment of media types was assembled for the announcements, and although I was familiar with all the categories and names of the nominees, I was still nervous about reading them aloud. As part of the surprise element, the CMA and the accounting agency who tallies the scores don't inform the announcer in advance of who the nominees are, so imagine my surprise when I opened the envelope and read, "And the nominees for the Horizon Award are: Dan Seals, Dwight Yoakam, Kathy Mattea, the Forester Sisters . . . and Randy Travis." I looked up and smiled as the cameras flashed. It was awkward, but nice.

I experienced something similar when I opened the envelope for the Single of the Year award and read: "'On the Other Hand,' written by Paul Overstreet and Don Schlitz, recorded by Randy Travis." I smiled nervously at the press again and shook my head in amazement. Then I read on: "And '1982,' written by Buddy Blackmon and Vip Vipperman, recorded by Randy Travis." I grinned sheepishly and shook my head as though to say, "I didn't write this stuff!"

But when I opened the envelope designated "1986 Male Vocalist of the Year," I nearly lost it. I tried to read the names on the card without choking up. "The nominees for Male Vocalist of the Year are . . . George Jones, Gary Morris, George Strait, Hank Williams Jr. . . ." I paused and gulped hard. "And Randy Travis."

I looked up, and my eyes blurred with tears. I was overwhelmed. *What in the world is my name doing there with those guys? George Jones? He's a hero to me, and now here I am nominated for the same award as him? I must be dreaming!*

The "dream" continued when I announced the nominations for Album of the Year, and right there among albums by the Judds, Reba McEntire, Ronnie Milsap, and George Strait, I read, *"Storms of Life."*

It was a strange but wonderful feeling, reading the nominations for the first time and seeing my name associated with five awards. It was a real shock to me, but one I wouldn't have minded in a million years!

In October 1986, Lib and I attended the awards show, held at the Grand Ole Opry House. I wore a formal black tuxedo with a white shirt, and she wore a formal gown. For two country pokes like us, that was really stepping out of our comfort zones, but we were honored to be there and wanted to reflect that in the way we dressed. Thanks largely to the success of *Storms of Life*, I received the Horizon Award, CMA's recognition of the best *new*, up-and-coming artist of the year. That was early in the show, and then I sat quietly and smiled as the three other awards for which I was nominated went to other artists. The expected acknowledgment, "It's an honor just to be nominated," was more than merely a cliché for me. I was like a kid gawking at his heroes. I genuinely appreciated my name being spoken in the same breath as theirs. I was deeply gratified, too, when Paul and Don won Song of the Year (Songwriter's Award) for "On the Other Hand."

It was a memorable evening. Reba McEntire was honored as the 1986 Entertainer of the Year, and in a poignant tribute to some of country music's greatest heroes, George Jones won the Music Video of the Year award for his song, "Who's Gonna Fill Their Shoes?"

Although I would never be so bold, the song posed a question for which many country music fans had a ready answer: "Randy Travis."

8 ————— HITTING THE ROAD

We had a number of gigs that had been booked before we really blew up on the charts, and although we were now in much greater demand for shows offering much more money and prestige, we honored every one of our earlier commitments. Now, however, some of those venues were not large enough to handle the crowds. In Conyers, Georgia, for example, we did four shows and cleared the venue four times to accommodate the number of people who showed up for the one show we had booked months earlier.

Out on the road, we worked hard to give people a good show. We felt that the people who came to our shows were hardworking Americans, so we were determined to give them our best every night. But we quickly realized that what I did onstage was only part of the equation. We needed an entire team to help book concerts and promote them.

When I first began touring, we had signed a booking agreement with the World Class Talent agency, which was owned by Barbara Mandrell and JoAnn Berry. Most of my dates had been scheduled by Allen Whitcomb, who booked me as an opening act for Barbara, T.G. Sheppard, and many other artists. Eventually Lib and I formed our own in-house booking agency, and we hired Allen as our sole employee.

Allen had also previously worked for Jimmy Jay, general manager of United Talent, one of the top agencies in Nashville, founded by country superstars Conway Twitty and Loretta Lynn. At one point Jimmy had handled the careers of twenty-six major acts, including Conway and, later, Loretta.

While working with United Talent, Allen had gotten to know Jimmy's son, Jeff Davis. Jeff had worked with his dad from the time he was old enough to jump on a tour bus, traveling regularly with Conway for more than eight years and gaining a wealth of practical tour-management experience.

As Jeff tells it, he and his wife, Cori, saw me on Ralph Emery's show, *Nashville Now*, and heard me sing "1982" and "On the Other Hand." That same night, Jeff called Allen Whitcomb and said, "Allen, let's get Randy Travis booked on some dates with Conway."

"We can sure do that," Allen said.

That weekend, when Jeff was on the road again with Conway, Jeff told the superstar about me. He later listened to some of my songs and called Jeff. "I heard that new guy, Randy Travis, that you were telling me about. We need to get him on a show someplace."

Jeff contacted Allen Whitcomb again, and they booked me for one show on May 2, 1986, along with Conway Twitty and Loretta Lynn at the civic center in Asheville, North Carolina. I was a huge Conway and Loretta fan, so I was thrilled about the invitation.

Lib and I drove from Nashville to Asheville in a van, followed by our band traveling in the converted bread truck we had purchased. (This was still a while before we bought our bus.) While I did a quick sound check with the band, Lib hauled in our one blue Samsonite suitcase filled with photos of me and T-shirts. Even though I had hit songs on the radio, my first album with Warner Bros. had still not been released, so we had only a few shirts and photos to sell at our small merchandise table at the back of the hall.

The show went well, and every so often, out of my peripheral vision, I noticed Conway and Jeff and several of their band members watching us from sidestage. I don't know how long they observed, but apparently they were pleased.

It was the first of many shows I would perform along with Conway and Loretta. We worked together throughout the summer and into the fall of 1986. Conway and I got along great, and working with the country-music icon was almost like going to school with a master teacher. He was open and readily forthcoming whenever Lib asked him for information about the music business. And she asked him a lot.

Before a show in Tempe, Arizona, in November, Conway called Jeff over to his bus. "I've been watching what's going on every night," Conway told Jeff, "and Randy is coming on strong. I think that tonight Randy should close the show." Conway suggested that I follow Loretta and him.

Jeff returned to our bus and informed me about Conway's request. "No!" I protested. "I can't do that." I didn't mean that I wouldn't be honored or that I couldn't do the job, but that I respected Conway and Loretta too much to be their closing act. But Conway was both a brilliant entertainer and a good businessman. He had an innate sense for what worked, and he never let his ego get in the way of a great show. He insisted that I close the show and so, with a bit of trepidation, I did. From that night on, for the remainder of that tour, I closed the show every night. The two gracious superstars provided me with the opportunity to be a headliner, and I appreciated it.

Eventually Jeff Davis asked about joining the roster of United Talent, but Lib had what she thought was a better idea. She invited him to join *our* camp to expand and grow our touring operations. I had been an opening act for the Judds, the Oak Ridge Boys, George Jones, and a number of other artists, but I really hadn't been a headliner. Jeff helped develop shows where I could be featured as the main event.

We were still working a lot of dates with Conway and Loretta, so the transition was relatively painless. Jeff's brother, Jerry, took over his responsibilities with United Talent, and Jeff climbed onto our bus.

Jeff became our in-house promoter in September 1987, booking the arenas and promoting the concerts. To support his efforts, Lib and Jeff formed a new company known as Special Moments Promotions, with Lib as president and Jeff as vice president. He worked at our makeshift office—the kitchen table at our home on Sixteenth Avenue South in Nashville.

Jeff showed up the first day, lugged in two file boxes loaded with his contacts, and set up, ready to work. I heard him talking outside my bedroom door, so I got up, still rubbing the sleep out of my eyes, and walked out in my robe and socks. "Good morning, Hoss," I said to Jeff.

A few minutes later, Lib came out of the bedroom, dressed in her robe as well.

Jeff just shook his head as if to say, "What have I gotten myself into?" and went back to work.

One of the first shows that Jeff promoted as part of our team was in Charlotte during Thanksgiving weekend of 1987. I had appeared along with George Jones and Patty Loveless at the Charlotte Coliseum the year before, and we had sold it out. It had been my first hometown concert since my songs started playing regularly on the radio. But this time I was returning as a headliner, and the response was gratifying. We sold out all ten thousand seats almost immediately, so we added a matinee for that same day, and more than seven thousand people bought the tickets. It was a fantastic crowd, and it felt great to be appreciated at home.

Jeff Davis continued to develop and expand our touring operations, and together with his lone assistant, Linda Ghaffari, he proved tremendously effective. In country music at that time, few flat-fee financial guarantees existed. Instead the artist assumed most of the risk. So for most shows, Jeff rented the venue on our behalf, and then, through Special Moments, he booked the opening acts, promoted the show, bought all the advertising, and sold the tickets.

Besides setting up bigger shows at better venues, Jeff brought a new precision to our tours. His itineraries were so detailed that the band members' wives could find us at any time of the day or night and know what we were doing. Having lunch, doing meet-and-greets, having dinner, doing sound checks—Jeff had it all on the itinerary.

It was always interesting to me to see how concerts came together. For instance, a relative of George Richey, Tammy Wynette's husband, owned a General Motors dealership. George put together a sponsorship package in which we were teamed with Tammy and the Judds for a series of concerts sponsored by GMC Trucks. We performed twenty-five shows a year, all over the country, for several years as part of that package. General Motors received great advertising; local dealerships received concert tickets to give away; and we had a secure income performing in major venues. It was a winning combination for everybody, and most of the concerts were sellouts.

We were still doing a number of concerts with Conway Twitty and

Loretta Lynn in 1987, working shows all up and down the West Coast. We played San Diego, Anaheim, and Oakland, and then we had a few days off before our next date in Portland, so we detoured through Reno. While the bus drivers slept for a while, the rest of us went inside a casino. I had never before been inside one, so I gawked around like a wide-eyed kid. I had never gambled, but the Twitty team taught me well. I didn't win anything significant, but I had lots of fun.

Later, when we stopped for fuel, Jeff went into a truck stop to find some videos we could watch on the bus while we traveled. One movie he purchased for us was *Airplane!*, a hilarious comedy loaded with memorable one-liners. At one point in the movie, the crew of a jetliner are incapacitated due to food poisoning and a traumatized war veteran turned taxi driver has to land the plane with help from the tower. As the vet struggles to follow the instructions from the ground, one person after another comes into the cockpit and tells him, "Hey, we just want to tell you good luck. We're all counting on you."

At the show that night, as I stood in the dimly lit backstage area waiting for the emcee to introduce me, Jeff Davis came over to me and quipped, "Hey, Hoss"—we all called each other Hoss—"We just want to tell you good luck. We're all counting on you!" I cracked up laughing.

Jeff would do that every night, every show, for the next twenty-six years.

9 ——————— LIVING THE DREAM

Shortly after I received the CMA Horizon Award in October 1986, Lib and I purchased a large farm out in the country near Ashland City, Tennessee, about thirty miles outside of Nashville. I'd always wanted a place where I could stable horses and ride, and I guess the farm was sort of a reward for both of us.

The main farmhouse was located down a winding gravel road and sat right alongside the bend in a stream running through the property. It was a log home with a rustic feel that I really liked. Lib referred to it as "the cabin," so I went along with that description too. But that cabin soon grew larger, thanks to renovations. Our tastes for Southwestern art and decorations created a warm, comfortable, homey atmosphere.

Besides making our house a home, Lib made life easy for me in many ways. She picked out my clothes, cooked special healthy meals for me, and even canned our vegetables. Lib fretted that I had allergies, so she encouraged me to avoid chocolate, nuts, pasta, and all sorts of other treats. She also didn't like for me to wear cologne or to buy her perfume—or to be around women who wore pretty perfume.

But in truth, I never had any serious problems with allergies. Certainly some foods adversely affected my voice if I ate them shortly before a show, because they bloated my stomach or created mucus in my throat. I never liked to sing on a full stomach anyway, because that impaired proper breathing for singing. So I usually ate after a show, not before. I didn't regularly use allergy medication, prescription or over-the-counter. Yet Lib constantly reiterated that I was allergy prone.

Because we now had some land, we kept several horses, and I loved to ride. Some days I'd ride six or eight miles. Riding was a great way to clear my head and get away from all the hoopla surrounding the music business. We didn't socialize much, except with Lib's friends, and I didn't attend a lot of concerts or sporting events. I was content riding horses, practicing my ambidextrous quick-draw techniques with six-shooters, and target shooting on the property. I loved to play pool, so we bought a gorgeous pool table that we put in my upstairs studio. Of course we also had a workout area, and I spent several hours a day there. We both loved movies, so we attended a lot at our local theater and watched even more at home. That was our life.

Around that time, Lib and I also bought the exclusive rights to the songs I had written. Early in my career, when we were trying to get a recording deal in Nashville, we had entered into a copublishing arrangement with Charlie Monk. Now we wanted to fully own the songs covered by that arrangement.

The negotiations were heated, and Lib and Charlie were often at loggerheads. Although I didn't get too involved in their contentious discussions, I allowed them to happen, and for that I later felt remorse. After all, Charlie had been good to me. He had been instrumental in my landing a recording contract, and he had believed in me when few others did.

Earlier in my career, everyone had told us, "If you want a better chance at a record deal, you need to write your own songs," so I was trying to do that. But I wanted to record the *best* songs, not simply something I had written. To me it was all about the song. So I ended up singing someone else's material as often as I did mine. Still Lib and I knew that we had some good songs in our catalog, so she threatened a lawsuit to get my songs back from Charlie.

But Charlie had been around the music publishing business quite a while, and he was not simply going to roll over. Although our accounting of the live-album sales was spotty, to say the least, Charlie knew he was rightfully due half of the publishers' royalties for every song on the album, and he hadn't been paid a dime. He spent more than thirty-five thousand dollars in legal fees negotiating with Lib, and eventually we paid him around a quarter of a million dollars to secure the exclusive publishing rights to my songs. Sadly, had Lib not been so adamant about things, we could have achieved the same results for less than half that amount, which was what Charlie originally had suggested. Charlie didn't go away broke, but he did depart with a lot of hurt feelings, and I felt awful about that.

Live and learn, but at least we now controlled the ownership of my songs. We also knew more about the value of song publishing, so I often met with writers at our log-cabin home to work on songs together. The farm proved to be an inspiring place for songwriting.

Don Schlitz and I had tried to write some songs together when Lib and I were living on Music Row. We'd never succeeded in coming up with anything great, but we'd had so much fun bouncing ideas off each other that we looked for opportunities to write together.

Although we had experienced very different upbringings, Don and I were both Carolina boys. He'd grown up in the Raleigh-Durham area and hung out around the university crowd. He used words such as *indefatigable* in ordinary conversations. Nevertheless, he understood my background, and our personalities clicked. As Don put it, "We both recognized early on that neither one of us had an accent." Maybe that's why he was willing to make the sixty-mile round trip out to the farm to write together.

Don and I would go upstairs to the third floor, where I had transformed the attic into a room large enough to include a cozy writing studio above my workout room. Meanwhile, Lib provided motivation. "I'm cooking a delicious lunch," she promised, "but you can't eat until you write a song."

By the time Don and I finished the first song, Lib had the table loaded with an elaborate spread of food. "Here you are, Don," she said. "Dig in. Randy's not allowed to eat most of these things because of his allergies." So I'd look on with hungry eyes and eat some bird food or something healthy while Don feasted on Lib's Southern-style home cooking. Then we'd go back upstairs to work on another song, though we usually wrote better before lunch than after.

In addition to the pool table, the studio held a couple of collectible saddles as well as an old-style Coke machine that dispensed a small, six-ounce drink when you put in a dime and pushed the lever. One afternoon Don and I were writing, and he was singing lyrics. He got thirsty, so he went over, put a dime in the machine, and retrieved a cold Coca-Cola. A short while later, he put in another dime and got another drink. And a while after that, he put in yet another dime and got another drink.

We were still working on songs, laughing, and sharing musical thoughts when Don walked over to the Coke machine, stuck his hand in his pocket, and then said, "Hey, Randy, I'm out of dimes. Can you loan me one?"

I looked at him with just a hint of a smile. "Why sure, Don," I said. "But there's a key right over there on top of the machine."

"You sorry rascal!" Don said. "You'd have let me plop dimes in that machine all day long, wouldn't you?"

"Yup," I said with a smile. "I sure would have."

♫ ♫

In November 1986, Warner Bros. threw a big party at the Station Inn, a well-known music venue in downtown Nashville, to celebrate the fact that my album *Storms of Life* had been certified by the Record Industry Association of America (RIAA) as "gold," signifying sales of more than five hundred thousand albums. "I have a feeling we're going to be doing this again soon," Jim Ed Norman, CEO of Warner Bros. Nashville, told the audience as he presented me a large, framed gold record.

While thanking the crowd of industry insiders and members of the media for attending, I also made the announcement that I had been asked to join the Opry. "I think that means more to me than anything else," I said. I wasn't denigrating the significance of the gold album; I just wanted everyone to know what really mattered to me. "Hal Durham told me they needed me on the show." I shook my head in disbelief, and my voice cracked slightly as I said, "Isn't that something?"

On December 11, 1986, I appeared on *Hee Haw*, the incredibly popular TV variety show hosted by Roy Clark and Buck Owens. I sang "Diggin' Up Bones" and cracked up while helping out with "Pfft You Were Gone." The *Hee Haw* stars made me laugh so much I had a hard time singing!

One of my favorites in the cast was Louis Marshall Jones, better known as "Grandpa Jones." A fan favorite on the Grand Ole Opry, inducted into the Country Music Hall of Fame in 1978, Grandpa was also famous in music circles for "keepin' it country." Besides his energetic banjo playing on the show, Grandpa was a mainstay in the Hee Haw Gospel Quartet. A good man, he always had a twinkle in his eye and a way with words. During a break while taping a segment "in the corn patch," Grandpa and I struck up a conversation. "Son, I sure like what you're doin' in country music," he said to me. "If those people in Nashville try to change you, just tell 'em to kiss you where it shows the most when you're pullin' turnips!"

"Grandpa!" I pretended to be shocked as I cracked up laughing.

When I returned to *Nashville Now* on December 12, the host, Ralph Emery, couldn't keep from having a bit of fun with me. Ralph replayed the clip of me shaking like a leaf in a storm when I had performed on his show a mere two years earlier. Now I was a gold-record recording artist, rapidly approaching platinum status and playing to sold-out crowds in concert halls all over America. I'd had little more than two weeks off the road all year long. That night I sang "Diggin' Up Bones" as well as my new single, "No Place Like Home," another well-written song by Paul Overstreet. It had debuted at #49 on the charts and would eventually land at #2 and #1 in Canada.

Ralph and I had developed a great relationship by then, and we had a lot of fun when I appeared on his show. Ralph knew that I loved Roy Rogers and anything having to do with the old West, so on one occasion we decided to open *Nashville Now* with both of us dressed up as gunslingers. We wanted to recreate a scene similar to the opening of the classic cowboy television show, *Gunsmoke*, which began with Marshal Matt Dillon quick-drawing on a bad guy at the end of the street.

The producers positioned Ralph and me about fifty paces apart at opposite ends of a field, and when the cameras rolled, we came at each other with guns a-blazing. The scene looked really good—until somebody noticed that I was wearing cowboy boots and Ralph was wearing his usual Nike sneakers. But we led right into the program's theme song and kept right on rolling.

Eventually Ralph retired from doing his daily morning and evening television shows and did only hour-long specials about once a month. For one special he wanted to feature Andy Griffith and his gospel album, which had already sold more than a million copies. Andy agreed to do the show but only if Ralph would bring the show to him in North Carolina. The company agreed and sent a film crew to North Carolina, as well as the sets.

I heard what Ralph was planning, so I called him. Ralph knew that I was a big fan of Andy, so he wasn't surprised when I said, "I'd really like to be on that show with you and Andy Griffith."

"Okay," Ralph said. "Where are you on that date?"

"Oh my," I said, looking at my calendar. "I'm playing in California."

"Is there any way you can get back here?"

"No, I'm afraid not," I said.

"Okay, I'll talk to management," Ralph said, "and see if we can beam you in by means of satellite, and you can join us that way." It was an incredible idea, and an expensive one, but TNN agreed to pay the fee for the satellite feed. That was a big deal in those days, and I'm sure it was only due to Ralph's significant clout with the network that they were willing to incur those costs.

Just prior to the show, while Ralph and Andy were in makeup, Ralph told him, "Andy, I know you don't like surprises, so I want to let you know in advance that one of your biggest fans, Randy Travis, would like to be a part of this show. He can join us by means of satellite. Would that be okay with you?"

"Why, sure," Andy replied. "That would be just fine."

Andy, of course, was the quintessential actor. As the show progressed, Ralph said to Andy on air, "We have a special person who really is a big fan of yours, and I'd like to present . . . Randy Travis."

At that point the network connected me by means of satellite and Andy looked humbly stunned. "Randy Travis!" he exclaimed. "What a surprise!"

Ralph ran a clip of one of his and my favorite episodes of *The Andy Griffith Show*, the one in which a number of Mayberry residents were singing in the church choir at a pie festival or something and the tenor was sick. Who was going to sing his part? Barney stepped up and volunteered, but Barney could only sing off-key. Andy told Barney, "You need to sing very quietly, because that microphone is real loud." They kept moving Barney back farther and farther from the microphone so he couldn't be heard. Ralph and Andy and I all laughed about the episode. "I think I know that sound man," I joked.

Andy went through the entire remainder of the show and never gave even a hint that he'd known I would be joining him and Ralph. He was an incredible actor and a true gentleman.

♫ ♫

On December 20, 1986, I was officially inducted into the Grand Ole Opry by Ricky Skaggs. At twenty-seven years of age, I was the youngest male artist ever to become a member. At that time, Lorrie Morgan was the youngest female member.

Even though I knew what to expect, I had plenty of jitters as I waited backstage. Then, during his portion of the show, Ricky paused and said, "Tonight is a very special night. We want to welcome the newest member of the Grand Ole Opry. We hope he's as excited to be here as we are to have him, because I know what it meant to me when they made me a member a few years ago. 'Cause I grew up listening to the Grand Ole Opry . . . just like he did. And he's the hottest new star on the horizon today. A nice hand for the great Randy Travis—the sixty-second member of the Grand Ole Opry!"

I walked onto the stage to an incredible ovation, thanked Ricky, and performed two songs, "Diggin' Up Bones" and "White Christmas Makes Me Blue."

"This is probably one of the biggest, happiest nights of my life," I told the crowd at the Grand Ole Opry House. "To tell you the truth, it's been an honor just to be able to come backstage and be around some of the great people here at the Grand Ole Opry—people that I've admired for a lot of years . . . and loved their music. It's great to be a part of the Opry family now." I felt then—and still do to this day—that being invited to join the Opry was one of the highest honors I could ever achieve. To be included in that exclusive "club" with all my heroes and friends was a dream come true for me.

In February 1987, the Grammy Awards were planning to feature some of the new "young guns" of country music, including Dwight Yoakam, Steve Earle, and me. I was invited to perform "Diggin' Up Bones" on the live telecast since I'd been nominated for that song in the category Best Country Vocal Solo Performance—Male. That was the good news. The bad news was that I was already booked with Conway Twitty for three shows in Pennsylvania and Virginia during the same time the Grammys were scheduled in California, and we had signed contracts on all those dates. Besides that, Conway had been so good to us. But this was the Grammys!

Lib, Jeff Davis, and Jeff's dad, Jimmy Jay, who still managed Conway Twitty, met with the superstar in his office. "I know we have signed contracts on all these dates," Lib said, "but this is a big opportunity for Randy. Is there any way you can let us off the hook so Randy can be on the Grammys?"

Ever gracious, Conway responded, "We really need Randy on the dates in Virginia, but you need this more. Go do the Grammys."

I played the date in Hershey, Pennsylvania, then took an early morning flight to Los Angeles so I could be on the Grammy show.

I didn't win the Grammy that year. That honor went to Ronnie Milsap for his performance of "Lost in the Fifties Tonight." Nevertheless, more than sixty-five million people watched the show, many of them hearing me sing for the first time. It was my initial appearance on the prestigious show, and just to be included on the roster with so many music heavyweights from all genres was an incredible honor.

The accolades continued coming faster than I could keep up with them. On February 10, 1987, *Storms of Life* was certified as a platinum album with sales of more than a million units.

Don Schlitz and Paul Overstreet received Song of the Year honors for "On the Other Hand" from the Nashville Songwriters Association International at a banquet at Vanderbilt Plaza Hotel ballroom on March 7, 1987. To be honored by their peers in such a way seemed especially meaningful to Paul and Don. I was thrilled for my friends and dreamed that maybe someday I could win such an award.

10 —————— ALWAYS & FOREVER

With the first four singles from the *Storms of Life* album still going strong, we knew it was time to get to work on the next album. That was easier said than done, of course, because we were touring so much. Kyle was great about working around my travel schedule, but there were times when I came in off the road almost too exhausted to sing. I tried my best to go into the studio fully prepared, but there were some days when Kyle would say to me, "Randy, this just isn't working today. You need to go home and get some rest."

Kyle knew my voice so well, he could tell when fatigue was affecting me and I wasn't able to sing my best. When my voice was healthy and rested, there was a certain quality that provided the "magic" for us. If my voice was tired, we could tell the difference, and no matter how hard we worked or how many times we rerecorded a verse or chorus, we were wasting our time.

Sometimes we worked for an hour or more, hoping my voice would loosen. If it didn't, Kyle was straightforward enough to say, "You're not in your best voice, Randy. Let's try it again tomorrow." And I trusted his judgment.

Often, when we did that, I'd return the following day, and we'd knock out three or four songs in a few hours.

The success of our first album naturally evoked higher expectations for a hit sophomore record, and this added to the pressure we faced. I understood the record company's anxiety and anticipation, but I tried to keep a clear focus and stay true to myself. All I wanted to do was to make the best music I could.

To select the songs for the second album, I met with Kyle, Martha, and Lib to listen to song demos. We spent hours and hours listening for songs we hoped could be hits. One day Martha was tremendously excited about a new song by Paul Overstreet and Don Schlitz, cowriters of "On the Other Hand."

As Don later told us, he got the idea for the song while listening to his little boy learning the Lord's Prayer. Don called Paul late one evening, wanting to write.

"It's kinda late, Don," Paul said. "I played thirty-six holes of golf today, and I'm really tired."

"I'd really like you to hear this, Paul," Don insisted.

"Do you want to do it tomorrow?" Paul asked.

"No, I want to do it now."

Paul knew the importance of going to work when the creative juices were flowing. "Okay," he said with a sigh, "come on over."

Don drove to Paul's place, and the two songwriters sat outside on Paul's porch and wrote the song. They were so excited they went into their publisher's studio that very night. They called James Stroud to play drums, and with Paul and Don singing and playing guitar, they recorded the demo. When they were done, they knew the song was meant for me.

When Martha first played it for us, I thought it might be a gospel song. That was okay with me, although I didn't see us putting out a gospel song to follow up *Storms of Life*. But when I listened more closely, I thought, *This is a song almost everyone can relate to.*

It was one of those songs that the first time we heard it, we all said yes. It was a song celebrating love and commitment and marital fidelity through the years—a major departure from country staples that touted "lyin', cheatin', and tears in your beer."

The new song was titled "Forever and Ever, Amen."

It was a once-in-a-lifetime song, the kind of song you can't expect to discover every day, the kind that some singers never find. I felt blessed that Don and Paul had sent it my way.

We recorded at Omni Studio, with James Stroud again playing drums, Paul Overstreet singing background vocals, and veteran studio musician Doyle Grisham, playing the steel guitar that featured so prominently on the song. But the song kicks off with a feature that caught everybody's attention. It was done on an overdub by Paul Franklin using his dobro—or, more precisely, what he called his pedalbro, a dobro with steel-guitar pedals that could bend the notes, creating a pleasant but unusual sound.

It was the first time Kyle had ever used Paul's pedalbro, and I'm not sure we ever used it again. But it sure worked. To this day, every time an audience hears that song introduction, it evokes applause.

I enjoyed working on the "Forever and Ever, Amen" video too. We filmed it at the University School in downtown Nashville, transformed to create the appearance of a real wedding reception. Pastor Skip Armistead of Hillcrest United Methodist Church helped the producer assemble a cast of everyday folks from the congregation, including various family members and children, along with several handsome fraternity guys from Vanderbilt University, and a few volunteers from a nearby seniors' center, all mixed in with some professional actors dancing. One of the female "extras" who danced solo in the video raised eyebrows when the bright studio lighting revealed she was not wearing a slip beneath her skirt. When the director told her that he could see through her skirt, she responded, "Oh, yes. I'm from Hollywood and I always get more camera time when I don't wear a slip."

"Ah, not in this video," the director replied.

Ironically, another woman who danced across the set several times was neither a member of the congregation nor an actor. When the producers later attempted to get her to sign a release, nobody could find her or even knew her name. She had crashed the video!

I've never been much of a dancer—probably because I've always been on the wrong side of the dance floor, performing the music so others could dance—so I didn't dance during the video, but it was fun watching even the older couples dance, hug, and kiss. The video, like the song, just seemed to have a touch of magic about it. We titled the second album, *Always & Forever* and put out the first single from it, "Forever and Ever, Amen," on March 25, 1987. It hit the charts a month later at #42 and kept on going higher from there.

Another surprise favorite from that album turned out to be a song I had written earlier, "I Told You So." I had included the song on my album recorded at the Nashville Palace, and a few people had heard it and liked it. Now millions of people were singing along to that song, and I was tickled to death.

The new album, *Always & Forever*, shipped more than half a million units the day it released, May 4, 1987—enormous opening day sales for a country album in those days. To celebrate the release as well as my birthday, Lib arranged for me to shoot a couple of games of pool with Minnesota Fats (Rudolph Walter Wanderone Jr.), one of the world's greatest billiards players. Fats had occasionally come in to the Nashville Palace when I worked there. He was now living at the Hermitage Hotel in Nashville.

We played three games and, amazingly, I won the first one . . . but I think Fats gave it to me. Then he started talking about playing for money, and I knew I was in trouble. Minnesota Fats nearly ran the table during one of the other games. The man was a fast-talking pool shark. The entire time we shot pool, he peppered me with his tall tales and entertaining banter. He was a character, and we had a great time.

When we first performed "Forever and Ever, Amen," out in public—at a concert in Kentucky—it had not yet been heard on the radio, nor had the video been shown. But the audience response was incredible. People were hootin' and hollerin' and wanting more. That night I thought, *Yep, we recorded the right song.*

A few nights later, we were playing at a club. The audience was enthusiastic throughout the show. I said, "We have a brand-new song we'd like to try out on you tonight." We launched into "Forever and Ever, Amen." When we got to the last line, I paused before adding the final "Amen." And the second I paused, the audience went nuts, banging on their chairs as though they were at a rock-and-roll concert. The response was unlike anything I'd ever experienced from a country audience listening to a country song. But I sure liked it.

By June 13, 1987, "Forever and Ever, Amen" was #1 on the *Billboard* charts. For some reason people connected with my voice and the lyrics of my songs—some of which included a wry smile behind them. Don Schlitz and Paul Overstreet were masters at inserting just a hint of humor in some of their songwriting, and that really appealed to me. Turns out, it appealed to a lot of listeners, as well. The album *Always & Forever*, which had been released the first week of May, hit the top of the charts, too, on June 20, 1987, and remained at #1 for forty-three straight weeks. That's ten straight months as the top country album in the nation!

Always & Forever received the Country Music Association's award for the Album of the Year in 1987. "Forever and Ever, Amen" won Single of the Year, and I was honored as Male Vocalist of the Year.

Bill Mayne, senior vice president of promotions for Warner Bros., later conducted focus groups that revealed that "Forever and Ever, Amen" had changed the perception in America about what country music really was. To me that was deeply gratifying. More important, everywhere we went, we heard heartwarming stories of what the song had meant to someone.

"That song reminded me so much of my grandparents, who have been married forever. So we played it at their fiftieth anniversary," a young woman said. "And Grandma and Grandpa danced."

"That's the kind of relationship we want to have in our marriage," a goo-goo-eyed engaged couple said. "Where we keep on loving each other no matter what happens."

"We were headed for divorce," one man admitted, "when the words of that song started running through my head. My wife and I sat down at the kitchen table and listened one more time to 'Forever and Ever, Amen.' We both started to cry, and we realized we were throwing away something truly precious. Then we went to see the lawyers and tore up the divorce papers."

Untold numbers of middle-aged couples smiled, I was told, every time the song played, as they looked adoringly at each other and declared their renewed commitment to each other, as they sang along to "I'm gonna love you forever and ever. Forever and ever, amen."

Letters poured in to our office and to Warner expressing how the song had been an encouragement and an inspiration to one person after another. One letter especially touched my heart. It was written by the mom of a young girl who had gone through chemotherapy treatments and had lost all her hair. When she heard the line in "Forever and Ever, Amen" that said, "I ain't in love with your hair, and if it all fell out, well, I'd love you anyway," she was encouraged to see herself as the beautiful person she was, with or without her hair. Eventually her hair grew back, but our music had helped her through the tough time. I was happy the song was on top of the charts and that we were selling albums, but you can't put a price tag on something like that.

The 1987 Academy of Country Music Awards were held in California in April, and we were nominated for four major awards: Male Vocalist of the Year; Single Record of the Year (for "On the Other Hand"), Song of the Year (also for "On the Other Hand"), and Album of the Year (for *Storms of Life*).

Because the album had done so well, I thought we might have a shot at winning the award for Album of the Year, but receiving the Male Vocalist award was really a shock for me. To my amazement I came home with all four awards! Prior to the show, I had tried to think of a few things I might say if I won something, but I hadn't thought of enough to cover four awards!

Juice Newton and Charley Pride presented the award for Song of the Year, the song we had put out once and had failed. Now that same song, "On the Other Hand," was hailed as the best song of the year in all of country music. Amazing!

Paul Overstreet joined me onstage to accept the award. I'd already made several impromptu speeches that night, so I gladly stepped aside and said, "Go ahead, Paul."

With his usual low-key sense of humor, Paul began, "I never think about what I'm going to say when I come up here, because I kinda like to wait to the last minute and surprise myself."

The crowd responded with laughter, and so did I.

After thanking the publishers and me, Paul said, "I'm just real happy to be in a business where people can thank their moms and their pops—'cause I love ya, Mom, and I love ya, Dad. And you can also thank God, and I love ya, Jesus. I thank you for this." Paul then went on to deliver a poignant statement: "About two and a half years ago, I was contemplating getting out of the business. I really put myself down a hard road. I just gave it to the Lord and said, 'What do you want me to do?'" Paul held up the award and said, "I guess this is what I'm supposed to do."

When it was my turn to speak, I said, "I don't know what to add to that." I nodded toward Paul, "Except that I'm glad you didn't get out of the business, and thanks for writing great songs!"

♪ ♪

Following the phenomenal success of my first two albums, movie scripts started showing up in my mailbox. Maybe the writers and producers saw something in my music videos that led them to believe I'd be able to convincingly portray a character on the big screen. I was intrigued with the idea of acting in the movies—especially Westerns—but most of the early scripts I received were either pretty bad or didn't appeal to me. Still, I thought that my appearing in some films could expand the audience for my music, so we kept looking. I hoped to find the right sort of movie, something in which I could feel comfortable. After turning down several scripts that didn't seem right, I accepted a tiny role in a cowboy movie.

Immediately after the 1987 ACM award show, I flew to New Mexico to shoot my part in *Young Guns*, a Western set in 1878 and starring Emilio Estevez, Charlie Sheen, Lou Diamond Phillips, and Kiefer Sutherland. Those guys really were young guns, and they all went on to great acting careers. But my part in the movie was so small, my character didn't even have a name; the credits would list me as "Gatling Gun Operator." I wore long sideburns and a droopy mustache, and my dialogue included profound lines such as "Git 'em!" and "Shoot 'em!" But it was a great experience, and it whet my appetite for acting in more movies.

At the CMA Awards that October (1987), Don and Paul again won Song of the Year, this time for "Forever and Ever, Amen," and they were also nominated in that same category for writing "On the Other Hand." During their acceptance speech, Don quipped, "I think we're the first people to ever win and lose at the same time." Schlitz deadpanned, "I'm not real sure how to deal with it, but I'm going to ask Paul to go home and be philosophical and resigned. And I'm gonna go out and party all night long!"

I laughed because that statement showed the contrast between the two great collaborators. While they shared many similar attributes, they were quite different personalities, yet they both brought something special to everything they created. They wrote many great songs, but one they wrote for me, "Forever and Ever, Amen," would become my signature song, known to millions of people all around the world.

♪ ♫

Thanks to the success of *Storms of Life* and *Always & Forever*, everything in my career surged forward, pedal to the metal; things were happening fast, and we were on a roll. At one point, of twelve singles the record company released, ten of them soared to the #1 position on the charts. Almost immediately I was in demand for more shows, and it seemed that I was living on the road, working at least five shows a week, plus promoting the albums all day. It quickly got tiring. One night in the middle of the show, I wanted to say something relevant to the local crowd, but I forgot where we were. I turned around and walked back to L.D. between songs. "L.D., where are we?" I asked him.

"Well, Hoss," L.D. said, "you just finished 'My Heart Cracked (But It Did Not Break),' and I think 'No Place Like Home' is next." He thought I had lost my place in the set list for our show. I burst out laughing, went over to our bass player, Rocky Thacker, and asked him the same question. Rocky informed me that we were in Atlanta, Georgia, at the Omni Coliseum.

On another occasion I woke up on the bus in a new town and found that our road manager had signed us in to our motel and left a room key for me on the front table. The other guys had already gone in to the motel the night before, but I'd stayed in bed. I took the key and got out of the bus. I saw a motel to the right of the bus, so I walked over and put my key in the door matching the number on my key. But the door wouldn't open.

To my surprise, a woman then appeared in the doorway. "Can I help you?" she asked.

I was a bit flustered that a woman was in my room. "Well, I think I might have the wrong room."

It was only then that I noticed that there was another motel across the street. "I think you might be looking for a room over there." The woman kindly pointed and closed her door.

Sure enough, when I went across the street and inserted my key, the door opened. Right place, right time, right key.

Eventually we got our travel routine down to a system that operated like clockwork—well, most of the time. We became so accustomed to our schedule that we sometimes failed to communicate when we diverted from the norm.

On one occasion in Las Vegas, our bus driver, Ron Avis, parked our bus at our hotel and checked in to his room to catch some sleep before our trip to Los Angeles the next day.

The following morning, Ron awakened and returned to the bus, right on schedule. The rear door was closed, so Ron simply assumed that I was in the back as usual. He fired up the motor and headed for Los Angeles, about a five-hour drive away.

Unfortunately, I was still in the hotel in Vegas! When I came outside, I thought that Ron was pulling a practical joke on us—the bus was gone. Imagine Ron's surprise when he discovered that so was I! It was too long a trip for him to come back for me, so I hurriedly grabbed a flight to LA to make it in time for that evening's show.

A few weeks later, Ron was sleeping in a hotel again, and I woke up early. Just to mess with him, I moved the bus around to the hotel's rear parking lot. So when Ron came out of the hotel, the bus was nowhere to be seen. Ron thought someone had stolen it—with me as a hostage. I had a good laugh when he discovered the bus sitting safely behind the hotel.

♫ ♫

From the time I first got free of drugs and alcohol as a teenager, I had started taking better care of my body by engaging in more exercise. I enjoyed working out, and I would do it for hours. I really got into weight training in a big way. I didn't lift enormous amounts of weight, but I did repetitions of seated dumbbell curls until my shoulders ached.

Working out with weights was such a personal thing. I could shut myself off from all the craziness of the external world and focus on myself, my thoughts, my plans—even though I wasn't quite sure where they might take me.

Of course, burning so many calories by working out intensely meant that I could eat as much as I wanted—and I did. Despite my ravenous appetite, I always had a hard time keeping my weight up. Some of my friends worried constantly about every calorie they put in their mouths, and that was probably good advice for a lot of folks. But for me, I usually needed to put on a few pounds. The trick, of course, was to turn all those calories, protein, and carbohydrates into muscle rather than fat, so I worked hard at doing that. I had to work a little harder than most people, because I loved ice cream so much—especially vanilla ice cream slathered in hot fudge!

In communicating with our team, I always tried to use the pronoun *we* far more than *I*. I wasn't merely being modest. I believed that I had a God-given talent, but talent can only take a person so far. Ours was a group effort, and I knew that the success I enjoyed depended on the excellent work of a lot of other people. In the same way, I avoided making demands of or even giving instructions to our band or crew. Instead, I chose to *ask* for their help.

As far as I know, I never said, "Okay, guys. Here's what I'm going to do, so you guys adapt."

I preferred to ask, "Would you mind . . . doing this or that?"

I had witnessed other artists start out in the business with great humility and appreciation for everyone who helped them succeed. But then, little by little, they adopted an entitlement mentality in which they expected people to cater to them. I did not want that to happen to me, and I hoped that anyone who ever worked with me would know how much I valued his or her contributions. Over the years I have admired artists—such as Ricky Skaggs, Charlie Daniels, Garth Brooks, and others—who have treated their teams well. They have maintained a genuine humility despite their enormous popularity and success.

For the same reason, we always tried to treat our opening acts well. On some tours, the opening acts do not receive the same respect as the headliner. Sometimes the opening act won't be amped as loudly as the headliner or have access to the full complement of lights or video complex. We didn't do things that way, though. We did our best to make sure our opening acts had every resource that we could provide for their portion of the show. Not only did we believe this was the right thing to do, we also owned the show, so it was in our best interests to make sure that anyone onstage with us was set up to succeed.

We usually parked our bus and checked in to a hotel in the city where we were performing, but often I would not use the hotel room. I had a full kitchen, shower, and bedroom in the back of my private tour bus, and I was perfectly content to stay there. Lib, however, often made use of the hotel business office, and I took advantage of the workout facilities. The band, crew, and bus driver also enjoyed the hotel facilities.

Our tour manager, Jeff, typically stayed at the venue during the day, making sure that everything was set up and running properly. Shortly before showtime, he returned to the hotel to drive our bus to the concert location in time for a sound check while our bus driver slept in preparation to drive through the night.

Whenever possible, I chose to do a sound check, not merely for my benefit, but also so the sound technicians could "tune the room," making sure our sound was the best it could be for whatever particular venue we were playing. Oddly enough, we didn't play many of our own songs during sound check. Instead, the band and I enjoyed playing some Hank Williams Sr. songs such as "I'll Never Get Out of This World Alive" or Merle Haggard hits such as "Swingin' Doors," "The Bottle Let Me Down," or "I Think I'll Just Stay Here and Drink." We obviously didn't have time or the need to do those songs during our regular show, but we sure enjoyed playing them during sound check.

Occasionally I might have a late radio or television interview to do or some other responsibility that interfered with doing the sound check. On those occasions I'd ask Jeff, "When we get to the venue, would you mind checking with Terry (our sound man) and find out if it would be okay if I skipped sound check today?"

I wasn't necessarily seeking permission—I was, after all, the boss—but I didn't want to disrupt everyone else's schedule or cause hurt feelings. Nor did I want to blow off the sound check if the building was difficult or required some unusual sound reinforcement to give our fans the best show possible.

We did our first European tour in 1987, beginning in Dublin and Paris, playing to sold-out venues everywhere we went. The auditoriums in Europe were much smaller and more intimate than those we were accustomed to playing in America, mostly around twenty-five hundred to three thousand seats.

We weren't really sure how the Europeans would accept our music, but at the show in Paris, the crowd was wonderfully enthusiastic. We closed to a standing ovation and did three encores, and the audience still wanted more!

"What are we going to do?" I turned to the band. "I don't have any other songs prepared!"

"You gotta sing something."

I looked to my right and saw Jeff Davis standing offstage. "Turn the house lights up!" I called to Jeff, thinking that the crowd would get the idea that the show was over.

"They *are* up!" he called back. The crowd continued to roar.

That's when all those Haggard songs that we enjoyed playing for sound check came in handy. With the crowd becoming even more rowdy, Jeff yelled, "Hoss, do 'I Think I'll Just Stay Here and Drink!'" I knew the song well, and so did L.D. It was the perfect call for the moment—a rowdy, upbeat Merle Haggard classic—and the French audience loved it.

It was an electrifying experience. That French crowd might not have understood English, but they understood traditional country music.

We also toured portions of Canada that year with the up-and-coming band Highway 101 as our opening act. As a prank one night, our drummer, Tommy Rivelli, poured baby powder all over the snare drum head of Highway 101's drums prior to the show. When the lights came up, every time Highway's drummer, Michael Scott "Cactus" Moser, hit the snare drum, it produced a puff of powder right in his face. We all got a good laugh out of it—everybody except Cactus, that is.

On the road no good prank goes unanswered, so the following evening, as I hit the high notes in the chorus of "I Told You So," I heard the audience burst out in laughter. *That's odd*, I thought. *Did I do something wrong?*

I turned around to look at our band, and when I did, I saw Phil Kaufman, Highway 101's tour manager, riding a bicycle all the way across the stage, right in front of the musicians. I tried to keep singing, but it was difficult to remain serious with Phil pedaling behind me, making his way back across the stage and out the exit. The crowd went nuts, and Cactus had the last laugh.

Back in the States, during that time, I worked a lot as the opening act for George Jones. George and I grew to be great friends. Oddly enough, I discovered that while George was the quintessential entertainer onstage, keeping an audience mesmerized with his voice and stories, he was actually kind of shy offstage. He didn't like to hang out—not with me, not with anyone except his wife, Nancy. But I knew he loved me because every so often, without informing me ahead of time, George would show up at one of my shows just to hear me sing.

"You are the real thing, Randy," he told me over and over. "You're gonna be big. You are bringing back real country music. I think you are gonna be one of the greatest ever!"

I'd smile sheepishly. "Oh, George, you're the greatest. I know that."

"Naw, son," George would say. "You got it goin' on. Keep it up!"

I loved performing at concerts with him, even though he could be a tad set in his ways. George always emphatically told the stage manager, "I want to be on by seven o'clock so I can be off by eight." Some people on tour thought it was because George wanted to perform while the audience was primed and ready. That wasn't it at all. George just didn't want to miss reruns of *The Andy Griffith Show* on TV.

One night there was a delay, and I didn't get on till late, so that automatically pushed George's time back too. Was George okay with that? Nope. In the middle of my set, I saw the stage manager waving at me frantically, motioning me off the stage. Apparently, George had been giving the stage manager a hard time, saying, "If I'm not onstage by seven, I'm not going on."

George went on at seven that night. He did his hour-long performance, and then I went back to finish my portion of the show.

After we had toured together for a while, George decided I should close the show. I felt the same sort of reluctance as I had with Conway. I sure didn't want to follow George Jones! So before one of our shows together, I went over to George's bus. "George, can I talk to you?" I asked.

"Sure, son," George said. "Have a seat." He pointed to a seat opposite his as he leaned back in his plush leather chair.

I sat down on the edge of the chair and leaned forward nervously. "George, I know you want me to close the show, but please don't do this to me. The people are all going to leave after you're done."

George smiled the smile that had given him his nickname, the Possum. "No, son, they ain't gonna leave," he said. "You're hot as a pistol right now. You'll do a good show. I ain't worried about it, so don't you worry about it."

"But George, you're the star."

"Oh, nonsense. There ain't no such thing as a star."

I hemmed and hawed and tried to talk my way out of closing the show, but George insisted. So I closed the show, and it went well. Meanwhile, as I was doing an encore, George was already back in his bus watching television.

If George was laid back, his wife, Nancy, was the opposite. She was spunky and outspoken, and when she and Lib went toe-to-toe, I knew that Lib had met her match. It happened at George Jones Country, an outdoor park and music venue owned by the Joneses in Texas. We were scheduled to appear on the Sunday lineup for a weekend festival that began on Thursday.

When we arrived at the venue, Lib noticed the marquee advertising all the performers' names throughout the weekend, including George Strait, George Jones, and me as the featured artist on Sunday. Lib marched right over to Nancy's on-site office. "Um, I need to talk to you," she said.

"All right, Lib," Nancy replied. "But I should warn you that I've been up since Thursday night. I'm tired, George is drunk at the house, and I have to go feed him to even get him to do the show."

"Well, I see on the marquee that you have Randy's name advertising the whole weekend."

"Yeah, but he only works on Sunday," Nancy said. "The sign says, 'Sunday, Randy Travis.'"

Lib cocked her head slightly in her managerial pose and said, "Well, we're going to need a little more money."

"For what?" Nancy asked.

"Because you've been using his name to advertise the entire weekend," Lib repeated.

"Lib, get out of my face and go back to your bus," Nancy said. "I have to go sober up a man just to get the show going."

"Well . . . Randy is not going on unless we get some more money."

"That's not Randy speaking," Nancy stated. "That's you."

"No, I've already talked to Randy," Lib said.

"Then leave," Nancy said. She gestured adamantly toward Lib, swiping against her hair. Lib had a penchant for wearing blond wigs, and when Nancy's hand flew past Lib, she inadvertently knocked Lib's wig right off her head.

Lib was horribly embarrassed and even more irate. "I'm going to get Randy," she yelled. "We're leavin'!"

Just then I walked into the office. "What's going on?" I asked.

Worse yet, somebody must have told George, because he staggered into the office and bellowed, "What's going on down here?"

"Nothin'," I answered quietly.

"Nothing at all," Lib said, suddenly demure in the presence of George as she tried to straighten her wig, not quite succeeding.

The Possum wrinkled his forehead and looked at Lib's crooked hair. "Well, I heard that somethin' was goin' on down here, and I need to know what it is."

"I was just talking to Nancy," Lib told him. "Everything's fine." Lib turned toward me and said, "Randy, we need to get back to the bus so you can get dressed for the show."

I did the show, and later, when we heard the full story, George and I had a good laugh about the incident. George knew that I would sing for him for free. But I'm not sure Lib and Nancy ever made up.

Between 1987 and 1988, I made the transition from being an opening act for George Jones, the Judds, Reba McEntire, and Conway Twitty to becoming a headliner myself. By 1989 we were headlining along with Tammy Wynette and the Judds for a number of shows sponsored by General Motors Corporation. By the end of that year, we were doing our own events, booked and promoted by our own company, with K.T. Oslin as our opening act. We were packing out arenas such as the Palace of Auburn Hills near Detroit and Reunion Arena in Dallas.

On the first day of fall, a warm Sunday afternoon in September 1987, we were scheduled to do an outdoor show at Red Boiling Springs, Tennessee, at the Deerwood Amphitheater, which was basically a hillside with a small stage at the bottom. About three thousand people had gathered to hear our show, which included the McCarter Sisters, who were my labelmates at Warner Bros. and with whom I had worked often. The folks who came for the show were real friendly. Most had brought their own lawn chairs or blankets to sit out on the sun-drenched hillside.

The whole atmosphere felt like a large church "singin' and dinner on the ground." Warner even hosted a picnic lunch for us and a number of guests out in a beautiful area where they had set up a small tent and picnic tables, away from the crowd and secluded by trees. Our publicist, Evelyn Shriver, was there, as was Martha Sharp and several other Warner Bros. representatives. After everyone had their food, Jim Ed Norman, head of Warner's Nashville division, announced that he had a special presentation he wanted to make. Kyle Lehning was traveling with us that weekend, and he caught the entire episode on video.

Dressed in a white shirt and khaki slacks, Jim Ed tried to sound formal. "We're here once again to recognize Randy's singular achievement," he began. "Today, we are recognizing another plateau." Jim Ed turned to me and asked, "Randy, do you realize that in the last two years, you have sold over three million records?" The picnic group applauded loudly.

"Today we would like to recognize your latest efforts," Jim Ed continued. "Your success has only been eclipsed by one thing. That is, that through all of this, you remain a gentleman and a kind man and a man who is willing to work with those people around you. Everyone at Warner Bros. is proud of your success, but we are equally as proud of the way you have handled your success." Jim Ed then presented me with a framed platinum album of *Always & Forever* in commemoration of sales of more than a million albums.

As I accepted the plaque, I was truly surprised. "I didn't realize that we had sold more than three million records with only two albums in such a short period of time," I said.

I noticed the twinkle in Jim Ed's eyes as he went on, "Randy, in our tradition of horsing around, we thought it would be appropriate that we hand the reigning king of the 'new tradition' the reins of this horse, named today as New Tradition." As Jim Ed was speaking, someone brought a fully-grown horse up behind us. Jim Ed handed me the reins of the gift horse and quipped, "We've checked his teeth, and you can look him in the mouth."

I took the reins and began running my hands over the animal's mane. "Well, thank you," I said, still stunned that the record company had given me a horse! "Man, he is beautiful."

"You can call him Platinum Harry," Jim Ed said. "Or you can call him Always and Forever or Forever and Ever, Amen, or whatever you want. Do you want to go ride?"

"Yeah," I said. I guided the horse into a clearing where I could walk him away from the group.

Platinum Harry was a beautiful, well-bred animal, but after we got him back home, nobody could ride that horse, not even me! He was bred as a racehorse, but he was the worst riding horse we ever had, continually changing gaits. I kept him for a while but finally gave up trying to get him to cooperate. My brother Dennis couldn't handle him either. We even took the horse to North Carolina to see if my dad—an expert horse trainer—could do anything with him. I'd never seen a horse like that before, one that was so erratic. It was almost as if he was trained to mess with me.

♪ ♪

On December 12, 1987, I volunteered for a hitch in the service—not as a soldier, but as a performer with the USO. My band and I would do a series of concerts for our troops before Christmas, hopefully bringing them a taste of home. The USO chose to send us to Fliegerhorst Kaserne, a US army base in Germany, to perform for our military stationed there. We took along the entire band, the sound guys, plus the McCarters. We crammed as much interaction with the troops as possible into the two days we were on the base. We toured the flight training facility with proud officers as guides. Later we performed a two-hour show in an aircraft hangar for a large crowd of soldiers, then I spent a long time talking and signing autographs for them. I hadn't realized so many of them knew and enjoyed my music. A number expressed heartfelt emotions that had surfaced after our show. To me, that is what country music is all about—touching people's hearts.

That was the first of five USO Christmas tours we did. Over the years we performed for service men and women at Guantanamo Bay, Cuba, and in Alaska, Japan, Turkey, Germany, South Korea, and a number of other places where there were US troops stationed far from home at Christmas. We also did a number of performances aboard American ships deployed at sea. Country star Patty Loveless joined me on several of those trips, which usually got us back home just in time to celebrate Christmas. Our soldiers, sailors, and airmen were always so appreciative and were fantastic audiences wherever we went. And of course, the song that they asked for over and over again was "Forever and Ever, Amen."

11 ——————————————— THE SHOW

The first two years after the release of *Storms of Life* were a whirlwind. With a tour schedule that kept me out on the road, plus magazine interviews and television appearances on everything from *Today, The Tonight Show Starring Johnny Carson, Good Morning America, Late Night with David Letterman,* and *Nashville Now* to *Sesame Street,* we were going all the time. Lib rarely turned down an interview opportunity for me, even if it meant foregoing rest, relaxation, or personal time. Add to that songwriting and recording, working with Bill Mayne of Warner's promotion department to do station identification spots for radio stations around the country, and visiting with key vendors along with Neal Spielberg of Warner's sales and marketing department, and there wasn't time for much else.

Our touring show expanded exponentially to keep up with the success of the albums. We had started by traveling with a few instruments in a bread truck and van. Then we bought a single used tour bus and, later, another bus for the band. By 1988 our tour had grown to five tour buses and four to five production tractor-trailers filled with equipment and merchandise. We had more than fifty people on the road with us at any given time—that's fifty people to feed, lodge, and pay—as our traveling troupe crisscrossed the USA.

My performance onstage focused on singing. I didn't shake, rattle, roll, or dance around the stage. In fact, I usually moved very little while I was singing, staying behind the microphone stand until near the end of the show. Then, I loved taking a handheld microphone so I could reach out and shake hands with members of the audience who were seated or standing up close to the stage. Occasionally, when it was possible, I really enjoyed going into the audience during a song.

I also liked adding a few lighter moments to the show. The team at Warner cringed a little when I told a joke or a life story, not because they were off-color—I never did that—but because they were usually corny. But I knew that, and I'd grin openly as the audience groaned or laughed along with me. I had stacks of joke books, and I scoured them, searching for just the right stories to tell our audiences. I didn't inject the jokes into the show arbitrarily, though; I planned strategically to put them where they would work best. For instance, I often tried to tell a good joke when the band members needed a little extra time to set up for the next song. I loved to laugh, and I figured the audience did too.

Prior to each tour, I spent a good amount of time working through the song sequence, deciding ahead of time what songs I wanted to perform at what point in the show and even where the jokes or stories might fit well between the songs. Although we liked including new songs, audiences always wanted us to play our hit songs they'd heard on the radio. That was okay with me. I felt that people were paying their hard-earned money to come out to our shows, so I wanted to make sure to give them our best, even if they had heard some of our material in previous shows.

Jeff Davis wasn't really a musician, but he had a great sense of what a good show should look and sound like. So I usually checked with him once I felt I had my plans for the show figured out. "Hey, Hoss, I'm gonna fax you our set list," I'd say to him over the phone. "Take a look at it and let me know what you think." As tour manager, Jeff could see the audiences' response—or lack of response—to various songs and stories almost as well as I did. Maybe, because he wasn't performing, he had a better perspective. So he had a good handle on what worked and what didn't, and I valued his opinion and advice. Together, I thought we constructed a pretty good show.

Every once in a while, though, something would go wrong. For instance, we were right in the middle of a sold-out show at the Silver Legacy Resort Casino in Reno, Nevada, when I forgot the words to the second verse of "I

Told You So." I had written the song and had been performing it for more than a decade, but try as I might, the words simply would not come to mind. I turned toward the band guys with a panicked "somebody help me" look. Several of them were mouthing the words, but I couldn't read their lips from my microphone location. I tried to fake it, but that only caused me to break up laughing.

The audience was wonderfully gracious to me, though. Everyone in the room could tell that I was lost, so I just admitted it. Porter Wagoner had once told L.D., "The audience loves to see you make a mistake—if you'll just admit it." So that's what I did. And Porter was right. The audience laughed along with me . . . and sang me through it, singing the lyrics to my song for me, and eventually, I remembered the words and got it right.

The following night, when we got to "I Told You So" again, the same thing happened! I simply could not recall the words to my own song—a song I had sung hundreds of times. Once again, the audience was kind to me. "If there's anyone here who happened to attend the show last night," I said, "this is not a regular part of our show, for me to forget the words to a song that most of you know." The audience cracked up and forgave me again.

Richard Logsdon, one of our exceptionally creative graphics guys on the tour who designed our sets, T-shirts, other merchandise, and some of our album covers, said afterward, "Hoss, that was special. The audience felt like they got something unusual. They loved that mistake so much, maybe we ought to put it in the show!"

Big things were happening fast as my career continued to skyrocket. On January 25, 1988, I brought home four "favorite" awards at the American Music Awards. And less than a month later, on February 20, 1988, I appeared as the musical guest on NBC-TV's *Saturday Night Live*. The show was hosted by the actor Tom Hanks, so Tom and I recorded a ridiculous but hilarious promotional spot. In what was an obvious play on *Hee Haw*'s Roy Clark and Buck Owens, I said, "I'm a-pickin'," to which Tom responded, "I'm a-grinnin'"—and we both stood there with goofy smiles on our faces. I had a blast doing the show and sang two songs, "Forever and Ever, Amen" and "What'll You Do about Me."

Our concerts were drawing huge crowds, too, and on February 25, 1988, we set an attendance record for a country music performance at the

Houston Livestock Show and Rodeo, drawing nearly fifty thousand fans. To concert promoters around the world, that was really *big*!

As much as I enjoyed the enthusiastic audiences that packed the Astrodome for the show, one of the biggest gigs in country music, it was a tough venue for me. The huge arena had one of the longest reverbs of any venue I'd ever played, and the deep rodeo dust on its floor adversely affected my voice, at times leaving me almost hoarse. So I either stayed on the bus or in the Houston Astros' locker room, where our makeshift dressing rooms were, until right before showtime.

Prior to the 1988 show, I was sitting on a bench with my guitar in my draped-off section of the tile-walled locker room, when I heard Bill Mayne call my name from outside.

"Come on back," I called. When Bill walked in, I quickly greeted him and said, "Man, Kyle sent me this new song, and I'm learning it. Tell me what you think of it."

I sat there in front of the lockers and played and sang an incredibly well-written song by Paul Overstreet and Don Schlitz that incorporated a number of images about love, all drawn from nature and the beauty around us. The song was called, "Deeper than the Holler."

Bill later said that was the moment when he had a country music epiphany. He realized afresh that the power in country music is a simple but powerful lyric.

"That song is a hit!" Bill said. "I'm calling Kyle. As soon as you get home, you need to get into the studio and cut that."

Bill was right. We put the song on our album called *Old 8 x 10*, and it shot up the charts.

I was thrilled with the acceptance of our "new traditional" style of country music, as pundits were calling my straight-ahead, stone-country style. That's all I wanted to sing and all I knew how to be. When I stopped in to the Warner Bros. offices one day, Neal Spielberg was really excited. "Randy, look at this!" he said as he opened *Billboard* magazine. I was shocked to discover that my new album was #5 on *Billboard*'s Top 100 pop charts. The folks at Warner were celebrating, but I was irate. "Pop charts? What's it doing on there? Get it off there," I said sternly. "I'm not a pop singer! I'm a country singer."

"Randy, they aren't saying you are a pop artist," said Janice Azrak, a Warner publicity representative who happened to be in the room. "They are saying your album is the #5 album in the USA in all genres."

"Oh. Okay. I guess that's all right then."

♪ ♫

In June 1988, we participated in the Country Music Association's giant promotion in Europe. Known as "Route '88," it was a two-week push in which various country acts played in and around London. The acts were promoted by Paul Finn, manager of a tremendously popular European group known as Level 42. Paul was the perennial winner of the CMA International Award for his work promoting concerts in Europe. We played Dublin, a city in Wales, and several other UK cities with magnificent old theaters. For the grand finale, we were performing in London's Royal Albert Hall along with our opening act, Kathy Mattea. When I took the stage, I looked out at the crowd in the majestic venue and could hardly believe my eyes. There, seated in "the Queen's box," were Mick Jagger and his then girlfriend, Jerry Hall. I rarely got nervous doing a show anymore, but to have a music icon like Mick Jagger in the audience made me really anxious.

Mick and Jerry stayed for nearly the entire show. Then, just as we came to the close, we started into "Forever and Ever, Amen," and the crowd roared its approval. By the middle of the song, I glanced up and noticed that Mick and Jerry were gone. I thought they may have left early to avoid the crowd.

Nope. Although I didn't know it at the time, they had made their way backstage, and Jeff Davis had bumped right into them in one of the narrow hallways. "Oh, sorry, Mick," Jeff apologized. "I was in a hurry to get to the stage and didn't see you there. I'm Randy's tour manager."

"No problem, mate," Mick said to Jeff. "In fact, you're just the person we are looking for. Is there any chance that we can say hello to Randy after the show?"

Jeff was always protective of me, but this was one time when he didn't have to think twice about a meet and greet. "Why, sure, Mick," Jeff said. He took Mick and Jerry back to my dressing room.

After the show everyone gathered in the dressing room. Jeff introduced me to Mick, and the two of us sat down in the corner of the room. "What a great show!" Mick said. "I love the soulfulness of real country music, not the cheap rock-and-roll imitators."

"Well, thank you very much, Mick," I said. I smiled as the fleeting thought crossed my mind that one of music's most famous icons enjoyed traditional country music, when for ten years or more in my early career, I was "too country."

Mick and I talked about the venue. "This is a fantastic old auditorium," I said. "Have you played here?"

"Oh yeah," Mick said. "About twenty years ago."

"You haven't played here since? Why is that?"

"Well, they had a big problem with a rock-and-roll show here one time, so they banned most rock-and-roll bands from playing here," Mick said, his eyes twinkling.

"Really? When was that?" I asked.

Mick smiled mischievously. "About twenty years ago."

I busted up laughing.

"Jerry and I are going out for dinner," Mick said. "Would you and Jeff and your lady like to join us?"

I looked at Lib and Jeff. "Can we do that?"

"Sure," Lib said. "We have a Warner media event to do first, but we'd be glad to join you afterward."

"That's okay," Mick replied. "We'll just go along with you, and then we'll go eat."

Mick and Jerry, Lib, Jeff, Evelyn, and I made our way to the huge British media meet and greet. When I walked into the room along with Mick Jagger, the British press went berserk. Mick soon realized that he was drawing too much attention and stealing our thunder, so as I fielded questions and shook hands with members of the media, he graciously whispered to Jeff, "Hey, mate, we'll go ahead to the restaurant and meet you there." He gave Jeff the name of the restaurant, and then he and Jerry slipped out of the room.

Meanwhile the media event dragged on and on. Everyone in the room, it seemed, wanted to talk to me. We knew it was an important press conference for country music, so I wanted to give it my best. But the British press just kept peppering me with questions and didn't show signs of stopping. Realizing that we were running extremely long and not wishing to be rude to Mick and Jerry, Jeff went outside to the pay phone and called the restaurant. But the person who answered the phone would not acknowledge that Mick Jagger was in the building and refused to pass along our message. We never could get in touch with them after that, and to this day Mick Jagger might think that we blew them off.

Sorry, Mick and Jerry, we really wanted to join you. Call me!

♫ ♫

Although my third album, *Old 8 x 10*, didn't sell quite as well as *Always & Forever*, on September 13, 1988, it was certified as both a gold album and a platinum album, indicating sales of more than a million units. One of the most popular songs from that album, in addition to the title song, was "Deeper than the Holler," the song I'd sung for Bill Mayne back in Houston. It had released as a single on October 21, 1988. A few weeks earlier, on October 8, another of my songs, "Honky Tonk Moon," had hit #1 on the *Billboard* charts.

Then at the 1988 CMA Awards, held October 23, I was nominated for the Male Vocalist of the Year along with George Strait, Ricky Van Shelton, Hank Williams Jr., and Vern Gosdin. My song "I Told You So" was also nominated for Single of the Year and Song of the Year. Dolly Parton presented the nominees for Male Vocalist in her own inimitable style. I was sitting on the front row when Dolly, wearing a white, low-cut dress, stepped down off the stage. To the amazement and delight of everyone in the audience, she sat down right in my lap! Now that sort of thing will get a fella's attention.

A lot of people may have thought that I knew what Dolly was going to do, that I had received advance notice so I could be prepared. Nothing could be further from the truth. I was as surprised as anyone in the building or the millions watching on television.

I couldn't help but laugh nervously as Dolly put her hand on my shoulder and said to the audience, "Folks, you know that this guy is single." Dolly playfully looked me in the eyes as she continued. "And I just want you to know that if I was twenty years younger, and I was single, and you liked little blonds with big hair and big . . ."—Dolly paused just long enough for effect, before saying "ideas," evoking a huge laugh from the audience—"I'd be giving you a run for your money, Randy Travis!"

A short time later, Dolly announced, "The Male Vocalist of the Year is . . . Randy Travis!"

I made my way onto the stage and stood behind the microphone. "After all that," I said, "I find myself trying to remember what I just won!"

12 ——— DEEPER THAN THE HOLLER

At the 1989 Country Music Awards show, I was asked to present the Female Vocalist of the Year award. Anne Murray graciously introduced me, saying, "Since Randy Travis sort of appeared out of thin air three or four years ago, he's been a superstar. He keeps recording one big hit after another, and he's won all the awards in the book, and that's great. But what's even greater is that he's still a very modest and shy country boy. Let me show you what happened last year to this shy country boy."

The onstage screen suddenly filled with a replay of Dolly Parton's show-stealing seat in my lap from the previous year's award show. When the clip finished, Anne Murray asked, "Do you suppose he's recovered yet? Ladies and gentlemen, Randy Travis!"

I bounded out onstage, ready to present my award. But what I didn't know was that Dolly Parton followed me out. I stepped up to the microphone, holding the award envelope in my hand, oblivious to what everyone in the audience saw—Dolly sneaking up behind me. "Thank you," I said to the applauding audience. I was waiting for the music to stop playing so I could announce the nominees for Female Vocalist of the Year, when in my peripheral vision I saw something. I turned to my left, and there was Dolly—again!

"Ah, hi, Randy," Dolly said.

"Oh no!" I said as I fell slightly back, with a laugh.

"I just wanted to come out and make sure that you didn't need me," Dolly said.

"Well, I might . . ." I said.

"I'm not really gonna horn in on your part," Dolly said. "I just wanted to come out and say hi."

I gave Dolly a brief hug and said, "Great to see you."

"The devil made me do it," she quipped as she retreated from the stage to tremendous applause from the audience.

I paused for a moment and tried to regain my composure before attempting to announce the nominees. "It's a tough job," I said to the audience with a big smile. Then, as each artist's picture and a sound bite of her singing filled the screen, I announced the nominees.

"And the winner is . . ." I opened the envelope and read, "Kathy Mattea."

♫ ♫

Like most big music tours, we carried enormous sound and lighting along with us in our four eighteen-wheelers, most of which were given over to staging elements. We constantly asked ourselves, "How can we make our show better?"

Most people who came out to our shows probably never anticipated that a Randy Travis concert would be cutting edge. After all, we didn't use pyrotechnics, lasers, dancers, or even background singers other than our guys in the band. We simply stood on the stage and played some great songs. But we were state-of-the-art when it came to sound and lights. In fact, we were the first country music show—and possibly the first in all music genres—to incorporate our own huge IMAG (short for "image magnification") video production in our tour on a nightly basis.

We had seen the technology used at big festivals and the Marlboro shows (huge concerts sponsored by Phillip Morris USA, the manufacturer of Marlboro cigarettes and other brands), using large-lens cameras and projection systems to put the performers' onstage images up on the big screens so the crowds could see better. Such technology is common nowadays, but in November 1988, we set a new standard in country music concerts by using the IMAG system in Starkville, Mississippi, at the arena on the campus of

Mississippi State University. Today, every major music tour carries their own similar technology.

On November 29, 1988, we left for another USO tour, this one taking us to Alaska, Japan, and South Korea, where we performed for the troops as part of a special pre-Christmas celebration. While we were in South Korea, one of our liaisons asked me, "Randy, would you be interested in going up to the demilitarized zone? It is quite a contrast from Seoul and some of the other urban centers of South Korea."

"Sure," I said, with no idea of the dangers surrounding such a venture. "Let's do it."

We traveled north toward the border with North Korea, and the liaison provided documents to the officials, who allowed us into the area. The moment we stepped into the DMZ, I noticed immediately that everything looked dark and dreary to the north. Then, when I looked up at a stark building ahead of us, I saw soldiers in every window wielding ominous-looking, heavy-duty rifles and AK 47s.

"Don't look at them," our guide said under his breath, "and whatever you do, do not try to take a picture."

That day was a stark reminder of the freedoms we often take for granted in America and the dangerous conditions in which our soldiers often serve—all to guarantee our safety and liberty. I've always had a great appreciation for our military, but seeing the danger up close made me understand their commitment even more.

On January 20, 1989, I performed in Washington for the inauguration of President George H. W. Bush. The formal gala featured a lot of country music by artists such as the Oak Ridge Boys, Crystal Gayle, Lee Greenwood, Loretta Lynn, and others. I was honored to be invited.

A week later, on January 28, "Deeper than the Holler" hit #1 on the charts. Then, on January 30, 1989, we picked up three more awards at the American Music Awards, including Favorite Country Album for *Always & Forever*. Although I wasn't quite as bashful now about being on national television, I was nonetheless overwhelmed and appreciative of the fans' acknowledgment of our music.

While working in California, I met Chuck Norris, the famous martial arts champion. Chuck was starring in movies at that time, but he was also still teaching martial arts to advanced students. Chuck taught me some basic karate moves, mostly kicks and punches, and he recommended lots of stretches for physical flexibility. He introduced me to his friends Hélio and Rickson Gracie, famed icons of Brazilian jiu-jitsu, who had a studio in Los Angeles along with their cousins, the five Machado brothers. All those guys were beyond tough. Even Chuck said they were some of the toughest martial artists he'd ever encountered. I had gotten interested in martial arts at that point, so Chuck invited me to work out with him and the Machado brothers.

One of Chuck's friends was a world-famous body builder and actor, Arnold Schwarzenegger, and the two of them often worked out together. When I first met Arnold, I asked him about his workout routine. Arnold told me that his diet was equally as important an element as his exercise program. "What you put into your body is more important than what you put out in exercise," he said.

I told Arnold that I had trouble maintaining my weight. While some people struggled with obesity, I was chronically underweight for my size.

"Well, what do you eat?" Arnold asked me. "And how much do you eat? Do you eat enough?"

I had never considered that. I'd assumed that as long as I worked out I'd be in good shape. But to Arnold, diet was the most important part of a healthy fitness program. Of course, he worked out pretty hard too.

During the week of the Grammys in Los Angeles, I went to a gym to work out with Arnold and former NFL defensive tackle Lyle Alzado.

"I'm a big country music fan," Arnold told me as muscles rippled all over him. It seemed that his entire body was solid rock. But he definitely wasn't muscle-bound. During our workout he moved so fast I could barely keep up with him. He didn't pause for a breather between sets; he just moved from one exercise to the other. Trying to follow his lead, I almost got lightheaded for a while, but I was determined to match him. Lyle was right with Arnold, too, keeping up with him step for step. He was even bigger than Arnold, yet his agility was incredible.

Afterward I had lunch with Arnold and his then wife, Maria Shriver. Arnold invited me to join him in the presidential physical-fitness campaign, "The Great American Workout," encouraged by President Bush to demonstrate the fun and benefits of exercise. I agreed without hesitation. Picking up on my workout enthusiasm, Warner Bros. put out a Randy Travis promotional T-shirt with the slogan, "I Worked Out." I don't know how many we distributed, but I know I worked hard to get one.

In 1989 I also filmed a really fun commercial for Coca-Cola, which was strategically planned to air during the nationally telecast American Music Awards show on January 20, 1990. In the commercial, two cute young women are in a gas station convenience store watching a video on TV of me singing, "You can't beat the real thing," when my bus pulls up out front. One girl remains enamored with the video and doesn't even see me when I walk in and say hello to the other. She responds with a smile and a starry-eyed, "Hi."

"Randy Travis," the girl staring at the screen coos. "He's the best. What a voice."

I smile at the second girl and reach for a Coke as girl number one asks, "Do you think he's as cute in person?"

Looking at me dreamily, the second girl replies, "Uh-huh."

"What I wouldn't give to meet a guy like him."

Her friend says to her, "Do you want to ring up this Coke Classic?" as I take a long swallow of my Coke and place the rest of my six-pack of Coke on the counter.

The first girl turns and sees me in front of her, her eyes widen, and she bites on her lip in surprise.

"Thank you," I say and head back toward the bus, leaving the girls standing together arm in arm.

That commercial was like a mini movie in thirty seconds. But it took a lot longer than that to film. Originally, I had written a short jingle for the commercial, but Coke came back to me and asked for something more of a country song. Don Schlitz and I wrote a short song, and Coke said, "We like it, but don't be so specific."

Okay. We tried again.

Coke and I went back and forth several times, and the night before I was supposed to record the song, I called Don and said, "I need help." It was about one o'clock in the morning. We started singing back and forth on the phone, working on the song. We finally finished, and I recorded the song when the sun came up.

Coke filmed a sixty-second version of the commercial and a thirty-second version, but it took us three full *days* to shoot all the segments. We shot getting off the bus, walking to the counter, and drinking the Coke. I took about forty swallows of Coke as we put it all together. But I loved the result.

I really enjoyed doing commercials. Later I did one for Folgers Coffee in which I sang a song describing life on the bus and, of course, "the best part of waking up." I also did a major advertising campaign for Discover credit cards, in which Discover asked me to create a piece of art they could print on their cards. I painted a picture of our ranch home in Santa Fe, and they featured it as one of their Private Issue cards, which showed off the creativity of a few actors, sports figures, and musicians each year.

Expanding my horizons through filming movies or commercials or engaging in other art forms sparked my creativity. Some people didn't understand that and thought that I was merely making some extra money or wasting my time. But I felt that my ventures outside the usual music avenues expanded my audience, so I just did what I thought was right for me. I learned early on that I couldn't satisfy everyone, no matter how much I tried, and that good people may have differences of opinion.

For instance, the Coke commercial ran on January 20, 1990, and people loved it. The next day, *US* magazine came out with an article stating that Dwight Yoakam and Clint Black were "in" and that Jerry Lee Lewis and Randy Travis were "out." And the day after that, for the third straight year, we led all country music award winners at the American Music Awards, bringing home three trophies, including the Favorite Country Single prize for "Deeper than the Holler."

Oh, the difference a day makes!

13 —————— HEROES AND FRIENDS

Even as an adult, I still felt like a kid who wanted to be a cowboy. I admired the cowboy lifestyle, and of course I loved horses. I also developed an appreciation for guns, target shooting at bottles on fences, and especially practicing quick-draw techniques, pulling a six-shooter out of a holster strapped slightly above my knee and returning it with various spins. I'd practice for hours at a time, and I got pretty good at it. I'd never been much of hunter—I didn't want to shoot an animal, much less dress it after I'd killed it—but I did enjoy target shooting.

From the time I was a kid, I'd loved Roy Rogers, my singing-cowboy hero. As a boy I watched Saturday morning reruns of *The Roy Rogers Show*, featuring Roy and his wife, Dale Evans. Even in the story lines, Roy and Dale were always models of integrity, standing for what was good and right and honorable. It wasn't until many years later that I learned they weren't really acting, that their personas on the show were almost identical to the way they functioned offscreen, in everyday life. Their character stemmed from their Christian faith. They didn't have to act like "good guys." That's who they were.

So when I began thinking about an album I wanted to put together called *Heroes and Friends*, on which I hoped to share duets with some of the people who had influenced me, Roy was one of the first people to come to mind. Roy was already pushing eighty years of age, but I really wanted to sing with him. I told him, "Roy, it would be one of the greatest honors of my life if you'd allow me to sing 'Happy Trails' with you." ("Happy Trails," written by Dale, had been the theme song of their show.)

"Why, sure, Randy. We can do that," Roy responded without a moment of hesitation.

When Roy came to Nashville to record his part on the album, he stayed at our home. After dinner one night, he and I went upstairs to my song-writing studio to shoot pool—one of my favorite things to do. We covered our cue stick tips with blue chalk, placed all the balls in the triangular rack, and I politely asked Roy if he wanted to break—that is, to hit the first shot on a game of eight ball. "Naw, you go right ahead," Roy drawled.

I leaned over, took a firm, straight stroke, and broke, sending billiard balls in every direction, with several landing in the various pockets. I was playing especially well that night, and in that first game, just by luck, I went on to run the table without ever giving Roy a single shot.

As the last ball dropped into the side pocket, I looked up rather sheepishly at Roy and almost wanted to apologize for playing so well. "I'm real sorry, Roy."

Roy Rogers just stood there for a few seconds, holding the cue stick in his hands as he shook his head. Then with his low-key, sardonic sense of humor, Roy said, "Son, signs of a misspent youth."

I chuckled. "Yeah, I guess so."

The next time Don Schlitz was at the house, I told him that story as we were shooting a game of pool. Naturally, we went back over to the writing area and wrote a song called "Signs of a Misspent Youth."

Not long after that, I asked Don if he could write a "little bitty song" that we could use as the lead-in to the *Heroes and Friends* album of duets. Don said, "Sure, let's do it." Don outdid himself, and he and I wrote the song, "Heroes and Friends," a simple, straight-ahead, "Randy Travis" song. Both of us had grown up watching cowboys on television, especially Roy Rogers, so we wrote the second verse with Roy in mind.

Don and I were just two buddies tossing around ideas that day and weren't even trying to create a hit song. When Kyle Lehning worked his magic on it, though, the song took on a whole new character. We not only used it as a lead-in to the album; we used it as a reprise, too, to close out the album. Additionally, Warner Bros. sent the song out to radio stations as a single.

The *Heroes and Friends* album was truly a work of love. In addition to Roy Rogers, I got to sing with Dolly Parton, George Jones, Conway Twitty, Merle Haggard, Vern Gosdin, Loretta Lynn, Willie Nelson, Kris Kristofferson, Tammy Wynette, and B.B. King. Even actor Clint Eastwood joined me for some commonsense advice in a duet: (You don't reach for the honey without) "Smokin' the Hive."

When the great B.B. King came in to do a song, he seemed unusually nervous. He said, "Randy, I'm not sure how you do things here in the Nashville studios, so I'm just gonna jump in there." B.B. jumped incredibly well and added a super cut to the album.

I was especially pleased that Vern Gosdin was on the album. I loved to hear Vern sing. He wasn't as well-known as George, Conway, or Merle, but he was a country purist who did things with his voice that I admired. We sang a duet of "The Human Race" on *Heroes and Friends*. Years later we would do a version of Vern's hit "Chiseled in Stone" that was released on a Starbucks compilation album.

We put thirteen songs plus a reprise of the title song on the *Heroes and Friends* album rather than the usual ten or at most twelve. To help make the profit margin come close to balancing, Lib and my business manager, Gary Haber, suggested that the songwriters and publishers take a lower percentage. That was not received well.

As a songwriter myself, I understood that every cut mattered, especially if it was your source of income. But there were a lot of people to satisfy, so Lib and Gary were looking for every way possible to lower expenses. They reasoned that because there were a dozen superstars on the album with me, the sales would be better than most compilation albums and that the songwriters would therefore make more than they normally would if their songs were on an album by a single artist. Eventually we worked out a compromise, and we were able to include all thirteen songs on the album, but I always felt bad about the way that happened.

Asking the songwriters to sacrifice was probably a mistake. Besides insulting some of my best friends in the business—the songwriters—when the news went public, it made me appear to be a selfish money-grubber. But all I wanted to do was to include thirteen great songs on the album instead of ten. They were all dynamic duets, and I didn't want to delete anyone's performance or deprive the fans of a sensational package.

The fans must have agreed. Warner released the album in early September 1990, and by Thanksgiving of that year, *Heroes and Friends* was #1 on *Billboard*'s country albums chart. Both the title song and "A Few Old Country Boys," a duet featuring George Jones, were big hits. So I guess it all worked out.

That same year, Reba McEntire and I hosted the CMA Awards, both of us for the first time. Everyone always says it is an honor to be nominated, and it is. Imagine what it feels like to stand on that stage looking out into the faces of so many of my heroes and introducing *them*, with millions of people watching on the CBS-TV network. It was really fun. Reba was a natural on camera and made my job much easier, and of course the teleprompters displaying our comments and jogging our memories helped a lot too. Music buffs noticed the nod to what they were now calling "neotraditional" country music every time they looked up and saw Reba and me. It wasn't new country to us; it was the same sort of music that both Reba and I had grown up with.

I love to laugh, and I especially enjoy making fun of myself. I learned early on that you might as well laugh at yourself because everybody else is gonna laugh at you at some point. So I've tried not to take myself too seriously. Like most country artists, I sing songs designed to touch people and tug at their heartstrings, but I especially enjoy singing songs that bring a smile to people's faces. I think that's what intrigued me about songs such as "On the Other Hand" and "Forever and Ever, Amen." They carried a message about real life but also included a dry, whimsical, subtle humor much like my own. Clever lyrics such as "I ain't in love with your hair" or "As long as old men sit and talk about the weather, as long as old women sit and talk about old men" really appealed to me.

Don Schlitz picked up on that part of my personality and looked for those humorous touches in life to put them into songs. Not all of those turned out to be hits, and some were never even professionally recorded, but I loved them.

One day, for example, I told Don about a conversation I'd had with Ron Avis, our tour bus driver at the time. At one point he'd said, "Oh, what a time to be me!" When Don heard that, his inner songwriter bells went off. We laughed our North Carolina butts off as we wrote a humorous song by that title about a fellow who'd lost his girl to me. According to the song, it was a sad time for him, but oh, "what a time to be me."

Something similar happened one day as Don and I walked through my house, getting ready to go upstairs to work on some songs. As Don passed a framed picture of a gorgeous young woman, he said, "That is a beautiful girl. Who is that?"

I looked at the picture, tilted my head slightly, and said, "Aw, she came with the frame."

"No, really," Don said. "Who is she?"

"I don't know," I replied with a smile. "She came with the frame."

"Oh man. Okay, let's go." We wrote the whimsical song about that frame, telling the story of a pitiful guy who kept a photo of a woman he didn't even know on the nightstand next to his bed. I never recorded the song on a major album, but we sure had fun writing it. I performed it once at a radio station with just a guitar and my vocal, and somebody had a video camera rolling. With a diligent search, the song can be found today online.

Don's lyric legal pads would eventually be placed in the Country Music Hall of Fame archives for safekeeping. This is good news and bad, because there's material on there that can cause trouble if it falls into the wrong hands.

Case in point: we were upstairs working on some songs one day when I received a phone call on our landline, located on the other side of the pool table, about thirty feet away from where we were writing. Few people in the world had that number, so I knew that when it rang, I'd better answer it.

Don continued working on the song while I took the call. After a few minutes, I called out to Don, "Hey, write this down."

"Okay."

The caller told me some numbers, I repeated them to Don, and he scribbled them down on his legal pad.

When I concluded the call, I walked back across the room to Don and said, "Now you have Arnold Schwarzenegger's private cell phone number." Arnold had been calling to recruit my help with one of the many charity events he spearheaded for the Special Olympics. I was always glad to lend a hand or my voice to one of his causes.

When Don's lyric sheets were later placed in the Hall of Fame, however, he completely forgot that Arnold's number was prominently displayed on one of the pages. So if you visit the Hall and see some of Don's lyric sheets, and if one happens to have a phone number on it, you may not want to call it. The person who answers might be the Terminator.

One of the things Don and I loved to do when writing was to kick around song ideas that we were absolutely certain nobody would ever record—including me. We just had fun bouncing around the ideas, and the process kept our creative juices flowing. One day when we were floating song ideas that nobody would cut, Don played a song that he said a lot of people liked but thought was too long. It wasn't a "boy-girl" song, more of a story like Don's famous song, "The Gambler."

As I listened to Don playing the song for me, for some reason it struck me. "I kinda like that, Don," I told him. "I think I want to record that."

Kyle loved it, too, so we recorded the song that nobody else would touch. It turned out to be "Oscar the Angel," which we put on my 1994 album, *This Is Me*. It's still one of our favorite songs, but few people ever heard it, at least compared to the more popular songs we recorded. It was never a single, nor was it a huge hit, but Randy Travis fans all around the world loved that song—and so did Don, Kyle, and I.

Being on the road as much as I was, I had lots of time for songwriting. But like many writers, Don was a homebody. He was also enormously successful and didn't need to be traipsing around the country on a tour bus, trying to find time in an artist's schedule to pen some songs. So when I was touring, my time with Don was very limited.

On one occasion, however, I talked him into hopping on our bus and traveling with us for a weekend trip to Toledo for some shows. "We'll have plenty of time for writing," I promised him. So Don reluctantly packed a bag and boarded the bus with us. But the trip turned out to be totally chaotic, with one distraction after another. People kept coming and going on the bus while Don and I were trying to write a song we had tentatively titled "The Kids Are All Country Now," an idea we had gotten by seeing so many young people in the audiences. Country music was cool again with younger crowds.

Adding to the distraction was a college basketball game. Born in Duke University Hospital, Don is a die-hard Blue Devil. Duke was playing

Kentucky during the time Don and I were trying to write the song, so we had the game on the bus television. Christian Laettner sank a last-second shot to give the Duke Blue Devils a dramatic 104 to 103 victory over the Kentucky Wildcats. That game, which sent Duke to the Final Four in 1992, was later heralded as one of the greatest college basketball games ever played. Don and I watched the end of it on the bus, and we never did finish the song.

Still glowing from the big Duke victory, Don brought his friend Doug Johnson out to the cabin to write with the two of us. Doug was producing music in Nashville and writing songs at the same time, and I liked him immediately. We wrote a couple of songs that day, but none of them ever caught on.

One of the great things about Nashville, however, is that it is a relationship-oriented town, particularly in the music business. That makes it especially good for songwriters and other creative types who could easily get frustrated by rejection if they lived somewhere else. Although Doug Johnson didn't write any hits with us that day at our cabin, he did become a friend. He would go on to write a song with Kim Williams that would have a major impact on millions of lives, including mine. The song was called "Three Wooden Crosses."

♪ ♪

A new, young artist being produced by Keith Stegall was our opening act in 1991 and 1992. His name was Alan Jackson. Since Keith was now working with Alan, he came out to a concert to see his new act. I was backstage in the catering area prior to my going onstage in front of about ten thousand people when I saw Keith. We shared a slightly awkward hug. The last time we had seen each other—except for the day he delivered the bus—Keith had told us he needed to stop producing my music and go back to just being an artist. That had nearly turned Lib's blond hair red!

Now, a couple of years later, I'd had a few hit records, our show was drawing large crowds, and Keith had decided to go back to producing. He had been working with producer Tom Collins when he discovered a new guy who, like me, just stood onstage and sang real country music. That was Alan Jackson, who also wrote some great songs. Working together, Keith and Alan would go on to have phenomenal success.

I smiled at Keith backstage and said, "Man, Keith, this is a lot of fun."

We were all totally enamored with Alan Jackson. Lib suggested that Alan and I write together with Don Schlitz, which made a lot of sense, considering Don's sensational success as a writer. But for some reason, Alan was reluctant. For a guy who performs in front of thousands of people on a regular basis, Alan is remarkably shy and reserved.

Since we were with each other on tour, Alan and I decided to write some things together. Unlike Don, Alan was accustomed to trying to write songs while surrounded by the bedlam of a tour bus. On the afternoon of August 17, 1991, with the crew setting up and preparing for our show at the Kentucky State Fair in Louisville, Alan came over to our bus, and he and I sat down with two guitars and some notepads. Within an hour we had written two songs, "She's Got the Rhythm (And I Got the Blues)" and "Better Class of Loser." That was a pretty good day of songwriting.

Alan ended up cutting that first song with Keith Stegall, I cut the second with Kyle Lehning, and both songs subsequently went to #1. I was especially pleased that after working so sacrificially to help get a record deal for me, Keith was now enjoying a bit of well-earned payback on his investment.

14 ——————— ALL-AMERICAN HEROES

In early April 1990, we were doing a show on the campus of George Mason University in Fairfax, Virginia, not far from the nation's capital. Our first show sold out, so we quickly added two more on consecutive nights at the same location.

While we were there, one of our hosts asked, "Since you guys are going to be here for a few days, would you like us to arrange a VIP tour of the White House?"

I'd met the president previously, when I performed for the inaugural gala, but I'd never been to his home, so I said, "Sure thing!"

Most days when we were on the road, Lib made breakfast on the bus for Jeff Davis and me. We had a phone mounted on the wall of the bus, and it rang while Jeff and I were having a cup of coffee. Jeff and I exchanged puzzled expressions. *Who has this number?* I wondered. Very few people did.

Jeff answered the phone. "It's the White House!" he whispered to me.

"Please hold for the president of the United States," the operator said matter-of-factly.

Sure enough, the next voice we heard was that of President George H. W. Bush. "Hey, I hear you're coming over," President Bush said as casually as if he were a neighbor talking to us over a fence. "Well, doggone, I'm not going to be here today. Can you come another day?"

"Yes," Lib said. "We'll be here for three days."

"Okay, we'll work that out. I'll send somebody to pick you up."

A day later, around nine in the morning, a plain brown car approached our bus, with six police officers on motorcycles following close behind. The car stopped, and a distinguished looking fellow got out. He knocked on the bus door and identified himself as Tom O'Neill, with the White House. We had met Tom at the inauguration of President Reagan, so we were delighted to see him again. A personable Naval officer with top national security and White House clearances, Tom often hosted celebrities with the president. President Reagan referred to Tom as "Merlin" because he could make magic happen. He sure made marvelous things happen for us.

Tom positioned us in the car with three motorcycle police officers in front of us and three behind us, and we took off. I mean we *took off*! Those boys were driving like I used to drive when I was a kid, except now we were speeding through busy Washington, DC, traffic. We didn't stop for anything. We roared into town with the police lights flashing and sirens blaring.

When we reached the DC-Virginia border, we were met by the Virginia State Police and the US Park Police. We stopped briefly, and the officers asked Tom if they could get a picture with me. "Sure," I said. We got out and took pictures for about twenty minutes.

One of the Park Police officers asked Tom, "Has Randy ever been around to the memorials?"

"I doubt it," Tom said. "Have you, Randy?" he asked me.

"No, not really," I said.

"Great!" the officer said, "just stay close to us, and we'll take him on a tour."

With lights and sirens, the officers led us on a high-speed tour of the various national monuments in Washington. When we got to the Washington Monument, we roared right up the triple-wide sidewalk in front of the monument and circled around at the base, lights and sirens still blaring. Tourists must have thought the president himself was visiting the Washington Monument!

We roared out of the monument area and headed for the White House. As we approached, one of the motorcycle officers pulled up next to Tom and said, "Hey, Tom. Do you see that big limo in front of you guys?"

"Yes, of course," Tom replied.

"Well, that's Michael Jackson. He's supposed to receive some sort of honor for his charity work from the president today."

"Whoa, whoa, whoa," Tom said. "We can't let Michael Jackson get in before us." To Tom, this was war.

One of the motorcycle police pulled Michael's limo off to the side of the road, and we swept right past them.

Later, as we pulled in at the side parking area of the White House, Tom asked one of the guards, "Where are they parking the Jacksons?"

"Right there on West Executive Drive," the guard replied.

"Oh no, no, no. Put them somewhere else. How about giving us that spot here?"

The guard knew Tom well. He smiled and said, "Yes, sir. I'd like you to park right here on West Exec Drive." He pointed at an open parking spot right in front of the White House entry area. We later discovered that he parked Michael on East Executive Drive, nearly a block away! Since he had a specific appointment, Michael did, however, get to see President Bush before we did, although not much before. We saw him exiting the building as we went inside.

A marine opened the door for us and smartly saluted Tom as he ushered us through the doorway. We walked with him as though we were royalty, straight to the Oval Office. Patty Presock, the president's executive secretary, opened the door for us, and the president was sitting in the office, waiting for us with a pot of coffee.

"Hi, Randy!" President Bush rose and greeted me. "Welcome to the Oval Office." I was thrilled. It's one thing to meet a president out in public somewhere, but it is even more awe-inspiring to be invited and welcomed by the president of the United States in the Oval Office. I was a long way from Marshville!

We talked for a few minutes and enjoyed a cup of coffee with the president. "Randy, I want to show you something," President Bush said. "This is where the real work gets done." We went into his private dining room, and the president walked over to a cupboard. He slid the door open, and there on the shelf was a row of cassette tapes of country music albums, including ones by Larry Gatlin, the Oak Ridge Boys . . . and Randy Travis.

The president had to go back to work, so Tom took us on a personalized tour of areas in the White House that the public rarely gets to see, including the White House Library, the Diplomatic Reception Room, and the Gold Room, which houses a collection of beautiful vermeil gold-plated dining ware that was donated to the White House. Lib seemed tremendously impressed by that.

We enjoyed our tour of the White House, and it was fun for me to think of the president as a country music fan. To me, President George H. W. Bush paid all country music artists and fans a compliment when he attended the Country Music Award show in 1991, the first sitting president ever to do so.

The president wasn't merely paying lip service to country music. He really loved it. We were working in the Dallas-Fort Worth area one evening about that time when President Bush arrived early for the concert. He came on the bus and visited with me for a while, then went backstage to say hello to the band members as they were doing a sound check. How many presidents would do something like that?

♫ ♫

At the award shows and onstage, from the time I could afford it, I always wore Manuel custom-made suits, jackets, and even tuxedos. One of my favorites by Manuel was a unique jacket that looked like an Indian blanket, with leather sleeves. I wore that jacket again and again.

As much as I loved horses and being a cowboy, I never wore a cowboy hat to perform, as did a number of other artists in the "new traditional" camp. I usually wore a dress shirt, black Wrangler jeans, a country-style sports jacket, and black cowboy boots. I developed a real affection for Stubbs shirts, handmade by Stubbs Davis in Dallas. The Stubbs shirts had a special "country" look, with great fabric, interesting stitching, and large, decorative buttons on a tape that made them removable and interchangeable. The shirts were sold in upscale boutiques as well as major department stores such as Nordstrom and Neiman Marcus.

Lib and I visited the Stubbs office every time we came anywhere near Dallas. On one such occasion in late 1990 or early 1991, Stubbs introduced us to his sister, Mary, who had moved back to the area and was working with him in his Western-wear company. A graduate of Baylor University, Mary had appeared in some movies in Los Angeles, been a flight attendant for Southwest Airlines, sold real estate in her family's business, and operated her own interior-design company prior to teaming up with Stubbs. A few years after our initial meeting, Mary married a Dallas-area dentist whose first name was Ritchie. She and Ritchie built a large, thriving practice in Plano, a suburb of Dallas.

We all hit it off instantly and became good friends, even though we lived in different cities. Any time we were doing shows near Dallas, the Davis clan was in the audience. If I had a free day in Dallas, we sometimes had dinner together. We made regular visits to Mary and Ritchie's home and eventually to their dental office as patients. Lib and Mary spent many hours shopping, and the four of us frequently enjoyed time together as couples. Once, when Lib had some surgery done in California, Mary even traveled to Los Angeles to help her during her recuperation.

Our friendship grew stronger and tighter over the years. When Ritchie and Mary had kids, I felt as though their children, daughter Cavanaugh and son Raleigh, were like family. I had always loved kids and had always wanted children, but didn't have any of my own, so I enjoyed watching them grow up, and they seemed to enjoy hanging out with me.

When Raleigh was eleven years of age, we invited him to go on the road with us for several weeks during the summer. Raleigh was a spunky, athletic sort of kid with a quick wit, so he and I had a lot of fun wrestling and working out together. He also kept up with the latest cell-phone technology, so Lib frequently asked him to assist her with her phone applications.

Raleigh had a blast on tour with us, so much fun that he forgot to keep up with his summer reading for school. When I asked him, "Raleigh, have you read your book yet?" I saw his eyes widen. I guessed instantly that he hadn't even started it.

"No," Raleigh said, as he held up a large book. "I gotta get a thinner book!"

Raleigh was always fun to have along on the road. He and I played pool together whenever possible at various towns where we stopped while on tour, and we even went fishing for huge Pike in South Dakota. One of Raleigh's favorite pastimes while traveling on the bus was to watch me practicing my quick draw techniques. Raleigh seemed fascinated that I could draw my guns from their holsters and twirl my six-shooters equally fast with either my left or right hand. He asked me to teach him how to draw, so I did. By the time Raleigh went back to school, he was getting pretty good at it. I loved having him travel with us and watched out for him as I would my own son.

♪ ♫

I've always had a tremendous appreciation and respect for the military, so when any opportunity came to visit Walter Reed Hospital in Washington, DC, I was glad to do it, even though those visits were often gut-wrenching.

Tom O'Neill and I were at Walter Reed one day after the first Gulf War when I heard some of my own music wafting out of one of the soldiers' hospital rooms. As I walked into the room, I saw a young soldier sitting up in his chair with a sheet over his lap and legs. My music was playing, and he was on the telephone. When he saw me, he was ecstatic. "Mr. Travis!" he called out. Still on the phone, he said, "Honey, you aren't gonna believe who just walked in here!" He practically yelled it into the phone, "He's here. Right here, in my hospital room. It's Randy Travis!"

Maybe she didn't believe him, because he said, "No kidding—he's standing right here! Wait. I'll give him the phone and you can talk to him."

"Well, I, er, ah, I don't know," I stammered.

"Mr. Travis . . . " He waved the phone toward me.

"Just call me Randy," I said.

"Yes, sir. Could you say hello to my fiancée?"

The soldier stretched out his arm in my direction, handing me the phone. So I took it and began a conversation with the woman on the other end. "Ah, yes, ma'am," I said. "He seems to be doing just fine. He's getting the best of treatment, and I'm sure he'll be coming home to you real soon."

When I finally got off the phone nearly thirty minutes later, I started cutting up with the soldier. He had a great smile and a fantastic attitude, and I enjoyed talking with him. I had come to encourage him, and he was inspiring me! After a while, I asked him the tough question: "How did you get here, son?"

"Well, sir, I was in an armored personnel carrier coming into Baghdad, and our chief had hooked up a CD player, so we were listening to some of your music. It was really hot inside the carrier, and some of the guys said, 'Get us some cool air back here!' So I made a mistake and opened the back door, and the enemy blew a rocket-propelled grenade right up the back of the carrier, right where I was."

Just then, the sheet came dislodged and dropped off the soldier's legs. I was shocked to see that both of the young soldier's legs were gone. They'd been blown off.

I was dumbfounded and didn't know what to say. I mumbled something about how sorry I was and how much I appreciated his sacrifice for our country's safety.

"No, no, no, sir. Don't start feeling sorry for me, Mr. Travis," the young soldier said. "I just have to change some of my priorities around. I'll be okay."

I tried to control my emotions, but I lost it and couldn't hold back my tears. I was so touched by the young soldier's attitude. He displayed not a hint of self-pity. He had lost so much, but he was still alive and grateful for every day. I said a heartfelt good-bye to the soldier and stepped out into the hall, trying to regain my composure.

Heroes have always been important to me, and I knew I had just met another one.

15 ——————— CONSIDER THE SOURCE

In late winter, early spring of 1991, the *National Enquirer* tabloid came out with a story claiming that I was still single because I was a closet homosexual. Granted, I hadn't dated a lot during my teenage years and had experienced only one real love interest during that time, a crush on a young woman in Marshville. By the time I was seventeen, I was with Lib, who was thirty-five at the time, and people often wondered about our relationship. At times, so did I. Throughout my early career, Warner had subtly pitched "my innocent sexuality" as part of my image. So maybe it wasn't surprising that the tabloid would print such a story. The trouble was, it just wasn't true.

Of course, the *Enquirer* cited no facts, sources, or incidents. Tabloids don't have to be factual or to base their information on credible people. They just print it and risk being sued. One unnamed person they quoted said of me, "If Randy Travis isn't gay, then my grandmother is Willie Nelson."

When I heard about the article and that quote in particular, I responded, "My advice is to buy your grandmother a red wig and teach her to sing through her nose." It was a silly comment, but I was angry and spoke my mind. I would have been wiser to have kept my thoughts to myself.

The false report went public during the annual Country Radio Seminar held in Nashville, where hundreds of top radio deejays and station managers gathered to hear the latest. They certainly weren't expecting to hear something like that about me. I felt I needed to confront the vicious rumor head on. I was scheduled to perform at the CRS opening, and as I was waiting to go onstage, the slanderous article continued to nag at me. I was as angry as I've ever been. "They can say they don't like me or the way I look or the way I sing," I ranted to Bill Mayne. "But this—this just isn't right!" I continued to lash out in a verbal flood filled with every expletive I'd ever heard.

Bill tried to calm me down. "Just let it alone, and nobody will even bring it up," he advised. "And if anyone does mention it, just say something like, 'As my grandpa used to tell me, consider the source.' They'll get the idea."

That was probably good advice. Too bad I didn't take it.

I normally let irritations slide, but I couldn't seem to do it this time. Still fuming, I went onstage and tried to do my set, but it was impossible. I stopped in the middle and vented to the crowd of listeners, many of whom were significant players in the realm of country music radio. I vehemently denied the allegations in the tabloid, repeating many of the things I had said to Bill.

I don't know whether the radio execs were more shocked or intrigued. I do know that somebody circulated a survey the following day, asking if they believed the accusations or believed me. What a mess!

After that I called my lawyer and asked what recourse we had. Not much, I discovered. Because I was considered a "public person," they could write pretty much anything they wanted about me, and the only recourse I had was to sue for malice or defamation of character. Showing malice is difficult, and it is impossible, it seems, to "defame" a public figure nowadays.

I was furious nonetheless. "There's no one on this planet who can substantiate any such claims," I told the press straightforwardly. And then, in an almost knee-jerk reaction to the tabloid story, we put out a statement on March 8, 1991, saying that I had been living with my manager, Lib Hatcher, for a number of years. I just hadn't wanted to get married.

Then I put my own spin on the situation. "I guess it could have been worse, though," I said with a twinkle in my eye. "I guess they could have said that I wasn't *country*." The members of the media chuckled, since most of them knew that for the first seven years of my career, prior to getting a recording deal, I had been dubbed as "too country."

After that I did my best to clear my mind of the article, because the following day, I needed to be in Washington, DC, at the renowned Ford Theater to debut a special song, "Point of Light," with President Bush and his wife, Barbara, sitting in the audience.

The song had been written by Don Schlitz and Thom Schuyler at the request of the president—to highlight his emphasis on personal responsibility, volunteerism, and community involvement. He had used the phrase "a thousand points of light" when he accepted his party's nomination to run for president and then again during his inaugural address.

After the election, the Bush White House had contacted the Country Music Association requesting that someone write a song with a similar emphasis. The CMA had passed along the request to some of the best songwriters in town, and Don and Thom took the challenge. The guys wrote the song and sent it to Sig Rogich, a member of the Bush staff. The president listened to it and sent it back to Don and Thom, saying, "I like it. It's really good. But the chorus needs to be a little more sing-songy."

So Don and Thom rewrote the chorus. That may be the first time a sitting president weighed in on the writing of a hit song.

Once "Point of Light" was completed, the next question was, "Who is going to sing it?"

Don and I were sitting in a couple of rocking chairs one day, and he mentioned the song to me. I was sold as soon as he played it for me. Kyle Lehning and I went into the studio and recorded it. Then I performed "Point of Light" live for George and Barbara Bush at the Ford Theater and later at the "Celebration of County" program which aired on ABC-TV in April. The double meaning in the title was deliberate, as it was a great evening of country music artists, including Alabama, Alan Jackson, Ricky Skaggs, the Statler Brothers, Clint Black, and Tammy Wynette celebrating our nation. As I sang the song, the audience got into it, rocking back and forth to the beat and waving miniature American flags.

I sang the song again on April 3, 1991, on the CBS-TV special "The All-Star Salute to our Troops," featuring Andy Griffith, Ray Stevens, Barbara Mandrell, Tony Orlando, and many other artists. Although I've never been overtly politically involved, our nation was in a patriotic mood, volunteerism was flourishing, and I was glad to participate.

I performed "Point of Light" yet again in 1991 at Andrews Air Force Base (now part of Joint Base Andrews) in Washington, DC, to welcome home our troops from Operation Desert Storm, the largest war effort Americans had participated in since Vietnam. The troops gave us a resounding reception, and at the close of the show, during an encore number, a huge American flag unfurled as a backdrop behind the band and me. The troops instinctively began cheering. It was truly one of the more emotional patriotic moments of my life.

In the spring of 1991, shortly after that, we traveled again to Washington, DC, where I was to receive the Bob Hope USO Award. My brother Dennis, Jeff Davis, and several Warner execs—Bill Mayne, Neal Spielberg, and several PR people—accompanied us, as did Barry Weinberg, the head trainer for the Oakland A's Major League Baseball team. Barry was an enthusiastic country music fan who often hung out with us and sometimes worked out with me. Barry had once arranged for Jeff, his brother Jerry, and me to work out in the Oakland A's training facility when we were playing a show at what is now the Oracle Arena and Coliseum. Lib liked having Barry around because he gave her free massages.

At the event in DC, I was introduced to General Norman Schwarzkopf and General Colin Powell, the victorious military leaders, as well as Dick Cheney and other political leaders. It was a magical evening and I was humbled to be the honoree that everyone had gathered to acknowledge.

Afterward our entire group returned to Lib's and my suite at the hotel. Dennis came in and said, "Hey, guys, there's a great band playing at a little club around the corner. Why don't we all go hear them?"

I was still running on adrenaline from the evening, so I piped up immediately, "Yeah, Dennis. That sounds great." Everyone seemed in favor of the idea except Lib. She was always wary about me going out with friends, especially to any place where there might be alcohol or attractive women. Although I'd never given her any reason to doubt my commitment to her or to stay away from negative influences, Lib made it her business to keep me from socializing with anybody but her—including both female and male friends, even within the music industry. Although I had lots of guy friends, I almost never went anywhere with them that was not work related.

Sitting across the room, Bill Mayne could see from my facial demeanor that I was excited to go out on the town. He nodded to Lib and gave her a look as though to say, "Don't worry, Lib. I've got this."

Lib ignored Bill. She moved closer to me and said, "Well, Randy, you know that saddle we looked at earlier today at that tack shop? I decided that I'm going to buy that for you, so we're gonna have to get up real early tomorrow morning."

I knew what that meant. My countenance dropped, and I felt crushed. I turned to the friends around me and said, "You all go on without me."

The group didn't seem surprised. They were accustomed to Lib's mothering, smothering, and controlling me and everything around me. I often acknowledged that Lib had saved my life by helping me break my addictions, so nobody questioned when I acquiesced to her desires. Still, some people had concerns.

"I've never been quite sure whether Lib is protecting Randy or herself," said one of our guys. "Is she protecting herself from losing him? Is she afraid that if he gets out in the real world on his own, he might be attracted to a younger, more attractive woman? Or is she protecting him from the temptations surrounding him—the same sort of things that follow any successful music artist?"

The one point upon which everyone agreed was Lib's domineering personality. Comparing her absolute control of nearly everything in my life to the domination of Elvis Presley by Colonel Parker, one friend quipped, "She makes Colonel Parker seem like a kindergartner."

Everyone left the suite except Bill Mayne, Barry Weinberg, Neal Spielberg, Lib, and me. Bill and I sat down and talked while Lib went into the bedroom to change. A few minutes later, she came out wearing only a towel and said, "Barry, I'm ready for my massage."

Barry and Lib went in the other room, and Bill, Neal, and I continued to talk as though nothing had happened. We all knew that this was about more than Lib's concern for me being around alcohol or other women; it was about her total control in my life. While I believed that Lib loved me and knew that she had poured her life into helping us succeed, the question of whether she was serving my best interests or her own popped up frequently and increasingly irritated me. It was always there, festering like an infected wound, even when fantastic things were happening in our lives.

And fantastic things *were* happening, make no mistake. Not too many months earlier, while Operation Desert Storm was still raging, I'd had the honor of participating in the compilation song and video "Voices That Care." A tribute to our troops still in the Middle East, the song had been written by David Foster, Linda Thompson, and Peter Cetera. When they'd asked me to participate, I'd quickly said yes.

Similar to the 1985 "We Are the World" effort, the video featured an odd but wonderful mix of musical artists from all genres, including Celine Dion, Garth Brooks, Kenny Rogers, Stephen Stills, Little Richard, Peter Cetera, Luther Vandross, and Michael Bolton, as well as a diverse chorus composed of famous actors such as Meryl Streep, Billy Crystal, Brooke Shields, Chevy Chase, Kevin Costner, Whoopi Goldberg, Dudley Moore, and sports stars such as Michael Jordan, Orel Hershiser, Marcus Allen, Magic Johnson, Brian Bosworth, Wayne Gretzky, and Mike Tyson, and many other celebrities—all expressing support for our troops in danger.

The video did not premier in a fancy Hollywood theater, but in the war theater in Kuwait. It was shown to our troops in the field, some of whom had tears in their eyes as they heard and watched the expressions of support from such an eclectic mixture of celebrities. It was an amazing, united effort, and the song reached #11 on the *Billboard* charts.

More important, it encouraged a lot of our soldiers. And that's what mattered most to me.

Being onstage, exchanging energy with my fans, has been my favorite place and the highlight of my career.

John Davisson/Invision/AP/Shutterstock

It was rare when we could get together for family photos, so this is a cherished moment for our family. Back row (l to r): Ricky, Dennis, David, and me; front row (l to r): Rose, Harold Traywick (Dad), Bobbie Traywick (Mom), and Sue.

Randy Travis personal collection

I was the second of six siblings.

Randy Travis personal collection

I started performing music shows with the Traywick Brothers when I was eight years old and began working at Country City USA in Charlotte at seventeen.

Randy Travis personal collection

My brothers and sisters and I all had our own horses by the time we were five, and some of my fondest childhood memories are those times when we saddled up and rode together through the woods, fields, and trails around our home. (Left to right: me, David, Rose, and Ricky)

Randy Travis personal collection

From the time I was a young boy, horses have been a big part of my life.

Randy Travis personal collection

It takes time and patience to teach a horse new tricks. It took a while to get Preacher on the blocks.

Photo courtesy of Mary Davis Travis

Home sweet home, relaxing next to our saddled bannister.

Photo courtesy of Mary Davis Travis

I enjoyed singing George Jones songs long before we met and toured together. Besides being good friends, both George and I fought our demons, the devil, and the bottle and found a renewed relationship with God in the process. Here, I'm presenting George an award during the 1992 CMA Awards show.

Mark Humphrey/AP/Shutterstock

One of my early appearances on *Nashville Now*, hosted by Ralph Emery, here with Minnie Pearl (Sarah Cannon), one of the sweetest and funniest women ever to grace the stage.

Photo courtesy of Ralph Emery, Jim Hagans photographer, used by permission

We pitched songs from my first full album, recorded live at the Nashville Palace, to every major record label in Nashville. They all turned us down, saying I was "too country."

Randy Travis personal collection

Many of the songs I recorded felt as though I had lived them—and most of them, I had!

Photo courtesy of Kelly Doherty, used by permission

My producer, Kyle Lehning, gave me some of the best musical advice I ever received when it came to selecting songs. Kyle said, "Don't record 'em if you don't love 'em." Kyle produced all but two of my albums, and he was brilliant.

Randy Travis personal collection

I've had the honor of working with most of my band and crew members for nearly thirty years. We were "family." This shot was taken right after we finished recording my last album.

Photo courtesy of Kelly Doherty, used by permission

I was honored to visit with President George H. W. Bush in the White House. The president loved country music and was a true friend to our industry and to me.

Photo by Jeff Davis

I loved appearing with Andy Griffith on his television show *Matlock*. He was everything I hoped he would be. Here we are between takes, playing music and having fun.

Randy Travis personal collection

Roy Rogers was one of the finest Christian men I've ever met. When I ran the pool table on him without giving him a shot, Roy simply smiled and said, "Signs of a misspent youth." And he was right!

Randy Travis personal collection

Dolly Parton surprised me at a couple of CMA award shows. Dolly is a small woman with a huge heart and a great sense of humor. Here, I surprised her at her Winstar show, less than a year after I'd had a stroke.

Photo courtesy of Mary Davis Travis

Three people who helped my career early on and became dear friends were Loretta Lynn, Conway Twitty, and Ralph Emery. I was still a cook at the Nashville Palace when I first appeared on Ralph's show.

Property of Ralph Emery, Jim Hagans photographer, used by permission

Alan Jackson and me taking a break from our 1991 Alaskan shows to model some warm hats. His had the rhythm, and mine had the blues. No, we didn't buy them!

Randy Travis personal collection

Just a few old country boys—rodeo champion Larry Mahan, Willie Nelson, me, Kris Kristofferson, and Jamey Johnson. We have some stories!

Photo courtesy of Mary Davis Travis

Three of my heroes and friends: me; Little Jimmy Dickens, who first invited me to the Grand Ole Opry; George Jones; and Charlie Pride.

Photo courtesy of Nancy Jones, used by permission

In the studio, working on a song for *Heroes and Friends* with Clint Eastwood. Who knew that Clint could sing?

Randy Travis personal collection

I loved talking about songs with the incomparable Merle Haggard aboard his bus. I played some of Merle's hits almost every night during my sound check, and one of his songs probably prevented a Paris crowd from rioting at the close of my performance.

Randy Travis personal collection

Josh Turner and John Anderson joined me on the bus before my *25th Anniversary* concert and album release. John's rendition of "Diggin' Up Bones" was a crowd pleaser. Josh's private concert for me in the hospital, when many people wondered if I would live or die within days, encouraged me not to give up.

Courtesy of Josh Turner, photo by Jennifer Turner, used by permission

My friend and songwriting buddy Don Schlitz (center) wrote "The Gambler" for Kenny Rogers (far right). At least five of Don's songs that I recorded were mega-hits for me.

Randy Travis personal collection

I was honored to welcome Carrie Underwood as the youngest member (at the time) of the Grand Ole Opry. Here, the Opry invited me to surprise her again on Carrie's tenth anniversary as a member, after I had suffered a stroke.

Photo courtesy of Mary Davis Travis

Mary Davis and I married in March 2015. We had hoped to wed before then, but our plans were postponed by the stroke and the long recovery period we both worked through.

Photo by Richard Krall, used by permission

I have always loved country music fans, and I enjoy being with them, from the youngest to the oldest. I'm convinced that fans of country music are more loyal than those in any other genre.

Photo courtesy of Mary Davis Travis

Working in films expanded my horizons and was great fun, but in *Texas Rangers* my character smoked small, dark cigars. Since I don't smoke at all, the strong cigars nearly turned my face green for every scene!

Randy Travis personal collection

Many people doubted I would survive the massive stroke. But Mary, Cavanaugh, and others prayed and believed. The helmet I'm wearing in this picture is to protect the area where a portion of my skull had been removed to stop the swelling.

Photo courtesy of Mary Davis Travis

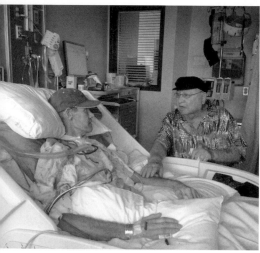

Near my lowest point during my six-month hospitalization, John Hobbs, original owner of the Nashville Palace, came to visit me. In his late eighties, John reminded me that I am fighter and that I could beat this thing.

Photo courtesy of Mary Davis Travis

I was feeling a little better when Raleigh spent many hours with me in the hospital, as did members of my band and crew, many friends and, of course, Mary, who rarely left my side the entire time.

Photo courtesy of Mary Davis Travis

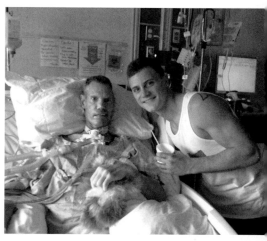

On the hospital rooftop overlooking Nashville, wondering if I would ever be able to stand and sing again.

Photo courtesy of Mary Davis Travis

Following the stroke, I had to relearn how to write, how to walk, and how to do a million other things. It was like starting life all over again—only slower.

Photo courtesy of Mary Davis Travis

I lost more than one-third of my body weight during my hospitalization. Getting back on my feet was a long, arduous journey.

Photo courtesy of Mary Davis Travis

I could form chords on the guitar with my left hand, but my right hand would not cooperate. Here, I'm working on learning how to play differently.

Photo courtesy of Mary Davis Travis

I went to rehab every day for four hours a day, for two and a half years. The staff and therapists were so kind and patient with me.

Photo courtesy of Mary Davis Travis

Immediately after being inducted into the Country Music Hall of Fame, I surprised everyone by singing all four verses of "Amazing Grace." Overwhelmed with emotion, Garth had tears in his eyes, as did Mary and most people in the audience.

Laura Roberts, Invision / AP / Shutterstock

Cavanaugh, Raleigh, Mary, and I have always been close, but through all the trials we have endured, we have become a truly blessed family.

Photo courtesy of Mary Davis Travis

Our family was together at the Country Music Hall of Fame induction ceremony. Being acknowledged as one of country music's all-time greats was an honor and a dream come true.

Randy Travis personal collection

Many people said that the opening to the 2016 CMA Awards show, featuring some of country's biggest hits sung by some of music's greatest stars, was one of the most moving and inspiring performances in CMA history.

Photo credit: John Russell/Country Music Association, Inc. © Country Music Association, Inc. All rights reserved.

Being back together with country music fans and artists has energized me. Here, Mary and I greet more than 17,000 cheering and applauding fans at a Nashville tribute concert held in my honor in 2017.

It was sheer joy being with our friends again and hearing them sing songs from my albums. The tribute concert was truly a night I will never forget.

Our good friend Garth Brooks joined us backstage before the show billed as "One Night, One Place, One Time, a Heroes and Friends Tribute to Randy Travis." Garth brought the house down by singing "Forever and Ever, Amen," and I added the last *amen*.

The tribute concert was even more special to me because Raleigh and Cavanaugh were with Mary and me.

I'm so grateful for the many people who prayed for my recovery, including my "big brother," Charlie Daniels, praying for me here, backstage at CMA Fest. | Photos courtesy of Mary Davis Travis

Later that night, I joined Charlie on stage. | Debby Wong / Shutterstock

After recovering from the stroke, I couldn't wait to get back to our horses. Here I am having fun with Preacher. Spending time with our horses was wonderfully therapeutic.

Photo courtesy of Mary Davis Travis

This was my first time back in the saddle after six months in the hospital and lots of rehab. Do you think I was excited? The look on my face says it all!

Photo courtesy of Mary Davis Travis

My youngest brother, Dennis, was afraid to ride with me when we were kids because I drove so fast. Here he and I share a special moment at a wedding we attended while I was still in a wheelchair after the stroke. We'd both come a long way from our rough childhood in Marshville, NC.

Photo courtesy of Cheryl Wiemeyer, used by permission

When I came home from the hospital, I couldn't walk, shave, take a shower, comb my hair, dress, or feed myself. Mary cared for me like a newborn baby. Today we laugh, sing, and enjoy every day as a gift.

Randy Travis personal collection

This is my favorite photo of Mary and me. I keep it on the kitchen counter and look at it every day. It reminds me that we are taking one step at a time into the great future that God has for us.

Randy Travis personal collection

16 ————————— STIRRINGS WITHIN

I don't know what it was. Maybe it was meeting those young wounded soldiers and realizing just how fragile life is. Possibly some of the false accusations hurled at me by the tabloids helped remind me that a good name and reputation must be guarded and backed up by a godly life. Maybe it was something about the turmoil in the Middle East that reminded me of the storms and turmoil I had known in my own life and caused me to turn my attention more seriously toward spiritual matters. Whatever the reason, I began to think more about God and my relationship—or lack of one— with Him.

For some people, spiritual conversion happens instantly, but for me it was more of a gradual process. It began when, without anyone prompting me, I started reading the Bible regularly during my early twenties. Even though I didn't always understand everything I read, I could sense it was having a positive impact on me. I was still drinking back then and using marijuana, but amazingly, when I'd read the Bible before going to bed, I would sleep and rest better. It brought a peace to me that I had never before known. I had always possessed a deep respect for the Bible and tried to live by the golden rule, treating others as I would want to be treated, living honestly and telling the truth. In my own way, I had trusted Jesus with my life, but I had never made any public statements to that effect.

For a while, I tried to clean up my act on my own. For instance, when Lib discovered that I was serious about breaking free from substance abuse, she helped me by rolling placebo marijuana-seed "joints." It was funny to watch her. Lib had never smoked a cigarette or imbibed alcoholic beverages as far as I knew. She was a complete teetotaler. Yet there she was sitting on our couch rolling joints for me! Using the placebo gave me a sensation that I was still smoking pot, but without the effects. After a few months, I was able to do without even the placebo.

Despite making some progress at being a better person, I still felt that if I were to die, I would not go to heaven. More likely, I suspected, I had a good chance of landing in hell.

Then in 1991, while we were still living in rural Tennessee, Lib and I went to the Sunday service at the Church of Christ in Ashland City, where we had been attending, and Pastor Dan Harless Jr. preached a powerful message. I don't even recall what the sermon was about, but I felt strongly that God was calling me to do something. I needed to respond. I didn't quite know how to express my desire to trust in Jesus and to follow Him, so after the service, I approached the pastor and said, "I'd like to get baptized."

The church had a baptismal pool on-site, so Brother Harless wasted no time. That same evening he baptized me, and it was a special celebration of my Christian faith. For me baptism was a powerful illustration of the statement that the old Randy was dead, buried in the water and gone, and that I was a new person. Thanks to Jesus, I had been raised to a new life here and now and eternal life in heaven to come.

Maybe the statements made about me in the *Enquirer* influenced my thinking, or maybe it was my growing spiritual awareness and understanding of the Bible—I'm not sure. Regardless, we decided that it was time to make a public commitment. On May 31, 1991, Elizabeth (Lib) Hatcher and I became husband and wife. She was fifty years of age and I was thirty-two. We were married in Hawaii, on the island of Maui, where we owned several homes, one in which we lived and four others that we rented. To seal the deal I gave Lib a four-carat diamond ring. The wedding ceremony took place in the courtyard of one of our homes, in front of a waterfall.

Despite the fabulous natural beauty all around us, the wedding itself was not a fancy affair. Lib wore a black-and-white checked dress, and I wore a casual shirt with black jeans. Only three people attended our outdoor wedding—the preacher and two people he brought along as witnesses. Not even my band members or our tour manager, Jeff Davis, knew that we had married. In fact, Jeff didn't discover it until our first show back out on the road, a gig with Alan Jackson at the Starwood Amphitheater in Nashville. Lib flashed the ring, and Jeff couldn't help noticing the diamond.

Early in October 1991, George Jones and I did a television special in which we shared singing some of George's greatest hits and a few of my favorites too. I loved George as a friend and mentor but also because he and I had both been through similar storms in life. When we sang about tough times, we could identify with them.

We led off with "A Few Old Country Boys," a song that George and I had done together on my album, *Heroes and Friends*, and then we moved to standards such as "The Wabash Cannonball"; one of my all-time favorites, "I'm So Lonesome I Could Cry"; and of course George's most popular song, "He Stopped Loving Her Today." It was such a fun show because we both enjoyed singing with each other so much. I think the audience sensed that George and I appreciated each other's abilities and that, rather than competing with one another, we were attempting to vocally complement each other. The results were truly a memory I will cherish forever.

A year or two before that, while listening to some songs at a publishing company in Nashville, searching for material for a new album, I'd heard a song that stirred some more memories. I started thinking about an incident that took place between my grandfather and me when he was seventy years old and I was seven.

Grandpa was sitting out under a mulberry tree in his yard, his hat on the ground in front of him. I was riding my bicycle around and around him, getting closer to his hat with each circle around the tree. "Don't you run over my hat, now, Randy," Grandpa warned.

I made several more rounds and, sure enough, I ran over his hat.

Grandpa's quick reflexes shocked me. Suddenly I felt strong hands on my shoulders, jerking me right off the bike's seat, with me hanging midair and the bicycle rolling out from under me.

A man of his generation, Grandpa felt that if a kid needed a punishment, he should get it then and there, rather than spending a half hour in time out. So he gave me a good whipping right on the spot. When he finally let go, I figured, *He can't catch me.* So I ran down the driveway about twenty or thirty feet away from him and started throwing rocks at him. Grandpa had a bit of a temper, so he picked up some rocks and threw them back at me. There we were—him seventy, me seven, both of us throwing rocks at each other—a picture of love!

The song the publisher played for me that day turned out to be "He Walked on Water," which did very well for us in 1990. I recorded it because it reminded me of Grandpa. Despite his sins, failures, and foibles, I thought that he walked on water. It was one of the first songs Allen Shamblin had written for a new publishing company that was owned in part by Don Schlitz. Allen would go on from there to write or cowrite a number of incredible hits, including "The House that Built Me" and "I Can't Make You Love Me."

One day the movie star Bill Paxton reached out to me with an unusual request. "Randy, I'm doing a movie called *Traveler*, and I want you to redo the classic Roger Miller song, "King of the Road," so we can include it in the movie.

"Bill, it's kinda hard to remake a Roger Miller song," I said. Roger was a one-of-a-kind, out-there sort of guy. I remember him telling me one day, "Never keep your pills and your change in the same pocket. I just swallowed thirty-five cents."

I didn't know if Roger was serious or not—but then, I don't guess anyone who knew him was ever quite sure.

Despite my misgivings about recording one of Roger's classics, I went in to the studio and cut my version of "King of the Road." The song became part of my regular show list for years. People just loved hearing it.

About that time, Lib wanted to get a special gift for me. I was unaware of it, but she'd been sweet-talkin' Roy Rogers for months, trying to get him to sell her a descendant of Trigger, Roy's famous steed. But she neglected to tell Roy that it was meant to be a surprise gift for me.

When Roy came to Nashville to be inducted into the Country Music Hall of Fame, Lib sat between Roy and me in the audience. Roy leaned across her and said, "Well, Randy, I guess you're gonna be getting one of my horses."

I had no idea what he was talking about, but one look at Lib's flushed face, and I realized Roy had spilled the beans on her efforts to surprise me. But my gift horse was beautiful, and I treasured the idea of having my own version of the horse of my childhood dreams.

Unfortunately, Trigger Jr. didn't respect me as highly as I respected him. While Roy's original Trigger had been sweet, docile, and peaceable, Trigger Jr. was cantankerous and mean as a hornet. If I walked by his stable, he'd lean over the stall and try to take a bite out of my shoulder. A lot of horses will do something like that at first, then mellow after a while, but Trigger Jr.'s personality never did improve.

That horse was real hardheaded. I was able to teach him some tricks, but he was never friendly. His daughter, Mariah, however, is a sweet horse, and Flash, his grandson, has a great disposition. I have both of those horses to this day.

Later Roy gave me a gift that I regarded as one of my most prized possessions—the original bill of sale from Hudkins Stables to Roy Rogers for one palomino stallion named Trigger in 1943. The price Roy paid was twenty-five hundred dollars.

♪ ♫

At the 1991 CMA Awards show, I sang "Heroes and Friends" along with George Jones and Tammy Wynette. George and I took the stage first, and the Possum sang the first verse, then Tammy walked out and joined us. We sang the chorus together and had started the second verse of the song when out walked Roy Rogers and Vern Gosdin, two of my heroes. The moment that Vern and Roy came out onstage, the entire crowd rose to its feet. What an honor to finish singing that song with so many of my own heroes and friends.

In February 1992, I appeared as a house painter on the hit NBC-TV series *Matlock*, starring another hero of mine, Andy Griffith. Andy was tremendously helpful to me during the filming of the show, encouraging me to put more emotion into my dialogue and helping me deliver my lines with much more punch and power. In between scenes we'd sit around talking and playing some music, and he'd offer suggestions to help me out since I was so new to acting. A few times I almost had to pinch myself because I felt as though I was talking to Sheriff Andy Taylor from Mayberry. It was all I could do to keep from laughing. But Andy made me feel welcome and comfortable on the set.

One day during a break from filming, I asked Andy about my favorite character on *The Andy Griffith Show* apart from Andy and Barney. "Andy, what was Floyd really like?" I asked.

Andy chuckled. "Why, he was just like the character he played on the show. He'd get us laughing so hard sometimes we couldn't stop."

I'd always held a deep admiration for Andy Griffith, and after working with him on his show, I was even more impressed with him as a quality person. He was exactly what and who I had hoped he would be and the kind of person I wanted to emulate.

Alan Jackson was still touring with us as we closed out 1991, and we were both having banner years. We would end up playing 108 shows together as Alan's career skyrocketed along with mine. That November, "Forever Together," another song Alan and I had cowritten while on tour, hit #1 for me on the *Billboard* country singles chart.

In October 1992 Arista Records released Alan's version of our song "She's Got the Rhythm (And I Got the Blues)" as a single. It quickly moved up the charts and hit #1 on *Billboard*'s country singles chart the third week of December. That was a nice early Christmas present for Alan and for me. My own single, "Look Heart, No Hands," was moving up the charts as well and would take over the top spot the third week of January, 1993. We were on a roll!

17 — TRANSITION TIME—THIS IS ME

Unlike performers in some other music genres, country music artists start touring early in our careers, and then we continue touring until we die. Part of the reason is that we enjoy it so much. Another reason for the longevity of country artists' careers is the fans' deep appreciation.

Simply put: country music fans are the most loyal in the music world.

I love what I do in front of an audience—whatever that is. I joke about that sometimes, because I don't really know what I'm doing musically. To this day I can't read a note of music. What I do is simply exercise a God-given gift, and I'm aware of that. When I have touched people through the music and they are moved, I feel so blessed to be able to do this for a living. I've been working in front of an audience since I was eight or nine years old, and I can't imagine doing anything else.

To me, there's nothing better than standing onstage and performing for an appreciative audience when everything is working right, when the band and I are in a groove and there seems to be a special feeling in the air. For a musician there's nothing else quite like that. And for years now, we had been going at it hard.

In 1990 we enjoyed our greatest year yet, touring with Shenandoah. In 1991 we worked an incredible, extensive tour with Alan Jackson as our opening act. Then, in 1992, another sensational young newcomer, Trisha Yearwood, opened for us in many shows. I loved having Trisha working with us, and she was a tremendous entertainer. The fans went crazy for her every night. More than that, she became like a sister to me. To this day, I regard her as one of the greatest female vocalists in country music.

Nevertheless, as 1992 drew to a close, I was ready for a break. I had been touring so much for so long, and I was simply wrung out. For the five straight years between 1987 and 1992, we had been the top-grossing country act in the world according to *Amusement Business*, the magazine and organization that tracks what acts are selling and at which venues. But despite my love of performing and our phenomenal success, I needed rest.

I didn't see myself as retiring—I was only thirty-three years old. But I was ready to take a hiatus. I gave Jeff a few months' advance notice, and we started making plans to bring our touring machine to a halt.

We were playing three or four straight Vegas shows in December during the rodeo season—which always drew huge crowds—when I announced my decision to the band and crew. I called everybody up to my suite at the hotel. Everyone gathered around in the living room. The mood was lighthearted but somewhat reserved since nobody but Lib, Jeff, and me had a clue what this meeting was all about. Usually, if I needed to talk with everyone, we'd gather backstage or in a dressing room at a venue. This was different.

I stood at one end of the room and slowly looked around at each of the faces. This wasn't a business meeting. These people were family to me. I spoke from my heart. "I love all you guys and appreciate you, but I'm spent."

Nobody made a sound, and the air thickened with emotion. "I'm going to take some time off," I continued. "I don't know how long. It might be a year; it might even be longer."

I paused and looked around the room again. This was difficult.

"I'm going to continue to make music. And I know that I'll be back at some point, but right now I'm not sure when."

Several of the guys' heads dropped. Some had tears in their eyes. Most nodded their heads a bit, giving me the impression that they understood my decision, but the news was still hard on them.

I knew the guys would be concerned about their incomes. Although they were all top-notch professional musicians and I was confident they could pick up work with other artists, I also knew that most shows were already out touring or bringing their tours to a close. It wasn't a good time for a musician to be looking for a job. So I had worked out a severance plan that would compensate each employee for several months even though we'd no longer be playing dates together. As I explained that to them, I emphasized, "If you pick up another job next week, that's great, but you are still going to get paid by me."

The meeting broke up with hugs and a few tears, and that night in Vegas we played our last show together. It was one of the best, yet most difficult, shows we'd ever done.

Following the last concert dates in Vegas, Lib and I retreated to Maui, one of my favorite places on earth. Lib busied herself searching for and acquiring more property there, and I enjoyed riding horses up in the hills overlooking the turquoise-blue waters of the Pacific.

Not surprisingly, the media immediately began reporting that I had retired. The reports included all sorts of false or misleading reasons for my hiatus. So in early January 1993, we instructed our publicist, Evelyn Shriver, to put out a press release stating that I was merely taking a break and not retiring. That may have squelched a few rumors, but not many.

Jeff Davis stayed on with us for a few months to field inquiries and to sell off all our buses, trucks, and sound and lighting equipment. Eventually, in February 1993, Jeff resigned and took another job with the country-rock band Brother Phelps, which had been formed by Ricky and Doug Phelps of the Kentucky Headhunters. I was sorry to see Jeff go; he was like a brother to me, but there really was little left for him to do with us once we were no longer touring.

I was a little discombobulated, too, especially at first. Ten months of every year for nearly eight years, I had awakened almost every morning in a different town. And as much as I loved my fans and enjoyed performing for them, I never wanted to tour that heavily again. But it took a little while for me to adjust to not doing it.

I did have plans, though. In addition to getting away from the rigorous tour schedule, I also wanted to explore acting some more. Performing in movies and television shows was a relatively stress-free activity for me once I learned my lines. It felt as though I was acting in a high-school play.

So even though I was out of the tour bus, I really didn't slow down much. I played in five movies that year, with some major Hollywood stars.

Four of the movies were Westerns. The fifth, *At Risk*, was sort of an artsy film about the tragic subject of AIDS.

The biggest-budget film I showed up in—and probably the smallest part—was *Maverick*, with Jodie Foster and Mel Gibson, an expanded remake of the old TV show starring James Garner. But I had a much bigger role in *Dead Man's Revenge*, a made-for-television movie in which I played a marshal trying to keep a land baron (Bruce Dern) from cheating everyone in town.

Bill Paxton and I became friends on the set of the movie *Frank & Jesse*—another Western about the notorious bank robbers, the James brothers. Bill played Frank James. Rob Lowe played his famous brother, Jesse. And I played Cole Younger, a member of the James-Younger gang, which had robbed and killed their way into Wild West infamy.

It was one of my first leading roles in a feature film, and Bill went out of his way to help me portray my character. He was such a good-natured guy and always so positive. "You're nailing this part, Randy!" he encouraged me. There was never a bad day on the set if Bill Paxton was there.

I especially enjoyed playing in *Frank & Jesse*, since the director allowed me to do my own stunts, most of which were done on horseback. I'd been practicing quick-draws and target shooting and riding horses since I was a kid, so I was happy to give some tips to some of my costars.

In preparation for working on the movie, I read quite a bit about Cole and the gang and discovered that Cole was a pretty rough character. I wasn't used to playing a villain, but acting like a tough guy was a lot of fun for me. I even had a full beard for a few weeks while on the set, but I never got used to it. As soon as I was done with the movie, I shaved that thing off.

In 1993, I also did a movie called *Outlaws: The Legend of O.B. Taggart*, a Western starring Mickey Rooney, Ernest Borgnine, Ned Beatty, Ben Johnson, Gloria DeHaven, Larry Gatlin, Nick Guest, and me. The story was about a reformed train robber who gets out of prison and tries to recover some stolen gold, but who has to battle his selfish sons (Larry, Nick, and me) to get it. The cast was remarkable—a collection of Hollywood greats. The script, however, supposedly written by Mickey Rooney, was notable for its horrible dialogue and the direction was even worse.

Prior to the first day of shooting, I had memorized all my lines, plus the lines of the characters with whom I was supposed to interact. I showed up on location the first day, and when the cameras rolled, I said my lines. Mickey started rattling off a bunch of lines in response, lines that I had not seen anywhere in the script. I stood there thinking, *I didn't read any of this!*

When Mickey stopped, I was still standing there staring at him.

"Do you know when to talk?" Mickey asked me.

"No, I don't," I responded, thinking that Mickey was going to give me some secret to great acting or some cue that I should play off. Then I saw it in his face: Mickey wasn't that profound.

"You talk when I stop," Mickey said.

That's how we did the entire movie—making up lines as we went along. When the movie came out, the lack of thought that went into each line of dialogue was all too obvious. The movie is sort of a grisly cross between *Of Mice and Men* and *Unforgiven*, but not in the league of those two great films. I loved Mickey Rooney, and I don't want to say that we were terrible, but few people saw that movie, and I'm kinda glad of that.

Outlaws premiered February 14, 1995, at the National Cowboy Hall of Fame in Oklahoma City. Thankfully, most people were out to dinner for Valentine's Day instead of in the audience.

One movie I did around that time was really unusual and a lot of fun. It grew out of my first visit to Santa Fe.

For several years, we had been doing tours with Tammy Wynette and other artists, sponsored by General Motors Corporation. During one of our sweeps out West, we played Albuquerque, New Mexico. While we were there, Tammy and her husband, George Richey, invited us to drive to Santa Fe for lunch. After eating a great meal of Mexican food, we started shopping—one of Lib's favorite sports—and exploring the area. We admired Santa Fe's landscape, its adobe architecture, and its laid-back cowboy lifestyle. Walking through town was like stepping back in time into a Western movie.

Out of that trip came a concept for an album and a movie to accompany it called *The Wind in the Wire*, a story about the making of a Western movie. The script included lots of fighting and lots of singing. My role, since the whole idea was to feature me performing some cowboy music, was that of a singer who gets to fulfill his dream of being in a movie about the Wild West—sort of a movie within a movie. Along the way my character befriends an orphan, and the rest is, well, downright hilarious.

For the leading roles in the movie, we called in favors from friends including Burt Reynolds, Lou Diamond Phillips, Denver Pyle, Charles Nelson Riley, and Melanie Chartoff. We even convinced Chuck Norris to do a cameo scene in which he kicked my butt for some reason I can't remember. Chuck plays rough! We had to do the scene several times, so the next morning I hurt in places I didn't know I had. I think even my feet were a combination of black, blue, purple, and green!

The movie itself was campy entertainment, but making it was a lot of fun. We filmed in New Mexico, Hawaii (with some real Hawaiian cowboys), and on a South Dakota ranch owned by our friend Ray Hillenbrand, who owned American Tourister luggage, which he sold to Samsonite, and Hill-Rom, a major hospital equipment company. Ray and his family also owned Batesville Casket Company, so we sometimes teased him, "Ray, between your luggage, hospital beds, and the coffins, you're gonna get us coming or going!" We had met Ray a few years earlier at a fair in South Dakota, and he'd invited us out to his ranch, where he had countless buffalo and other animals. It was the perfect set for a Western movie.

Lib received an executive-producer credit on *The Wind in the Wire* (as Elizabeth Travis) as well as a coproducer credit (as Lib Hatcher), along with Mark Kalbfeld. Gary Haber, our business manager, got a production credit, as did bus driver Ron Avis. We even managed to include my brother Dennis for a small part in the movie. It was definitely a family affair.

To accompany the movie, we went into the studio and recorded an entire album of special Western-style songs. It was one of the few albums in my career that Kyle Lehning did not produce; Steve Gibson, one of Nashville's premier studio musicians, guided the sessions. We used some of Nashville's finest musicians, including Charlie McCoy on harmonica, Gary Prim on keyboards, Eddie Bayers on drums, Sonny Garrish on steel guitar, and David Hungate on bass guitar. Acclaimed orchestrator Bergen White jumped in and sang background vocals. For the Hawaiian songs we incorporated the help of the Pahinui Brothers, who were famous in the islands for genuine traditional Hawaiian-style musicianship.

Despite our best efforts, *Wind in the Wire*, my eighth album for Warner Bros., was the absolute worst-selling record I ever did for them. We didn't even chart a single from it higher than #46 on the US music charts, although one song, "Cowboy Boogie," peaked at #10 on some Canadian charts. The guys were all great, but I guess the timing, the content, and the style worked against us.

Overall the movie and the album were both unsuccessful, but they accomplished one thing: they triggered our move from the Nashville area to Santa Fe. We bought a home and immediately began looking for property where we could build something to our own specifications.

At the same time, I began thinking about a new album—a different type of album. Kyle Lehning and I got together and found some great songs, and before long we were back in the studio again. The album turned out to be a more introspective work called *This Is Me*.

We were in the studio together one summer day in 1993 when Jeff Davis came by looking for some recordings for Brother Phelps, a group Jeff now managed with his new company Sum Management. I hadn't seen Jeff or even talked with him since he resigned from our company, so our reunion felt a bit awkward at first. But Jeff said, "Hey, Hoss, how're ya doin'?" Within minutes the uneasiness fell away, and we were back to our old selves. That was a good thing, because Jeff would be back in our lives sooner than any of us suspected.

A few years earlier, we had met Richard Sturm, who headed up the entertainment division at the MGM Grand Hotel in Las Vegas. Back then the hotel had been located where Bally's is today, but construction was already under way for a new MGM Grand. Richard had picked us up and taken us to the site on the strip where the huge "green T" version was being built. "When we get this place finished," Richard had said, "it is going to be a fantastic venue with an enormous arena, and I want you to be the first country-music artist to perform here." We'd shaken hands and smiled a lot back then, but we hadn't made any kind of formal agreement.

True to his word, however, Richard called me late in 1993. The new venue was set to open soon, and he wanted me to appear when it did. I agreed to do it—which meant I needed to put the show back together.

In December, we called Jeff Davis and left several phone numbers where we could be reached. I was doing a movie in Arkansas, so Jeff returned the call to our hotel room there.

Lib and Jeff talked briefly, and then I heard her say, "Do you want to talk to Randy?"

I jumped on the phone and talked with Jeff for a few minutes before handing the phone back to Lib. "I guess you heard that we are going to open the MGM Grand in February," she said to Jeff.

"No, I hadn't heard that," he said. "But congratulations. That's fantastic."

"Well, it won't be the same going out there without you," Lib said.

The phone remained quiet for a few long seconds before Jeff said, "Well, you don't have to." His voice was heavy with emotion.

"Really?" Lib seemed excited that Jeff might consider joining us for the Vegas dates.

"Well, yeah," Jeff said. "I'll be happy to help you if you want me to be involved."

"I sure do," Lib said. "Do you want to send us a proposal?" Jeff was no longer on our payroll, so we hired him as an outside consultant. We knew he would be a blessing because at that point we had no band, no crew, no set design, no production manager, and no sound and light people.

"Do you have anyone on board yet?" Jeff asked.

"Ah . . . not really," Lib admitted. "Evelyn Shriver has been talking to a few people, but we really need to rebuild our entire show." Jeff was the perfect man for the job. He pulled together some studio session players from Nashville to play the Vegas show and even talked Kyle Lehning into playing keyboards. A stellar producer, Kyle is also a fantastic piano player, and, of course, he already knew my songs.

We opened at the MGM Grand in Vegas during President's Day weekend in February 1994. When the industry heard that "Randy Travis is back," our phones started ringing off the desk again. Within two weeks we were back playing huge arenas such as the Houston Livestock Show at the Astrodome. On March 1 we played at the Warner Bros. showcase at the Country Music Seminar in Nashville. Over the next few months we gradually put most of the old band back together. Drew Sexton had been having some health problems, so he chose not to come back out with us. But L.D. was able to rejoin us— thanks to Porter Wagoner.

At the time, L.D. was playing full time at the Grand Ole Opry with Porter and freelancing a bit as well. He'd been a regular staff musician on the Opry for more than eighteen years. But he talked with Porter and told him I wanted him back out on the road, and Porter was kind enough to let him tour with me and still play the Opry whenever that worked out with everyone's schedule. I knew it wasn't easy to replace a guitar player with the expertise and experience of L.D., so the next time I saw Porter, I thanked him for being so gracious. L.D. came back on the road with me in 1994, but he still did every Opry show with Porter and his band any time we were in Nashville.

Meanwhile, as our touring schedule geared back up, I continued work on the new album. In 1994, I wrote a song with Buck Moore called "The Box." The song was about a father who loved his son but didn't do well with "love out loud." Yet he saved special pieces of memorabilia about his family and kept them all in a box. When the father died, the son found the box. As he riffled through the keepsakes, he realized for the first time in his life that his father had loved him and been proud of him. That song tore me up almost every time I sang it—I couldn't help thinking about my fractured relationship with my own dad. We put "The Box" on the *This Is Me* album.

When *This Is Me* came out in 1995, it had been more than three years since my last new studio project—with two greatest-hits albums and the *Wind in the Wire* cowboy-music soundtrack released in between. Although some reviewers didn't care for the scaled-down, back-to-the-basics approach, I thoroughly enjoyed making the record. In some ways, I felt it represented a reinvention of myself musically.

Kyle, Martha Sharp, and Lib and I considered more than one thousand songs for *This Is Me*, looking especially for story songs and some with a wink of humor. It took us more than a year to find what we wanted, but the extra work was worth the effort. The first single, "Before You Kill Us All," went to #1. The final single from the album was "The Box," and it reached #7 on *Billboard*'s Hot Country Singles.

We pushed ourselves hard promoting the album. On one occasion we worked three shows at the MGM Grand Resort in Vegas, and then, as soon as we were done, Jeff had a Gulfstream II jet waiting for us. The jet whisked us to Salem, Oregon, where we performed an evening show at the state fair, and then on to Los Angeles, where we set up early the next morning for rehearsal at *The Tonight Show with Jay Leno*, which taped around four o'clock in the afternoon. We did shows in three states within twenty-four hours. It was life in the fast lane, and we were riding high again.

On April 27, the day after the album released, TNN devoted an entire evening to my music, with me hosting *Music City Tonight*, followed by a special viewing of *The Wind in the Wire*. Then, on April 29, I appeared on *Late Night with David Letterman* to promote the new album.

I was glad to dispel the rumors that I had retired.

I felt as though I was back.

18 —— FANS, FLOWERS, AND FOOD

When we went out on tour in 1995, Sammy Kershaw opened our show, followed by George Jones and then me. We started with an outstanding series of concerts at the Palace of Auburn Hills in Michigan and the Rupp Arena in Lexington, Kentucky. Sammy would get the crowd stirred up, and then George Jones would leave them standing on their feet every night. He always had that playful smile on his face backstage after his show, as though to say, "There ya go, youngster. See if you can follow that!" It was tough, but I did, and the crowds were fantastically enthusiastic. These were show dates that Jeff promoted with his new company, and they were super successful.

Lib and I eventually talked Jeff into coming back to our company full time and working out of our office. He continued as our tour manager as well as helping promote our events.

One day Allan Baggett, one of our truck drivers, brought Jeff Davis a recording of a song he thought I should hear. It was called "Old Pair of Shoes." Jeff thought it was good, so he gave it to me. I listened and said, "Yep, that's a good song, and that's a great singer too."

About that time, a couple of the guys in the band told me about a new guy they had heard performing in a Nashville club. "You gotta hear this guy," the guys agreed. "He has a fantastic voice, and he loves traditional country music."

His name was Daryle Singletary, and the guys were right. I loved what Daryle did with a song. Lib quickly signed Daryle to a management deal to help develop him as an artist. She had done something similar with Gene Watson in the mid-1980s. But by now we were much busier, so Lib struck a deal with Jeff to comanage Daryle. We put him onstage with us as part of our band and then later as an opening act, singing a few songs before I came on. Daryle hung around with us for a couple of years before we finally wrangled a recording contract for him with Giant Records, a joint venture with Warner Bros. now headed by my longtime friend James Stroud.

James, David Malloy, and I produced Daryle's first self-titled album, and it landed two songs on the charts, "Too Much Fun" and "I Let Her Lie." We booked Daryle with us on a number of dates that we promoted in-house, and he was always a crowd-pleaser.

We loved to tease Daryle on the road too. At a venue in New Jersey, he opened the show for us. While he was onstage, L.D. and I slipped over to the side of the stage, where Paulie, our stage monitor engineer, was working the console. I leaned over Paulie's shoulder and pressed the button on the board so I could speak and Daryle could hear me through the monitors, but the audience couldn't hear me.

When Daryle went down deep to hit a low note, I said, "Good *try*." Daryle responded as though he'd heard the voice of God speaking to him, but he kept on singing. Then the next time he went for the low note, I said through the monitors, "Almost."

At that point Daryle realized it was me who was messing with him, and he started laughing in the middle of the song. Later that night, when I came onstage, Daryle found an opportunity to get even, sneaking out onstage with a microphone and joining us on our remake of the Brook Benton classic, "It's Just a Matter of Time."

L.D. and I were talking one night after a show about another artist we had recently seen. The artist seemed almost rude and uncaring about the fans and so arrogant. I was certain I must have gotten the wrong impression, so I asked L.D., "Did that artist seem cocky to you?"

L.D. nodded and said, "Yeah, Hoss, an ego is a heavy thing to carry."

I thought that was a simple yet profound statement. After that, any time I felt tempted to get cocky, I recalled, "An ego is a heavy thing to carry."

I loved meeting the fans, and I tried to take as much time as possible after every show simply to connect with as many as I could. I'd stay half the night if Lib or Jeff didn't come along and say, "Randy, we have to go. The bus is ready to roll." Folks usually understood if I didn't get to speak to them personally or sign their albums or photos, but I always hated to let them down.

I particularly remember a time when we were at the Rosemont Horizon (now known as Allstate Arena) near Chicago, playing to a sold-out crowd of more than ten thousand people. At the conclusion of the concert, Jeff and the security team whisked me out the back door of the venue and onto our bus. We grabbed a couple of water bottles and flopped down exhausted onto the couches in the front of the bus as the audience poured out the exits. There were metal barricades fencing off the exit doors from where our buses were parked, but the fans were in close proximity. They sounded so excited and happy, and I suddenly felt sad that I had not been able to spend any time interacting with them. I was too tired to talk, but I could hear the enthusiastic voices outside.

I looked down at the floor, then back up in the direction the fans' voices seemed to be coming from. Finally I nodded toward the bus windows nearest the venue and asked, "Jeff, can I go out there?"

Jeff looked surprised. "Yeah, I guess so," he said. "If you want to."

"Will you go with me?"

"Well, sure," Jeff said, then repeated, "If you want to go."

"I do."

Jeff and I stepped off the bus, greeted by cheers from the crowd. I walked over to the barricade and began signing autographs for the people coming out of the exit. Within seconds we had gathered a crowd. I talked with folks as I signed, and even though it was late at night, the group kept growing larger. We stayed out there signing autographs till somewhere between three and four o'clock in the morning—until the last person got an autograph. We had no security guards or "people handlers" trying to move folks along. It was just Jeff and me and a few thousand of our friends.

I never wanted to forget what it felt like to be a fan going to shows, so I went out of my way to sign an autograph or talk to someone who wanted to speak to me if at all possible. I knew what it felt like to admire an artist, and I still enjoyed going out to hear other artists any time I could. Even at television tapings or award shows, I wanted to go where I could see and hear the other performers. Although many were now friends, they were still heroes to me.

From the earliest days of my career, fans often brought or sent me stuffed animals. I kept most of the gifts in good shape throughout the year. Then, each year around Christmastime, we would pack up most of them and send them to a shelter for homeless children who otherwise might not receive a gift at Christmas. The kids loved the stuffed animals, and my fans knew their presents to me would also bless some children who would treasure them as well.

Fans also brought flowers to our concerts and either laid them onstage or gave them to me personally. That always meant so much to me, and I appreciated the beautiful bouquets and the thoughtfulness that accompanied them. I collected the flowers from our fans and kept as many as possible on our bus. Sometimes, when the fans were especially generous, we'd take the floral overflow to hospitals or nursing homes in towns where we were playing and pass along the fresh flowers to the patients.

Still other kind folks brought food to me prior to concerts or after the shows. I guess they felt that if I couldn't go home with them for a meal, they'd bring "home" to me. So we always had a ton of food backstage. I was trying to stay in shape, so I wouldn't eat much of it, but the band members ate well.

Lib always cooked delicious, healthy meals for us at home, and she and I ate well on the bus, too, whether fans brought us food or not. Our concert date rider—the part of a show contract document describing food and beverage details—was rather simple, with no big extravagances, but we did request good, commonsense food for our guys at each show. We also had a tradition called "Sundaes on Sunday." Every Sunday, in other words, we'd have an ice cream sundae bar with all the trimmings along with the dinner. And people wondered why I worked out so much!

I had long ago discovered that eating before a concert didn't work for me, so although we always had plenty of regional catered food backstage for the band and crew, on show days I would not eat anything after three o'clock in the afternoon. Certain foods no longer worked well for me on concert days, either. I loved ice cream, for instance, but eating it clogged my throat and negatively affected my vocal cords, so I passed it by.

The guys in the band often scooped up extra portions of food at the backstage catering service that they'd keep for "after the show." I'd often see them scurrying out of the arena with armloads of food they were saving for later. Knowing that I couldn't or wouldn't eat before the show, the guys would playfully call out to me, "After the show, Hoss!"

"After the show, Hoss!" became a saying on the road with the guys. Usually we were referring to what or where we were going to eat.

Daryle Singletary was a pretty hefty guy, so Lib was doing all she could to help him get his weight down. She hired a trainer to come out on the tour with us, and he had Daryle working out every day, trying to lose a few pounds and getting into better shape. Daryle was frustrated with the rigid diet and exercise program, and by the time we got to the Strawberry Festival in Plant City, Florida, he was practically begging Steve Hinson and L.D. for some real food.

"I'm so tired of this diet," Daryle said. "Please get me some of that home-cooked catering!"

Daryle didn't realize the humor in his statement, but it worked nonetheless. Steve and L.D. gave in and filled a plate for Daryle. They loaded it with fried chicken, mashed potatoes, green beans, and corn bread. Daryle ate every bit of it, and I don't think Lib ever knew.

19 — CLOSED DOORS, OPEN DOORS

After four singles in 1996 and 1997 didn't do as well as we hoped, frustration set in. In January 1997, however, my album *High Lonesome* earned platinum status for sales of more than a million copies, and ten days later *Old 8 x 10* was certified by the RIAA as double platinum. So the executives at Warner Bros. were thrilled. But Lib, unhappy over the failure of the singles, started talking more frequently about exploring other possibilities and maybe even signing with another record company.

We entered into serious discussions with Warner Bros. about my future there. At the same time Lib engaged in conversations with other music company executives, especially people who were telling her what she wanted to hear—that somebody was willing to give us more, that more of my songs would be recorded, that they would do a better job of promoting the albums and me, and that oh, yeah, they'd give us a ton of money too.

It all sounded almost too good to be true—which I assumed it was.

Why would we want to leave? I wondered. We had a great track record of success with Warner Bros. and they with us. Although Jim Ed Norman was still the head of Warner, many of the people who'd been there when we started were gone, and Lib was convinced that Bill Mayne and others at Warner had lost confidence in me and were no longer promoting my music as they had done in the past. It would be years before I found out that accusation wasn't true. But at the time, with the minimal response of radio to my last four singles, it seemed to make sense.

In one meeting with the Warner execs, we were discussing songs that I planned to record. Warner expressed concern that some of my selections weren't as good as some others we were considering. Lib countered with her concern that she, Kyle Lehning, and I didn't have as much say as we used to in which songs were being released as singles. One thing led to another, and soon the meeting devolved into a dispiriting discussion of how Warner Bros. was or was not promoting my music to radio stations.

Things got real personal in that meeting and some of the things that were said were offensive. Lib was irate. "You don't believe in Randy as a songwriter," she said.

"No, that's not what we're saying," Bill Mayne responded. "We just want the best songs to win."

Of course, that had always been my desire as well—not simply to record something that I had written, but to record the *best* songs that I could convey to the listener in the most believable fashion.

"I'm just saying we need hit records right now," Bill continued. "So we need to be careful about what songs we put on the album and even more intentional about what we put out as a single to radio stations."

Lib proceeded to imply that Warner was purposely trying to hurt my career. Jim Ed Norman and Bill Mayne countered with, "Why would we ever want to do such a thing? We'd only be hurting ourselves."

We left that day with a lot of hurt feelings all around the table. In late April 1997, after eleven years with Warner Bros. Records, I made a change, signing with DreamWorks Records, a new music and entertainment company owned by multimedia moguls David Geffen, Steven Spielberg, and Jeffrey Katzenberg. The DreamWorks Nashville subsidiary, which specialized in country music, was headed up by my longtime friend, James Stroud.

James and I went way back together. James had even played drums on "Forever and Ever, Amen." Now, with the help of the Hollywood heavyweight investors, he had developed DreamWorks Nashville, and I was the first major artist signed on the label. Some people guessed that I was signing with the Hollywood guys to enhance my acting career, but I had already worked in more than a dozen films and had appeared on several television shows, including *Matlock*, with Andy Griffith. Certainly there was potential for more film work, but that existed regardless of my record label.

Making my decision a little easier, Kyle Lehning had taken a job as president of another new label, Asylum Records in Nashville. As the boss of the label, he needed to be careful about conflicts of interest, so he couldn't continue producing my records.

Kyle and I never really talked seriously about my moving over to Asylum. One of the best producers in the business, he might have sensed that he wouldn't be happy sitting behind a desk and didn't think it wise to bring me to Asylum if he wouldn't be there long term. And that's exactly what would happen. Kyle would do a great job with Asylum, but he eventually got out of the business office there so he could spend more time in the studio.

Meanwhile, however, while he was at Asylum, Kyle was not available to me. So part of the deal for my moving to DreamWorks was to have James Stroud producing me, along with stellar producer Byron Gallimore, who was enjoying enormous success with Tim McGraw.

We made two great albums at DreamWorks, the first of which was *You and You Alone*. I was nervous when we put out the first single from that album, "Out of My Bones." After all, I'd been off the radio for a couple of years, with a hitless streak of nearly three years and four failed singles in a row. I fretted whether the deejays and program managers would even remember me, much less play my new music after so long. But "Out of My Bones" quickly landed in *Billboard*'s top five. Not bad for being out of the game for so long! The songs "Stranger in My Mirror" and "Spirit of a Boy, Wisdom of a Man" also did well and let radio know that I was back.

The second DreamWorks album, *A Man Ain't Made of Stone*, shot out of the gates as well in 1999, with some well-written songs and a slightly different sound than people were accustomed to hearing from me. I was excited and felt as though I was starting my career all over again.

But then the boys in Hollywood pulled the plug. In 2005 DreamWorks Nashville would be sold and sucked into Universal Music Group. James Stroud became cochairman of UMG Nashville, along with Luke Lewis.

I'd had fun working with my buddy James, and I'd enjoyed creating music with Byron Gallimore on the DreamWorks albums. But when the label went under, I went for a while without a recording deal. Eventually I would reunite with Kyle Lehning, my longtime friend and producer. Kyle and I shared a special chemistry in the recording studio that I never experienced with anyone else in quite the same way.

In the meantime I stayed busy doing shows on the road and also kicked my movie career into high gear. A film I had done with Patrick Swayze, *Black Dog*, premiered in Nashville—with Patrick on hand for the debut showing—a few days after the release of my first DreamWorks album in April 1998. The story was about a truck driver (Patrick) and his sidekick (me) hauling some illegal materials in an eighteen-wheeler. The action movie is loaded with chase scenes, truck crashes, and a villain (Meat Loaf, another musician/actor) who spouts Bible verses while he tries to highjack the truck. Patrick was one of the nicest, most unpretentious and down-to-earth actors I'd ever met. He was quick to help me with my lines and with the action in my scenes—and he could sing too! He came to Nashville in 1998 and recorded a song with me called "I Did My Part," and it turned out fantastic.

I played a cowboy-type gunfighter named Frank Bones in *Texas Rangers*, a movie based on actual events surrounding Leander McNelly, a Ranger hired to stop marauding Mexican bandits in 1875. I didn't have a lot of dialogue in the film, but my character smoked a lot of those small, dark cigars. Since I don't smoke at all, those strong cigars nearly turned my face green for every scene.

As soon as *Texas Rangers* wrapped, I traveled to Mississippi to work on another movie, *John John in the Sky* (later retitled *I'll Wave Back*), an independent film designed to be shown at the Sundance Film Festival. In this movie I played a man who appeared to be a fine, upstanding Christian, a churchgoing husband and father, who was all the while abusing his wife.

I was no sooner done with the abuse story than I signed on to do *The Trial of Major Reno*, a fascinating historical documentary about General George Custer's second in command, Major Marcus Reno, who was accused of failing to come to Custer's assistance when the horrendous massacre at Little Bighorn began. It was hard to imagine a uniformed officer not seeking to help under such critical circumstances, but as the story shows, not all men have courage under fire. Although Major Reno was officially exonerated of the charges, his reputation was ruined.

Charlton Heston narrated the documentary, and I served as the host, introducing various segments. The program aired on PBS. I enjoyed working on the educational project, and in the process I learned a lot about the frailties of even the strongest men.

I was reminded again, along with the entire country-music world, of how fragile our lives can be when we gathered at the Ryman Auditorium in Nashville early in April 1998 to say good-bye to one of music's greatest icons. Tammy Wynette had died unexpectedly at only fifty-five years of age. Mourners lined the streets all around the "Mother Church of Country Music" on a gray, windy day, but inside the auditorium the stage was lined with large, colorful floral arrangements and beautiful photos of Tammy.

I was one of a number of artists privileged to sing and speak at the service. Having toured with Tammy for nearly five years, I had gotten to know her well. "She was a lady who enjoyed laughing," I told the crowd. "I always loved her sense of humor." I sang the old gospel song, "Precious Memories," one of Tammy's favorites. Dolly Parton spoke and sang as well, and Naomi and Wynonna Judd also shared stories about one of the female pioneers of country music, who was also known as "the queen of heartache." Lorrie Morgan brought the memorial service to a fitting though somewhat ironic close by performing Tammy's signature song, "Stand by Your Man," as specially requested by Tammy's fifth and final husband, George Richey. I'd been to a few funerals and memorial services in my lifetime, but I'd never experienced anything comparable to the way country music artists and fans rally around our fallen heroes.

On May 23, 1998, we were scheduled as the headlining act at a huge festival in Palm Desert, California, when I received word that my mom had passed away from congestive heart failure back in North Carolina. Lib called Jeff and said, "Bobbie just passed away. I don't think Randy can do the show this weekend."

"Absolutely not," Jeff said. "Everybody can understand that."

"But what about the promoters?" Lib asked.

"They'll understand," Jeff said. "Trust me. I'll take care of it."

I went to Mom's funeral that weekend, and Jeff contacted Rod Essig at Creative Artists Agency, who was now assisting us with booking. Together they brought in somebody they thought could fill the bill, an up-and-coming artist I had once met when he was a waiter at a seafood restaurant in Jacksonville, Florida. His name was Tim McGraw. The fans and promoters loved Tim, and I appreciated him stepping in for me at the last minute.

Going to my mother's funeral and being with my father again evoked so many memories, most of them unpleasant. My dad had always been unpredictable, angry, and hateful, especially when he drank too much, and he hadn't improved in recent years. He'd often show up drunk and become belligerent at my concerts, brandishing one of his pistols. When we knew Dad was coming, we hired extra bodyguards just to keep an eye on him. He usually had a bottle of Kessler "smooth as silk" Whiskey in the trunk of his car, and when there was a break in the action, Dad went out to visit his trunk. When he returned to the venue, he was usually looking for a fight—with me, with a fan, with one of our crew guys, or especially with Lib.

There was a constant tension between Daddy and Lib. After all, in Daddy's mind, she had stolen me from my family when I was only seventeen. In reality, she had successfully kept me out of prison and helped me to get away from alcohol and marijuana. Now, here was my father almost flaunting his alcohol in front of me. He was a passionate country music fan, and I felt sure he was proud of me, yet he'd never say so. Instead, he persisted in causing trouble and more heartaches.

The home folks in the Carolinas were mighty good to me, though. In March 1999, North Carolina governor James B. Hunt Jr. officially pardoned me for four offenses I had committed as a teenager between 1975 and 1977. The charges included breaking and entering, carrying a concealed weapon, and larceny. Governor Hunt didn't stop there, though. On May 14, 1999, he declared "Randy Travis Day," and I was inducted into the North Carolina Music Hall of Fame. I sure appreciated the honor and the fact that the governor had cleared my name of those offenses. Few things in life feel better than forgiveness, even if it is a long time in coming.

In September 2000, I performed my first-ever concert backed by a full symphony orchestra at the Hollywood Bowl, a huge outdoor venue in Los Angeles. The sound on the stage was incredible as our band joined with some of LA's finest musicians to create a night of music we would always remember. Then in December we were back on the West Coast again where we recorded a new album, *Live: It Was Just a Matter of Time*, at the Sun Theatre in Anaheim, featuring our biggest hits and a few other favorites too. The album title was sort of an inside joke, since we'd been talking about doing another live album for years. The last one had been when I first started out at the Nashville Palace.

Onstage during the taping of the new album, I joked that I really missed the people in Tennessee—my brother Dennis and his wife still lived there—and I really missed the fried catfish, along with the amazing homemade pies and cakes. I was starting to get hungry just thinking about it when I heard one of the guys in the band call out, "After the show, Hoss!"

In May of that year, I appeared with Faye Dunaway, Lulu Roman, Delta Burke, and John Schneider in a special two-part story on CBS-TV's hit show *Touched by an Angel*. I had been on the show several times previously, filming in Salt Lake City, and I always enjoyed working with the great cast and crew. From the first time I worked with her during the inaugural season of the show in 1994, producer Martha Williamson put my mind at ease on the set. "Randy, just be yourself," she encouraged me. "That's why I wanted you to play this part. The character is a lot like you." Martha created two recurring characters for me to play on the show, Wayne Machulis and Jed Winslow. I was Jed in the 2001 episodes.

Part of the role included my character losing his temper in front of the angels, Monica and Tess, played by Roma Downey and Della Reese. But the story lines on that show inevitably included something redemptive, and that's why I always said yes when they invited me back.

20 ——————— BORN-AGAIN MUSIC

I remained an artist without a record label for a while. DreamWorks had closed, and I had not yet signed another recording deal. I was talking with Kyle Lehning one day, when Kyle suggested, "Why don't we make a record and you own it. Then you can pitch it to any label." Kyle had recently left Asylum and was ready to get back into producing music full time.

I liked his idea, so we went into the studio and began working. But we didn't want to create my usual "country" album. Instead, we hoped to record country music with subtle Christian themes. I didn't want to do the typical "country music artist sings the hymns" approach, although I always appreciate those kinds of albums. We weren't really thinking in terms of gospel music, either, but merely music with a message that would cause people to consider a relationship with God. We were shooting for a real low-key musical presentation with the vocals way out in front so the lyrics would come through strong.

After several months we were nearly done with the album, which we had titled *Inspirational Journey*, and we planned to present it to Peter York at Sparrow Records. Peter had heard the music and had begun negotiations on a deal with us for the album.

Kyle was on the board of the National Academy of Recording Arts and Sciences (NARAS), the organization that awards Grammy Awards and works in the best interests of music artists. Barry Landis was also on the board. Barry was now working with Word Records, which at the time was owned by Warner Bros. Barry asked about my next album, and Kyle told him that I was getting ready to sign with Sparrow.

"Wait a minute!" Barry said. "You can't do that! Please don't do that."

"Well, the paperwork is already done," Kyle said, "and is on the desk."

"Can I hear the album?" Barry asked.

"Sure, I guess so," Kyle said.

When Barry heard the new music, he did something highly unusual. He went to Peter York at Sparrow and begged him to allow Word to release and distribute it. Peter York is such a great guy that he said, "Look, if that is what you want to do, go ahead with my blessing." In one of the most rare and unselfish acts I've ever experienced in the music business, Peter allowed Barry to take the album.

Released in 2000, *Inspirational Journey* contained the typical blend of electrical and acoustic guitar sounds found on most of my other albums, expertly balanced by Kyle's adept producing skills that kept the background music laid back and my vocals up front. The most significant change, however, came in the song lyrics. Songs such as "Dr. Jesus" and "The Carpenter," a song on which Waylon Jennings and his wife, Jessi Colter, helped me out, expressed more overtly gospel messages than I had recorded previously.

One of the sensational songs on that album was simply titled, "Baptism," written by Mickey Cates. I had previously sung it as a duet with Kenny Chesney on his album, *Everywhere We Go*. The song describes the baptism of a young man in a muddy river, indicating that the old way of his life was over and something new had started. I could relate to the lyrics, so I performed the song in both my "Christian" shows and my regular ones, even the casino shows. No matter where I performed it, when I reached the part of the lyric that said, "down with the old man, up with the new," describing the old, sinful person dying to the former way of life and being raised to a new, rejuvenated kind of life, the audiences inevitably broke out in spontaneous applause.

Perhaps the most meaningful song of all on the album was the classic version of "Amazing Grace," a song written in the 1700s by John Newton, a former slave trader whose life had been transformed when he trusted in Jesus

Christ. God's power, love, and mercy turned Newton into a different quality of person. Although I couldn't explain it, I knew that something like that had happened to me. God had changed my life for the better. So singing the lyrics of that song has become a testimony for me—and an overwhelming, emotional experience every time I sing it.

Much to the surprise of many naysayers in the music industry, *Inspirational Journey* received critical acclaim as well as a Grammy Award nomination and two Dove Awards from the Gospel Music Association.

Rise and Shine was my second foray into music with an overtly Christian message. I had enjoyed writing and performing the songs from *Inspirational Journey*, so for the new album I cowrote six of the thirteen songs we included. The first time we played "Rise and Shine," we did it with just my guitar players and me at an Easter celebration, so the song fit in perfectly with the message of the Resurrection and the effects it had on believers' lives. Obviously that first audience had never heard of the song before—it wasn't yet on an album and hadn't yet played on the radio—but the crowd gave us a long standing ovation. The first four times in a row that we performed the song, we received similar responses.

The only other song that I remember evoking that kind of response night after night, with people who had never before heard it, was "Forever and Ever, Amen." I knew we had struck a chord musically as we played "Rise and Shine," and the lyrics struck a spiritual chord in people's hearts as they heard it.

Rise and Shine included some serious songs such as "Jerusalem's Cry," drawn from the book of Revelation, and some upbeat, guitar-pickin' songs such as "Keep Your Lure in the Water," a whimsical encouragement about witnessing for the Lord. And then there was, "Pray for the Fish," a song about a fella whose life was so dirty before he met the Lord that when he finally got baptized the fish in the water were in danger.

That song brought smiles to faces every time we played it. I knew it was not a life-changing song, but I like to laugh, and I like people who enjoy a good sense of humor. So I seek out those off-the-wall sort of songs that convey their messages with a touch of humor. "Pray for the Fish" was certainly that kind of song, and people loved it.

Another unselfish act helped put the album over the top. Michael

Peterson, a great singer, was recording an album for Sony, produced by Kyle Lehning and Blake Chancey. Near the end of the recording process, Michael found a new song. Michael took the song to Kyle and told him, "I really think this is a great song and it would work well with Randy's voice."

When Kyle heard it, he agreed. But he asked Michael, "Are you sure you don't want to record this yourself?"

"No, I don't hear it for me," Michael said. "But I do hear it for Randy." Just to be sure, Kyle let Blake Chancey hear the song. Blake checked with the label heads, who said that Michael had already recorded extra songs and didn't need that one. Only then did Kyle send the song on to me.

I was on a treadmill the first time I heard the song about a farmer, a teacher, a hooker, and a preacher who are all on a midnight bus to Mexico when it collides with an eighteen-wheeler. Just when I thought I knew where the story was going, the lyrics took an intriguing twist. The last verse of the song revealed a preacher telling the story, blessing the farmer, and the teacher, and the preacher who gave the blood-stained Bible to his mama—the hooker—who had read it to him.

That is an amazing piece of writing! I thought. I stopped the treadmill and went back and listened to the song again to get more of the details. The point of the story was that it's not what you take from this world, but what you leave behind when you go. When I heard that line, I immediately called Kyle. "I understand why you like this song," I said. "I know we're already done with our album, but let's record this!"

The song had been written by Kim Williams and Doug Johnson, the writer who had come to my house with Don Schlitz more than a decade earlier. We had failed to write anything worthwhile that afternoon, but apparently he hadn't let that discourage him. I was so glad!

The incredible song that Kim and Doug wrote together and that came to me due to Michael Peterson's generosity was titled "Three Wooden Crosses." It was the last song we cut for my *Rise and Shine* album. We released it as a single, too, and we had high hopes for it. Although it was a tough sell at first when it went out to small-market radio stations, the song soon caught on. Radio stations began to get more and more requests for it, and the label pushed it into larger markets. It continued to rise all the way to the #1 position—not merely on Christian radio, but on country music stations as well. It was the first song released by the Christian music industry ever to hit the top of the country music charts as well as the pop charts. Some wag also noted that it was the first successful gospel single ever to contain the word *hooker*.

The record label gave me an award for the song's unprecedented success, having reached the #1 spot simultaneously on the *Billboard* chart, the *R & R* chart, and the *MusicRow* chart. The success of the song thrilled all of us, and we were knocked out that a song with a clear Christian message would connect so well with such a broad audience.

Perhaps because of the gospel albums and my more public expressions of my faith, I received numerous invitations to perform at what the guys in the band affectionately referred to as "church gigs"—concerts sponsored by churches or held in church sanctuaries. We played at some of the largest churches in America. The pastors always checked me out thoroughly before inviting me into their worlds and onto their platforms, and that seemed right to me. After all, my rowdy, sinful past was rather well known. I didn't blame the pastors when they wanted to know for sure that I had trusted in Jesus, genuinely repented, and turned away from my former lifestyle.

For most church dates, I scaled back on the band a bit. I took only guitar players—usually Lance Dary and Robb Houston and sometimes L.D.—which lent to doing a more acoustic show. Occasionally we brought along Herb Schucher on drums and Bill Cook playing bass guitar. In many instances the pastors interviewed me at some point during the event, and that often led to them extending an invitation for people in the audience to meet Jesus Christ, to put their trust in Him, and to experience a spiritual transformation similar to what I'd had. Many people responded to those invitations, and I was always thrilled that God could use my story to help someone else.

At one of the first church gigs we did, a mother, concerned that her son's constant drinking would get him killed, talked the young man into coming to the concert because he liked my music. When the pastor extended the invitation, the wayward son walked forward to the front of the sanctuary and committed his life to Christ. Or, as evangelical Christians like to say, he was "saved" that night—saved from sin, saved from hell, saved from the demons that plagued him, and saved from himself. Better yet, he was saved *to* God. Eventually he was baptized, and he made a complete turn toward a much healthier, safer, and more productive life.

When I later heard about this story from the pastor, it really touched me. In all my years of performing music, I don't think I'd ever before had that sort of impact. I didn't know how to explain it or even how to describe it. But it was a very humbling thing—and rewarding.

That young man's transformation really got to me. I had never imagined that I might play even a small part of helping somebody find God, that I could influence someone like that in a good way. But similar stories started showing up after our gospel stops across the nation, where some of our country-music fans who might not have been regular churchgoers ended the evening at the altar rather than a bar.

My new "ministry" events created some tension in my own mind, however. After all, I was still playing in casinos and other places where there was drinking, gambling, and carousing. We'd do gigs like that on Saturday, and then on Sunday we'd play at a large church somewhere and people would get saved.

The disconnect created some confusion in my own heart and mind, so I talked with some of the pastors of the churches where we played about the dilemma I felt. They all said basically the same thing: "Randy, we know your heart is in the right place. So it is okay that you are performing there in the casino, because you have the ability to bring people here to our churches. Your influence might bring people through our doors that otherwise might never come."

Some pastors turned that idea around as well, saying, "And you can have an influence for Christ right there in the casino." I'd never considered that, but when I thought about it, they were right. As one pastor put it, I might be the only "Bible" some people would ever read.

I'd always included a gospel song in every show, whether in a casino or any other venue—songs such as "Have a Little Talk with Jesus," as well as other songs with strong spiritual messages that I'd recorded on my albums. Later I included "Baptism," "Shallow Water," and "Pray for the Fish." The lyrics in that last song described a fella who sounded a lot like the former me, so regardless where we performed it, the audience got the message.

My Christian witness continued to expand when my full album, *Rise and*

Shine, debuted in October 2002. That same week I was a guest soloist for the Billy Graham Crusade at Texas Stadium in Irving. Despite congested traffic and torrential downpours of rain for two days, the evangelistic crusade set consecutive stadium attendance records of 82,000 and 83,500 that weekend.

Dr. Graham was extremely kind to me. He was a courteous gentleman and became almost like a father figure. I was honored to perform at several more of his crusades and to hear his straightforward words of wisdom. Those words were music to the souls of the sinner and the saved alike.

At the Grammy Awards in February 2004, *Rise and Shine* won the award for the Best Southern, Country, or Bluegrass Gospel Album. No doubt the success of "Three Wooden Crosses" had a lot to do with the recognition given the entire album. Thanks to that song, I'd also been nominated in the Best Male Country Vocal Performance category. I didn't win but applauded enthusiastically and sincerely when Vince Gill received a well-deserved award for his recording of "Next Big Thing."

♫ ♫

Some folks seem to think that being a Christian means nothing bad will ever happen to you. I haven't found that to be true in my life. But I have discovered that even when difficult times come or unexplainable events occur, Jesus never leaves or forsakes us.

We were scheduled to play a show in Lakeville, Pennsylvania, located in the Poconos, a popular northeastern resort area. The winter thaw was barely beginning, and while the main roads were clear of snow and ice, many of the rural roads remained treacherous.

As he usually did, Jeff Davis traveled with the crew bus early Sunday morning to check out the venue and plan how he would get my bus to the location later in the day. The roads were still frozen at that hour, but since there was little traffic, the crew bus and trucks managed to safely drive in the middle of a narrow access road that led to the backstage entrance of the mountain resort. Later Jeff returned to the hotel where we were waiting in our 1997 Prevost XL, a beautiful coach with a gorgeous painted mural of the area around our Santa Fe home on the side. A side door in the middle of the coach led into our living area.

At about one o'clock that afternoon, Jeff took the wheel of the Prevost and started down that same road he'd traveled earlier. By now, however, the temperature had risen, and there was much more two-way traffic. Jeff expertly steered the bus as far to the right as possible, moving at about fifteen miles per hour. But then suddenly the road gave way beneath the bus! The beautiful Prevost bus lurched to the right and into a ditch and came to a stop, tilted precariously on its side in the mud and gravel, in front of a farmhouse.

Lib and I had been in the back of the bus getting ready while Jeff transported us to the venue. I had just gotten out of the shower, and Lib was sitting at a makeup table. Suddenly we felt as though we were in a Ripley's Believe It or Not museum. Everything was turned upside down or leaning to the right. Then the bus began to fill with smoke.

Someone from one of the vehicles following the bus came running to the driver's side window, yelling, "Turn off the motor." Apparently, because the bus was still in gear, the wheels were still spinning and grinding against the ground, burning rubber. Jeff shut down the engine.

Several men ran to the bus from the farmhouse, carrying shovels, and they immediately dug out around the door so Jeff could get out. They were able to open our side door enough for somebody to slide inside.

Meanwhile, Lib and I crawled up toward the door of the bus on our knees, holding onto anything stable. Jeff worked his way through the side door on his hands and knees. He saw us and called, "Are you guys all right?"

"Yes, we're okay," I said. "What's going on?"

"The road gave way, and we are almost on our side in a ditch," Jeff said. "We need to get out of here."

We slid out the side door of the bus while Jeff and the rescuers wedged it open for us. Once outside, I could see how close we'd come to a catastrophe. Had Jeff tried to turn the bus back onto the road, it would have certainly tipped over completely. As it was, we were still in a mess, with a show to put on later that evening, but the bus was intact—although leaning over precariously to one side—and we were all safe.

A number of motorists who had been right behind the bus parked and came running to help. "The road caved in under you guys!" somebody said. Sure enough, when we looked at the asphalt, we saw that it was cracked and buckled.

Nobody was injured, but it took two monster tow trucks more than four hours to pull us out of the ditch. We checked under the bus to make sure everything was functioning, and except for being caked in mud, the engine and undercarriage seemed to be okay.

Jeff was beside himself with worry about the bus. I walked around the coach with him, inspecting everything. "I'm so sorry for wrecking your bus," he said over and over. He knew well that it was valued at well over a million dollars.

"Hoss, this ain't your fault; there's nothing you could have done," I tried to console him. "That road just crumbled and didn't hold us."

Lib was upset and furious about the whole affair, but in one of her more gracious moments, she looked at Jeff and said, "Jeff, it's *only* a bus." (She later vented her anger to me and to one of our other bus drivers.)

Once the tow trucks got us out, Jeff drove the bus the rest of the way to the resort. We arrived in time and the show went off without a hitch. Afterward our regular bus driver, who had been sleeping at the hotel the whole time, drove that bus all the way to Santa Fe.

Never one to miss a publicity opportunity, Lib shared the story with media and dramatically added, "And Jeff Davis saved our lives." It was just another day of life on the road.

We were certainly thankful for the Lord's protection and were doing our best to give Him credit for all the good things happening to us and the people around us. For instance, in late May 2004, Doug Johnson and Kim Williams, the writers of "Three Wooden Crosses," received the Song of the Year award at the Academy of Country Music Awards.

Later that year I attended President Bush's eightieth birthday party—a gala affair with a guest list loaded with musicians and other celebrities as well as politicians. I was glad to honor our former president, joined in doing so by the Oak Ridge Boys, the Gatlin Brothers, Michael W. Smith, Wynonna Judd, Vince Gill and Amy Grant, and pro golfer Greg Norman.

Then in September I was honored to receive a star on the Hollywood Walk of Fame, not only for my music, but also for the many movies in which I had appeared, songs performed in movies, and my roles on numerous television shows—everything from *Frasier* to *Sesame Street* and, most notably, *Matlock* and *Touched by an Angel*.

♫ ♫

Given Lib's and my interest in movies and my desire to become a better actor, it was natural that we should encounter opportunities to become more involved in the film industry from an ownership perspective. Actor David A. R. White, a Mennonite pastor's son who felt called by God to pursue a film career, had appeared in numerous movies and television shows. Working in Hollywood, as a believer who had committed his life to Jesus Christ, he soon saw the need for—and the challenges in—making more wholesome films.

Partnering together with movie producers Michael Scott and Russell Wolfe, David, Lib, and I formed a new film company in 2005 known as Pure Flix. Our stated mission was "to uplift and bring people to higher levels of insight to who God is and the purposes He has for them." While none of us viewed ourselves as preachers or evangelists, we hoped the movies we helped create would change people's lives in a positive direction. We started out producing movies that went directly to DVD and gradually increased our budgets and filmmaking expertise to compete with major feature films.

In addition to heavily investing money in the company, I lent my acting abilities to some of the early films, such as *The Wager*, a story about a man who was the focus of a Job-like bet between Satan and God. A few years later, I also appeared along with Lee Majors, Stacy Keach, and Jaci Velasquez in the Pure Flix film, *Jerusalem Countdown*, a "possible end of the world" scenario based on a novel by San Antonio pastor John Hagee. In that film I played a hard-nosed CIA operative trying to keep Israel and America from being destroyed.

Starting from scratch, Pure Flix would go on to become the largest independent faith and family film company in America, shocking the industry status quo with such movies as the 2011 sixty-five-million-dollar-grossing *God's Not Dead*.

Musically, we started off 2005 by winning a Grammy Award for my album *Worship & Faith*, produced by Kyle Lehning. Two years after that, we won another Grammy for my album *Glory Train*, again produced by Kyle. Both of those albums contained overtly Christian messages, so we were pleased that our work could find acceptance in the mainstream music arenas.

In between the Grammy wins, I was asked in August 2006 to appear on a brand-new television show that Country Music Television wanted to do, called *CMT Cross Country*. The idea of the show was to pair two artists who were similar yet different. For the debut show, the producers tapped Josh Turner and me.

I loved Josh's music, and I respected him immensely as a person. Josh is known as a sincere Christian man who doesn't flaunt his faith or constantly quote Bible verses, but he lives his life in a way that points people to Christ.

Josh had opened for me at a show in Michigan, and we'd just hit it off. After the show he and his wife, Jennifer, had come onto our bus, and it had been obvious that we all connected. Lib took off her manager's hat for that evening and allowed herself to enjoy "girl stuff." She showed Jennifer some of the new jewelry I had recently bought her. We talked and laughed and had a great time together.

When we first met, Josh told me, "The first song I ever sang in public— other than in church—was 'Diggin' Up Bones.'" That cracked me up, since there are some lyrics in that song that a kid might not yet understand. "And *Storms of Life* was one of the first country albums I owned," Josh went on. "I still have it in a shadowbox. The album was like a soundtrack for my life."

I appreciated Josh regarding me as something of a musical role model, but by the time we worked together on the *CMT Cross Country* special, I regarded him not as an understudy or a protégé, but as a peer. Not only did we share a passion for traditional country music, the guy could flat out sing!

Josh handled a lot of the interview segments on the show, guiding me in talking about our friendship, our rural backgrounds, and our faith. We also had a great time singing each other's songs. Performing in front of a live television audience, we shared verses on "Your Man," "Forever and Ever, Amen," "Deeper than the Holler," "On the Other Hand," and of course, Josh's megahit song, "Long Black Train." We had a ball and, in many people's opinions, that inaugural edition of *CMT Cross Country* was one of the best CMT ever did. The special had a magical quality about it, and to this day, many people still talk about Josh's and my performances. It was during that show that Josh and I became more than fellow artists. We've remained really good friends ever since.

♪ ♪

In May 2006 I recorded a Christmas concert in one of the most unique and fascinating venues on earth. Actually, it was 830 feet *under* the earth—deep below the Chihuahua Desert in Carlsbad Caverns of New Mexico. We filmed some of the songs on a stage set, but we recorded two special songs in what is known as the Big Room, a giant underground chamber about a dozen football fields wide, naturally carved out of the rock and magnificently decorated by God with spectacular stalactites and stalagmites. The sheer enormity and grandeur of that space was awe-inspiring.

It was chilly down inside the earth—about fifty-six degrees—and quite humid due to the constant dripping of mineral-rich water from the cavern roof. I wore my favorite yellow leather jacket with a burgundy pullover sweater and black jeans. Santa made an appearance, and so did some of his "elves," about a half-dozen young kids I invited to sit on the front of the stage. We opened the show with "Santa Claus is Coming to Town" and then performed "God Rest Ye Merry, Gentlemen," and we kept rolling from there, doing Christmas classics.

I even included some of my jokes. I asked the kids sitting on the edge of the stage, "What does a snowman have for breakfast?"

One little boy raised his hand, so I put the microphone in front of him. "Frosted Flakes," he answered correctly.

I posed another question and the same kid answered. And then he provided the answer to my third joke.

About that time, I noticed the kid had a crib sheet off to his side. Each time I set up a joke, he would glance at his paper before answering.

"Let me see that," I said with a stern face. The boy gave me the paper, and I unfolded it. There on the page were the answers to all my jokes. "Where'd you get this?" I asked.

"From your wife," he answered. The audience roared in laughter.

"Well, maybe you better go sit with her," I quipped. "Maybe she'll sing to ya!"

It was all in the script, of course, but it was fun for us, and the audience loved it.

Later in the show, I read a beautiful poem, "The Christmas Guest," by Helen Steiner Rice, as the musicians played softly behind me, and it was a touching segment. But by far the most meaningful moment of the show came when I sang "Silent Night" in the Big Room. I used only an acoustic guitar to perform it, partly because of the subtle nature of the song, but also because the natural acoustics in the cave created quite a challenge to the sound engineers.

A national park guide had cautioned us, "One word with a loud voice will carry about a quarter of a mile in every direction." Sure enough, when video director Charlie O'Dowd called "Action!" to film the first take, we had to wait about five or ten seconds before beginning because the sound of Charlie's voice kept reverberating off the rocks. After that, Charlie resorted to hand cues to give instructions.

Despite the acoustical issues, the sound in the cavern was too sensational to simply sing by myself, so we had the sanctuary choir from the Carlsbad First Baptist Church accompany me after the first verse. The sound of their voices echoing off the rock formations must have resounded all the way to heaven. Then, still accompanied by the choir, I also performed the old hymn "Rock of Ages" in the Big Room, right next to a huge, ancient rock formation known as the Rock of Ages.

Legend has it that when the great humorist Will Rogers first saw that rock he said, "I'm glad they gave God credit for these underground wonders." No kidding. Only God could create such majestic artistry. About twenty-five crew members, forty members of the church choir, and even a couple of park rangers squeezed around the Rock of Ages for that unique portion of the video.

We released the DVD of that concert under the title, *Christmas on the Pecos*—my first-ever Christmas video. Our fans loved it, and the performance in the spectacular Carlsbad Caverns produced one of the most memorable musical experiences of my career.

21 ——————————— I TOLD YOU SO

On March 15, 2008, I stopped by the Grand Old Opry House for a special visit with Carrie Underwood. A few days earlier, Carrie had turned twenty-five years of age. A mere three years earlier, she had been the winning contestant on season four of the TV show *American Idol*. Now she was a superstar on the rise.

In late 2007, Carrie had called me and said, "Randy, I really love your song 'I Told You So.' Would you mind if I recorded it on my new album?"

"Mind?" I joked. "Are you kidding? I certainly wouldn't mind, and I have several hundred other songs you are welcome to record too."

That night at the Opry, Carrie had just finished singing "I Told You So," one of the first songs I had ever written, and she had done a stellar job on it. The Opry audience was already giving her a rousing response as she stood smiling, cute as could be, when I slipped up behind her without her knowledge. The crowd roared in surprise and appreciation, and more than four thousand people rose to their feet almost simultaneously.

It was then that Carrie noticed I had walked up on her right side and was standing next to her. Her surprise was obvious and real as she jumped to the left, squealed and raised her hands to her face with a laugh. She hugged me, and we both laughed. Then she turned to the audience and quipped, "I thought you guys were standing up for *me!*"

They were, of course, as Carrie turned and laughed robustly, jumping up and down at the same time.

"That's great," I said. "That was wonderful," referring to Carrie's rendition of my song. "I was going to do that song tonight," I joked with Carrie.

"You should anyway!" she responded.

"Oh no," I said. "No way." I laughed. "The first time I heard Carrie's version of that song," I told the audience, "I knew that it was far better suited for her vocals than mine." Then I turned toward Carrie. "That's a better performance than I will ever do of that song. Thank you. I'm honored." The crowd responded with enthusiastic applause.

I went on to say to the audience, "The rest of y'all here tonight . . . maybe you already know this . . ." I paused and looked at Carrie as I continued, "but I heard that this is your birthday week. Happy birthday! And to end your birthday week, I was asked by the management here at the Grand Ole Opry to come out here and ask you if you would like to be their next member."

Again Carrie's hands flew to the sides of her face, and her bright eyes lit up the stage. She put her index finger up to her head and joked, "Let me think about it." But she quickly shook her head and said, "Yeah!"

Carrie's response was so heartfelt and genuine. She leaned over to hug me as her eyes welled with tears. "What a surprise!" she said.

I then announced that Carrie's formal induction would be on May 10. She would be not only the newest member of the Grand Ole Opry, but also the youngest person ever inducted to the Opry at that time. I finished my announcement with "Carrie Underwood, everyone." The crowd at the Opry House, still on their feet, applauded in a another long ovation.

It was one of those rare, memorable moments that seem to happen more naturally in country music than in other genres. I know it was special for Carrie and for me, and I think it was for all country music fans.

Then, since I was already onstage, I followed the announcement by singing "Forever and Ever, Amen," to the audience's delight. What a night!

Of course, God always has a humorous way of keeping me humble. Carrie later told me that when her version of "I Told You So" was at the top of the charts, a woman came up to her gushing about how much she loved "that song of yours that Randy Travis sings."

♪ ♫

A few months later, on July 15, 2008, we released *Around the Bend*, my first country album in eight years. It wasn't that I had avoided making a new country album for all that time. We had just been busy following up some of the Christian albums that had been so well received. I had great success with "Three Wooden Crosses," on my Grammy Award–winning *Rise and Shine* album—the first overtly Christian album to reach #1 on mainstream charts—but I had not really recorded a country album in a long time.

I was excited to get some new music out and went on tour promoting the first single from *Around the Bend*, a song called "Faith in You." I went everywhere from *The Tonight Show with Jay Leno*, *The Late Show with David Letterman*, and ABC's *Good Morning America* to *Live with Regis and Kelly*. But one of the first places I went to talk about the album was on one of the most entertaining radio shows in Nashville history—*Coffee, Country, and Cody*, the morning show on WSM-FM radio, hosted by Bill Cody and his sidekick, Charlie Mattos. Bill had been on the air for more than four decades, and he had been a great friend to me for more than twenty years. He knew more about country music than most people who performed country music for a living, and he genuinely loved it. He was also a regular host on the Grand Ole Opry. Performers like me really appreciated the fact that, unlike a lot of radio and television personalities, Bill actually listened to the entire album, not merely the songs the record labels were pitching.

We had a lot of fun that morning on the program. At one point, referring to my well-known aversion to modern technology, Bill quoted a line in "Faith in You" that said, "I don't have faith in technology, but I do have faith in you." Bill quipped, "I hear that you are a no-tech redneck."

"That's right," I admitted. "I couldn't download anything if you paid me. Of course, I could learn if I wanted to, but I just don't care!" We both laughed, then Bill added, "As long as the listeners download the new song, that's all that matters."

Bill went on to feature one of my favorites off the new album, a remake of Bob Dylan's hit, "Don't Think Twice, It's All Right." We also talked about my early days, and Bill asked me about our early disappointments.

"I don't know why, but my wife and I never really got discouraged," I said. "All through those years, neither of us said, 'This isn't going to work,' even though I'd been turned down by every record company in town. But we always believed I'd make it eventually."

"That's a gift. That's a God gift, don't you think?" asked Bill. "The ability to withstand that and then look back on your life and the success you've had."

"It is," I agreed. "Having a certain amount of knowledge from the Word of God certainly helps."

On November 9, 2008, along with Trace Adkins and Martina McBride, I was honored to receive a star on the Music City Walk of Fame in Nashville. It was a humbling experience to see my star on the pavement along with Elvis Presley, Michael McDonald, Little Richard, and Jo Walker-Meador, the former executive director of the Country Music Association, also honored that same day. My buddy Josh Turner presented the award to me, and we tried to be serious—which was no easy matter, considering that Little Richard was sitting right behind us and cutting up and cracking jokes.

In 2009, "I Told You So" hit the charts again—this time by *American Idol* winner and new Opry member Carrie Underwood. Her version of the song topped out at #2 on country charts and was a top-ten pop hit for her. When Carrie appeared as a guest artist on a March 2009 episode of *American Idol*, she invited me to sing "I Told You So" with her.

Our duet, released as a digital single, became a Top 40 country hit, and our collaboration brought Carrie and me a Grammy Award in 2010. I'd known that song had legs when I wrote it and included it on my live album back at the Nashville Palace before I ever signed with a major music label. Of course, Carrie's "legs" gave it new life, and millions more people heard her perform it so well.

22 —————— THE IRISH GIG

My band and I toured Northern Ireland for several weeks again during the summer of 2009. Lib, Jeff, and I flew in on July 28, and the band and crew flew in a day later. We set up for two nights in Belfast at the UTV Country-Fest, a two-day indoor festival along with Martina McBride, Connie Smith, and other performers.

Because we had been to the island previously in 1988, we knew better what to expect upon our return. We couldn't use our big tour buses there, so Lib, Jeff, and I traveled all over the country to the venues and hotels in a fine Jaguar automobile. The car was driven by an Irishman named Eamonn McCrystal, who worked with the concert promoter and had been assigned to us as a valet to escort us, run errands, and take care of our needs.

A young fella in his early twenties who had recorded an album of Irish music, Eamonn, told us that he hoped to one day earn his living as a music artist. He gave Lib a copy of his live album. Lib became enamored with Eamonn, and the two of them talked nonstop any time we were in the car. They continued talking as I got out and went inside to the venue for sound check. Eamonn was with us most every waking hour during the entire twelve days we were in Ireland.

We flew back to the US on August 10, 2009. Shortly after that Lib decided that she wanted to sign Eamonn to a management deal, bring him to America, and promote him as a new artist. So almost before I knew it,

Eamonn was living at our house, eating every meal with us, and traveling on our tour bus to shows. We couldn't even go out to the movies—something she and I had always enjoyed doing—without Lib dragging Eamonn along. I understood that she was invested in him as an artist, but I hadn't really planned on adopting the young man as though he were our child.

Lib wanted to promote Eamonn in every way possible, so she decided it would be a good idea for Eamonn to sing a couple of songs during my shows. She would literally call me offstage and have Eamonn go out and sing a few songs—in the middle of my show! It was ridiculous. Why would anyone want to hear an Irish pop singer in the middle of a country music set? It messed up the rhythm of my show. But things had not been going well between Lib and me for some time. She seemed bored with me and restless, ready for some new venture. So to keep her happy, I reluctantly acquiesced to her demands.

At first I tried to make it seem like a natural progression in our show, telling the audience, "We were touring Ireland a few months ago and discovered a great new talent. Let's bring him out!"

It was nonsense. So one night, I refused to do it. Eamonn was dressed and ready to come out onstage, but I simply kept on rolling right through our show. Eamonn was disappointed, and Lib was livid.

That night Eamonn posted an open Facebook message apologizing to his fans. He told his followers that he had been ready to go onstage, but that I had been angry about something and had not permitted him to perform. Since I did not engage personally in any social media, I probably wouldn't have known about Eamonn's negative message if one of our bus drivers hadn't called it to my attention. When I saw it, I was appalled by Eamonn's arrogance. After all, it was *my* show.

Back in Nashville, Lib took Eamonn to Warner Bros. in an attempt to get him a recording deal. They passed, but that did not deter Lib. She later hired Kyle Lehning—and paid him—to record an album on Eamonn. Kyle did his best, but the album did not evoke any offers.

Wanting to enhance Eamonn's appearance, Lib took him to Ritchie and Mary's dental office in Plano, Texas, to get his teeth fixed. Later she and Mary went shopping, and it seemed that everything Lib bought was for Eamonn. She wanted to get him a bright emerald-green tie to wear to the upcoming

Grammy Awards show, an event I would be attending. But she couldn't find the tie she wanted, so she had one custom made from the same fabric as the green accent inlays on her black dress, which Mary had helped her design. Eamonn wore the matching green tie to the Grammys, and I wore a black tie.

By that point it was clear that Lib was doing everything with the young Irish singer that she had once done with me, back when she had first taken me under her wing as a seventeen-year-old. It all seemed way too familiar.

The next time Mary and Lib were together, Mary tried to gently broach the subject of Eamonn. "Doesn't Randy get tired of having Eamonn around all the time?" Mary asked. "Even a big bus can get pretty small when you have a third wheel."

Lib brushed her off. "Oh, Randy will never leave me," she said.

Maybe not, but Lib's and my relationship had been rocky for years. I chafed at her controlling ways, and she may have had her own issues with me. The subject of going our separate ways and divorcing had come up on several occasions. We had thought that counseling might help, but we had never pursued it. Then, when Eamonn came into the picture, the situation became even more tense and much more complicated.

Meanwhile, Lib's actions were messing with my mind, not to mention my heart. She was the type of person who always liked to have a new project, and Eamonn was her new pet project. Everything else paled in comparison, including our marriage. She seemed to be constantly looking for opportunities to promote him, much as she had me when she first became my manager. And I would have been fine with featuring him at another venue or taking him in a different career path, but I balked at inserting him into my career and my relationship with my wife.

By the fall of 2009, Lib's relationship with Eamonn was driving a stake right through the heart of our marriage and a wedge between her and me. Lib had Eamonn riding on our bus and at our house constantly. At night we would sit on the couch and watch movies—with Eamonn and Lib on one end of the couch and me on the other. They whispered to each other incessantly and obviously did not want me involved in the conversation.

Somewhere in the midst of the horrendous emotional stress I felt, I began to drink wine again. Lib had successfully weaned me away from alcohol more than twenty years earlier, and she had meticulously kept me away from it throughout my career. Now, she didn't seem to care.

Drinking for me became an escape, but also a badge of freedom. When some friends visited and saw eight bottles of wine in our pantry, one asked, "I thought Lib didn't allow you to drink?"

"I drink when I want to," I responded.

Before long Lib was traveling to various locations along with Eamonn, promoting him around the US and even in a few foreign countries, and leaving me alone at our 220-acre ranch and home in Santa Fe. We had purchased the property in 2002 from New Mexico's former governor, Bruce King, and it had taken a couple of years to build the house and bring the property up to Lib's demands. We had a bus garage on the property as well as a well-equipped gymnasium and swimming pool, a bowling alley, and a shooting range. We kept horses and cattle and even had a pet buffalo.

The main house, though huge—with more than nineteen thousand square feet of living space—had only three bedrooms, but it was decked out with ten fireplaces, a large kitchen, a fabulous living room, a library, and a well-appointed recreation room. The doors were all hand carved, and our wood-beamed kitchen ceiling was covered in stitched leather. Lib had decorated the house in classic Western style, with crosses everywhere—on the front gates, on the refrigerator, and even on the cabinetry.

I appreciated such a beautiful house. But to me at that time, it was basically a large, empty echo chamber where I stayed all by myself and fumed over Lib's latest project—her obsession with making Eamonn a star. I spent much of the holiday season that year home alone. Lib and Eamonn came in for a few days or so, and then they were gone again.

Throughout the winter, tensions ran high between Lib and me—and with good reason. Sometime during that season, our personal assistant and house manager in Santa Fe, Dolores Hessinger, discovered an email between Lib and Eamonn describing the intimate details of their relationship. Although she did not immediately inform me about the correspondence, Dolores printed the note and confronted Lib with it. "You need to come clean with Randy about this," she said.

Lib not only refused to inform me about the email; she fired Dolores. Her husband, Kurt, who also worked for us in Santa Fe as our ranch manager, left at the same time. Lib then arranged for a judge to place a gag order on Dolores so she was not permitted to speak to me or anyone else about the matter or the reasons for her employment dismissal.

When I asked Lib why she fired Dolores, Lib told me that Dolores had misused her email account. That seemed odd to me since part of Dolores's job description was to handle mail, email correspondence, and phone calls, to send Christmas cards and gifts, and to help with all sorts of other personal matters. She did everything for us and took great care of us. It was perfectly appropriate for Dolores to be monitoring emails—until she found that salacious note between Eamonn and Lib. Then, suddenly, it wasn't okay.

Dolores and Kurt had worked for us for a number of years and were good, salt-of-the-earth folks with impeccable integrity. I trusted them completely and loved them as family. But it would be a couple of years before I discovered the real reason why Lib had fired Delores.

23 —— ARE WE IN TROUBLE NOW?

On Saturday, March 6, 2010, I was scheduled to play a show at Billy Bob's, a large club venue in Fort Worth, Texas, but Lib did not attend. I was told that she was in Mississippi with Eamonn. Our good friends Mary and Ritchie had a business meeting nearby and knew that I was playing in Fort Worth, so Mary called Jeff Davis and said, "Hey, we heard that you guys are in town, so we're thinking about running over to see you before the show." She said that Ritchie had a few friends he wanted to bring along.

"Great," Jeff said. "Come on over."

I wasn't going onstage until ten o'clock that night. So Mary and Ritchie arrived prior to the show and spent some time visiting with Jeff and me aboard our bus. Mary seemed surprised that Lib was absent. The couple had known us for twenty years and had never before seen me at a show without her. When they asked about her, I tried to be upbeat as usual, but I really wasn't all that convincing.

When I stepped onstage that night, I felt as though a five-hundred-pound barbell was pressing down on my shoulders. My facial appearance was sallow, my demeanor was sullen, and I didn't talk much during the show or tell any of my usual corny jokes. I basically sang my songs and walked off the stage. My presentation was far from normal.

Afterward I visited briefly with Mary and Ritchie and their guests, shaking hands, taking pictures, and going through the motions, but hardly breaking a smile. After a short time, I excused myself, went to the bus, and headed back to Santa Fe, an eleven-hour drive. When I arrived at home the following morning, the house was empty. I was as alone there as I'd been in the back of the tour bus.

Mary called later that day, on Sunday afternoon, March 7. She was shocked when I answered the telephone—which I rarely did. Either Dolores or Lib usually answered all our calls at home and I didn't have a cell phone. Lib carried two cell phones with her, but she did not think I should have one. Now both Dolores and Lib were gone, so I had picked up.

"What are you doing answering your phone?" Mary teased.

"There's nobody else here to get it," I replied.

"What? Where's Lib?"

"I have no idea. I think she's running around Mississippi somewhere with Eamonn."

"You've got to be kidding!" Mary exclaimed. "And you are all by yourself?"

"Yup, " I answered despondently.

Mary had no idea that Dolores had been fired, but she must have sensed the despair in my soul. "I'm real worried about you, Randy," she said. "You weren't yourself last night. I've never seen a concert like that from you. I was concerned, so I'm just calling to make sure you are okay."

I took a deep breath and slowly exhaled. "No, I'm not really okay," I said. At that point Mary had no idea that Lib's and my marriage was falling apart. But now, as we talked, I felt safe enough to open my heart to her. We'd been friends for years, so I admitted that Lib and I were estranged and that I had been alone in Santa Fe by myself over much of the Thanksgiving and Christmas holidays and the early part of 2010.

"So have you been there all that time by yourself?"

"Lib and Eamonn come in for a few days and then leave again. It's been that way pretty much since I stopped touring last year in November."

"Do you mean you spent Christmas Day alone?" Mary seemed shocked.

"No, they came in for Christmas morning and then took off again."

We talked further, and Mary told me that she and Ritchie had been having intense troubles in their marriage as well, especially after a tragic house fire the previous August destroyed their home and most of their cherished possessions. Added to that, Mary's mother's health was declining and she was trying to care for her, which drained her emotionally and kept her away from home and the couple's dental practice for long periods of time. Ritchie had been demanding her presence at the practice. Mary felt that his demands implied that the business was more important than the loss of their home or her mom's deteriorating health. To Mary that was the breaking point. After several months of counseling, their marriage counselor regarded them as a lost cause and had recommended they divorce.

Mary and I talked for more than an hour that Sunday afternoon. Before we said good-bye, I said to her, "I'm heading back to Nashville, and we'll be stopping in Shawnee, Oklahoma, on March 10. Will you meet me there?" It was an impulsive statement coming from me, and I was surprised that I had been so bold.

Mary hesitated for a few moments, then said, "Yes." I think she was as surprised at her response as I was.

I gave her the details of where we planned to stop so John Williams, our bus driver at that time, could get some sleep before driving the rest of the way to Music City. Mary said she would be there, but I wasn't sure our meeting would really happen. Although I didn't know it at the time, neither was she.

That Thursday Mary drove to Shawnee, about a three-hour drive north of her home in Texas. She found our bus, which was parked in the hotel parking lot overlooking a wide-open field. I was excited to see her, and we quickly fell into lighthearted conversation, visiting like the longtime friends that we were. "I worked out and went out for a run over that way this morning," I said, pointing toward the open area.

I fixed lunch in the bus for both Mary and me, and we enjoyed a special time together. We talked and talked, about important things and about nothing, but it all seemed so refreshing and energizing. Around five thirty that afternoon, Mary headed back to the Dallas area. A short time later, John returned to the bus, and we pointed the coach down Interstate 40 East. Nobody had seen Mary and me together or had heard our conversation—or so we thought.

I appreciated Mary's sensitivity and her willingness to encourage me during one of the deepest troughs of my life, even though she had been trudging down a difficult, emotionally laden, land-mine-strewn road herself. We were both fragile and vulnerable at that juncture of our lives. Initially we were simply two good friends commiserating in the midst of unraveling marriages. But our relationship soon became much more.

We had been friends for so long, we felt that we understood each other well. We were both Christians, yet I couldn't help thinking of the lyrics to "Are We in Trouble Now?" a song written by Mark Knopfler that I had recorded on my 1996 *Full Circle* album. The song describes a couple irrevocably moving toward falling in love, and that's where Mary and I were headed. We both recognized that we were crossing a line that would produce negative repercussions. Nevertheless, we were committed to moving forward, and neither of us doubted the ultimate good we'd find in the direction we were going.

Looking back, though, we know we should have done some things differently. First of all, it was wrong for us to fall into each other's arms when we did. We should have gotten legally divorced, taken the time to date, settle our emotions, and clean up our messes, then get engaged and married. But we were both so beaten down emotionally, it felt good to have someone simply offer kind words, affection, and encouragement. Before long we were head over heels in love. And unfortunately we were both still married to other people.

A short time into our new relationship, Mary gave me a special present—a cell phone of my own. Now, in 2010, at fifty-one years of age, I finally had my own personal cell phone. Prior to that, if I wanted to make a call, I had to use the phone on the bus or make a call on Lib's cell.

Lib discovered I had my own cell phone, and shortly thereafter, Jeff Davis got on the bus carrying a package with a new cell phone identical to the one Mary had just given me. "Lib sent this phone for you," Jeff said. "And she said she doesn't want to talk to you on the phone that Mary got for you; she wants you to call her on this one when you communicate with her."

That seemed strange. At first, I naively thought the gift was simply a kind gesture on Lib's part, until someone on our team suspected there was a special tracking application on that phone so someone could tell where I was at any time of day or night. No wonder Lib demanded that I answer her calls on *that* phone, not another. Sometimes I'd notice that she had called and I would return her call from another device. Her first response was, "Answer my call on the phone that I gave to you."

Interestingly, not long after that, our longtime business manager, Gary Haber, called me on Mary's phone and said, "Get off the bus and walk at least fifty feet away. Leave the phone that Lib gave you in the bus. Then call me back on Mary's phone."

I followed his instructions and called him on Mary's phone. "Why am I doing this?" I asked Gary.

"Because every time we talk, within ten minutes of our conversation, Lib calls my office and grills me with questions about everything we just talked about."

Clearly Gary believed that both the bus *and* my phone were bugged and everything I said and did was being monitored. Sure enough, when we had the bus swept by a security company, they discovered where a surveillance camera had been installed that filmed my every move and another electronic device that recorded every conversation—potentially including what Mary and I had said to each other during our first meeting on the bus and possibly every one after that.

We investigated who had access to my tour bus. Although we couldn't confirm who had installed the surveillance equipment, according to one of our bus drivers, Eamonn often came onto my bus while I was onstage. He usually stayed about thirty minutes and left. Nobody else ever came onto my bus uninvited. Eamonn, I later learned, was a trained gadget guy, so I wondered whether he was checking on the surveillance equipment during his brief, unaccompanied visits. He had no other reason to be on my bus, especially since by then Eamonn and Lib traveled together in their own bus—at my expense.

Interestingly, on March 9, 2010, the day before Mary and I met in Oklahoma, Gary Haber submitted a contract on a condominium in Nashville. Lib and Eamonn had the condo decorated real pretty before I even found out about it.

By April 2010 I couldn't take any more. I filed for divorce from Lib in Albuquerque, New Mexico. I talked to my divorce attorney only twice—once by phone, and once while sitting on the tailgate of a pickup truck. Gary Haber handled all the financial dealings, including inventory and appraisals, and since my attorney had been selected by Gary, he did no research, appraisals, and evaluations about how our assets and liabilities should be divided. Gary gave both attorneys all that information. After the divorce was finalized on October 28, 2010, my attorney presented me a file barely an inch thick.

Not surprisingly the divorce was not in my favor or even equitable. I just wanted the nonsense to stop, and I didn't have the information regarding our businesses to ask many questions.

Gary Haber had determined that most of the businesses in my name were depreciating or losing money, but the ones that were in Lib's name were prospering. My accountant later discovered some intriguing financial maneuvers, done by my management team in the fall of 2009, that accelerated payments eliminating debt on the properties Lib ultimately received. There were also some curious claims that moved properties into Lib's name prior to our marriage, apparently taking advantage of my naiveté and my allowing others to sign documents for me. Of course, we had always considered our businesses as mutual property—until it came time to divorce.

Although we were severing our marriage ties, I wanted to take the high road as much as possible in my dealings with Lib. I said to her, "We're going to end it right here, but we can still work together if you want to." I suppose that was naïve of me, but I said she could stay on as my manager and I would continue to pay her as usual.

Lib countered with an offer that she would continue as my manager for 33 percent of my gross income. She placed a contract in front of me and urged me to sign it, implying that Gary Haber had already agreed on the deal.

I immediately called Gary and asked him about the new percentages. "Absolutely not," Gary said. "That's ridiculous. Do not sign that document." Eventually Lib and I agreed to function as we had in the past, with her receiving 25 percent of my gross income—an arrangement that was already considerably higher than the industry norm of 15 percent.

We settled in to give that plan a try, but that soon proved awkward. So when we played a date in Arkansas in June, I had Jeff Davis help Lib remove the rest of her personal belongings from the tour bus. They went through it stuffing Lib's belongings into a white plastic trash bag while I sat up front and calmly strummed my guitar.

We traveled to shows in two separate tour buses—Lib and Eamonn in one, and Mary and me in another—both paid for with income earned by me. It was a ridiculous arrangement and especially awkward for our band guys and crew, who tried their best to be kind and courteous to Eamonn and to Mary while the tension between Lib and me permeated every action and conversation. Fortunately the guys were such professionals that most fans never knew the tension existed. The show went on most nights without a hitch, we played all our hits, and the fans went home happy.

I soon had my doubts that Lib and I could maintain business as usual with her as my manager after we divorced. There were simply too many shady, gray areas. For instance, when I began looking into my financial matters, I discovered some padded expense reports. At one point I had been billed fourteen thousand dollars for a private NetJet flight on which I had not traveled. Years later I received a charge for more than nine thousand dollars on my American Express credit card.

"What is this expense?" I asked. We discovered that the charge was for the lease of a tour bus used by Eamonn McCrystal. The bus leasing company reversed the charges, but the incident highlighted the challenges I had trusting Lib.

In retrospect it would have been much wiser for Lib and me to simply go our separate ways. But Lib had been my guardian and manager since I was seventeen years old, long before we married, so we both thought we could separate our emotions from our business relationship.

We were both wrong.

After the divorce settled, in December 2010, I bought a ranch about forty-five minutes from Denton, Texas, just outside the little town of Tioga, the hometown of cowboy singer and actor Gene Autry. Boasting a population of fewer than a thousand people, Tioga was a tranquil, friendly town where everyone knew and watched out for each other. The surrounding countryside was known as "horse country" for its wide-open pastures, dotted with beautiful grazing horses. Mary and I felt it would be a great place for healing and for starting over again. Mary had a one-hundred-year-old home in Salina, Texas, about twenty miles away.

Lib never permitted me to return to the beautiful ranch estate in Santa Fe to pack up my belongings. She informed me that she had hired security guards at both gates, ostensibly to keep me out. Then she sent box after box of my memorabilia to me in Texas. A lot of the contents, including cherished awards, pictures in frames, and other priceless keepsakes arrived shattered in pieces. Many items had not been wrapped—just thrown into the boxes and shipped.

Looking back, although Lib's and my relationship was unusual, I truly believe that we had loved each other with as much love as we knew at the time. In many ways we had been good for each other, and I'd always expressed my appreciation for her dogged determination in steering my career.

On the other hand, the comparisons between Lib's and my relationship and that of Colonel Parker and Elvis Presley were apt. The Colonel helped make Elvis's career, but he controlled Elvis to the point that he had also helped destroy him. In a similar way, Lib had controlled everything about our business and about our lives from the time I was seventeen years old, and I had been content to allow her to do that for nearly thirty-three years.

Johnny Cash forged his own destiny. Eddie Arnold was in command of his career. Dolly Parton took charge of her own career from the beginning, and so did Garth Brooks. Taylor Swift and her parents were the key decision makers in her career.

Not me. I was never in charge. Lib was. And I let her.

Lib decided who my friends would be, where I would go, and what I would do. She seemed especially cautious or insecure around attractive females, particularly those younger than her. She didn't permit most of the wives of guys in our organization to get near me or attend company functions, nor would she approve my doing shows with certain sexy female artists. She restricted my recreational activities with male friends, too, unless we were working. And I allowed her to do that. As I mentioned, prior to 2010, I didn't own a cell phone, nor did I possess a computer. As long as I had in my pocket the twelve hundred dollars per month "allowance," I didn't care.

Even in most of our business dealings—and we had several companies and all sorts of written agreements, some filling twenty-five pages or more— Gary Haber and Lib took care of just about everything. Lib would ordinarily give me a brief description of the deal, hand me the last page of a contract, and say, "Sign this." And I would sign, usually without even reading it.

I trusted her and thought I knew what she was doing. I guess that made me a willing accomplice, comfortable in not having to worry about the details regarding our businesses. I abdicated all responsibility to her, and it wasn't until the divorce that I realized what a vise grip she had on me from the time I moved in with her when I was seventeen till the day I moved out as a fifty-one-year-old man.

Some have suggested that the way Lib treated me was psychological or emotional abuse. Maybe so, but I was culpable for allowing her to control me. For a long time I was simply happy to sing, ride horses, shoot pool, work out, and practice quick-draw, leaving everything else to Lib. That was not smart from a business perspective, nor was it good for our marriage.

24 ——————— HAPPY ANNIVERSARY

Throughout 2010, in the midst of the divorce proceedings, ironically, we were also putting together my twenty-fifth-anniversary album, *Anniversary Celebration*. We had all sorts of promotional events planned to promote the project, and lots of country greats had agreed to sing with me on the album. But Lib and I found it incredibly difficult to work together creatively during the time that our relationship was disintegrating.

I should have seen what was coming when, early in the song selection and recording process, Lib lobbied hard for me to include Eamonn McCrystal on the album, singing along with me on "Someone You Never Knew." The poignant lyrics of the song described a man in a relationship with the wife of another man, with the lover telling the husband things about his wife—"Someone you never knew." The song was a not-so-subtle message and a blatant insult to me, especially with Eamonn and me singing it in the same studio under the cloud of Lib's and my divorce, but Lib demanded that it be on the album.

When she had first suggested it, I didn't understand why we would want a relatively unknown Irish singer on an album composed of well-established artists singing along with me on my hits. But Lib was still my manager at the time as well as Eamonn's. Once I realized that Lib and Eamonn had more than the usual manager-artist relationship, however, her demands that Eamonn be on the album—and singing that particular song—seemed downright devious and malicious. Nevertheless, against my wishes, the song stayed on the album.

Despite the issues swirling around "Someone You Never Knew," all the other songs on the anniversary album were a delight to record, and making it was sheer fun. Alan Jackson and I sang a compilation of a couple of songs we had written together, "She's Got the Rhythm (And I Got the Blues)" and "Better Class of Losers." Both songs had been #1 hits for us, so Kyle arranged for us to do them together on the twenty-fifth anniversary album.

My friend John Anderson also appeared on the album. Earlier I had been at an award show when John came out and sang "Diggin' Up Bones" in his own style. Kyle Lehning leaned over to me and said, "Man, I wish we'd have thought of doing it that way!"

I nodded and chuckled. "Yeah, I know. John is incredible." So on the anniversary album, he sang "Diggin Up Bones" and killed it!

As a total surprise, Don Henley of the Eagles fame sang harmony on "More Life." We were recording at Sound Emporium Studios in Nashville and ran into Don in the hallway. He was recording in the smaller, more intimate studio across from the large one where we were working. I asked him if he'd sing on my anniversary album, and Don said, "Sure, absolutely!"

When Don heard the song, he said, "Man, that's a one-man song, so I'll just harmonize with you." He sang harmony on the choruses, and Kyle recorded the session. When Don came out of the vocal booth, he said, "Man, what a voice."

I thought he was talking about someone else, but I guess he was talking about me.

The finished album featured sixteen collaborations with country greats Brad Paisley, Josh Turner, George Jones, Carrie Underwood, Alan Jackson, Jamey Johnson, Tim McGraw, Kenny Chesney, Willie Nelson, Kris Kristofferson, Shelby Lynne, Zac Brown, Kristen Chenowith, and James Otto. One song was especially meaningful to me, since it featured Joe Stampley, Gene Watson, Connie Smith, Lorrie Morgan, Ray Price, and George Jones. The song was appropriately titled, "Didn't We Shine"—and they sure did. Fifteen of the sixteen songs on that album were incredible performances. Warner released *Anniversary Celebration* on June 7, 2011, almost twenty-five years to the day from the release of my first album, *Storms of Life*.

Once the album came out, I hit the road hard promoting it. And that involved daily interaction with Lib and Eamonn and Lib's office, because she was still handling most of my public relations and interviews. She weighed in on all concert dates as well, since she still received a sizable percentage of that income.

Because Lib's and my divorce was so contentious, many of our closest friends found it difficult to be around us, perhaps feeling they had to pick a side. Others apparently thought it was safer to say nothing at all. This was a time when many pastors, friends, and fellow artists disappeared from my life. That created a volatile situation for me. As a kid, my rebellion against my dad's control and abuse led me to lash out in anger, to escape into alcohol and drugs, and to get into a lot trouble.

Looking back, I can see that maybe I had never fully dealt with all that pain, so although the circumstances in my breaking away from Lib's influence were much different, the way I dealt with it was similar. That was especially dangerous for me, since I now had no one to whom I was strictly accountable for my actions. I had gone from a rigid "no drinking at all" standard with Lib for more than thirty years to a greatly relaxed attitude of freedom. Consequently, I was drinking more and more frequently, and more often than not out of anger.

Mary hadn't been around during my rebellious years, so she didn't recognize the seriousness of my situation.

Only a few friends tried to intervene with what they regarded as my self-destructive behavior. One of those was my longtime buddy and record producer, Kyle Lehning.

Cris Lacy, an A&R person from Warner, had shown Kyle a video of an interview I'd done in New York, one in which I was really off my game. When he watched it, he was crushed by what he saw. I looked tired, wrung out, and it was obvious that I had been drinking so much that I was almost incoherent during the interview.

Cris asked, "Is there anything you can do?"

"I don't know," Kyle said. "But I'm going to try."

Kyle came to Mississippi to see me perform. That in itself wasn't unusual. Kyle had seen me onstage many times before. But he rarely made those kinds of visits anymore at this point in our careers, so I felt that something serious might be on his mind.

Before the show we sat together on the bus, and Kyle said, "Man, I need to talk with you."

Mary asked, "Do you want me to leave?"

Kyle said, "No, actually, I think you ought to stay." Kyle had brought a DVD of my disastrous interview in New York along with him. "Have you seen this?" he asked.

"No, I haven't," I replied.

"You need to look at this," Kyle said somberly.

"No, I don't want to see it," I said. I recalled that interview, and I knew I hadn't been functioning on all cylinders. So I told Kyle the story of what had happened.

I had been keeping up a whirlwind schedule promoting my twenty-fifth anniversary album, doing concerts as well as radio and television interviews all over the country. I had been in Florida the night before the interview Kyle had seen, yet Lib had scheduled me to do interviews the next day on *Fox and Friends* and the NBC-TV morning show *Today*. My plane arrived in New York City around midnight, and I was supposed to be at NBC at four in the morning.

I did the interview and performed a song from the *Anniversary Celebration* album, and although I was terribly tired, hosts Hoda Kotb and Kathie Lee Gifford were real pros, so that interview went okay. Walking down a narrow hall after the interview, I passed Lib and Maureen O'Connor, a publicist with Rogers & Cowan public-relations agency. Lib scowled at me and said, "You looked and sounded like s—t."

I was furious and went ballistic. I punched the wall in the hallway so hard that my fist made a dent, damaging the wall.

The friction between Lib and me had intensified beyond toleration. She had wanted to stay on as my manager, even though our marriage and personal relationship had gone to pot. And why not? Apart from Eamonn, I was the only gig she had going. It was in her best interests to maintain the status quo. But it seemed to me that she was purposely setting me up for failure by arranging inadequate time for travel and booking such close events in the midst of an intense touring schedule. And right now, in that hallway, I let her know how I felt about it. "Why would you do that to your talent? If you're the manager, then manage!" That was probably the first time I had spoken so bluntly to Lib, but my patience and tolerance were totally depleted.

I left the studio after that and spent the next few hours drinking. I had another interview scheduled that afternoon, but by the time I arrived at the next studio, I was in no condition to answer questions about the new album. That was the interview Cris Lacy had shown to Kyle. It had been a disaster and I didn't want to see it again.

Kyle and I talked for nearly three hours on my bus that afternoon, and he begged me to get some help to combat the resurgence of my drinking problem. "The decisions you make in your personal life are none of my business," Kyle said, "but you can't keep doing this, buddy. I don't want to see you hurt yourself."

I knew Kyle loved me, and he was a dear friend. But whether or not that was a wake-up call for me, I can't say. I do know how important it was for someone who deeply cared for me as a person to look me in the eyes and say, "You've gotta stop this, Randy. It's gonna be okay, but you can't keep going in the wrong direction." Kyle was the only person who did that.

George Jones tried. I later learned that George had made an emotional phone call to Kyle Lehning, asking him for my contact information and expressing his concern for me. George was worried about how I was taking care of myself. He called me several times during that time. "I've been there," George said. "You need to be careful. Divorce and alcohol nearly killed me. Just get through this and you are going to be fine."

"I appreciate that, George," I replied. I could tell that George was sincerely worried about me and I knew he loved me as his own son.

♬ ♬

Although Lib had made a fortune off me—receiving 25 percent gross of everything I earned, plus expenses, plus another 10 percent gross for agency and promotions fees—I had always felt that she had my best interests at heart. After all, when I succeeded, she thrived too. But now, for a number of reasons, some blatantly obvious and others more obscure, I no longer had that same sort of confidence in her.

Matters came to a head on Monday, August 8, 2011, when I fired Lib as my manager.

The next day at noon—the time agreed upon by Lib's and my attorneys—Jeff Davis and his assistant, Rob Harrer, who had worked with us since the mid-1990s, arrived with a four-man moving crew at our Nashville office on Sixteenth Avenue. They moved all Jeff's and my belongings out of the office as Lib and her staff looked on, with Lib pointing out items to be removed or left behind and making sure that Jeff and his crew took only what belonged to me.

Jeff did not storm the building like an FBI investigative team, an impression that was foisted upon the media in the days following. He arrived at the prearranged, appropriate time with his truck and crew and proceeded to do precisely what the lawyers had outlined, taking only items she allowed that belonged to him or me. Jeff and his crew hauled out loads of my career memorabilia, including gold and platinum framed albums, photos, and even my last thirty-dollar check from *R & R* for cleaning the office twenty-five years earlier.

Knowing that at least two men who worked at the office kept weapons in their desks at all times, Jeff did take the precaution of bringing two armed security guards along with him. Although they didn't draw their guns or even show them, their presence no doubt added to the tension.

During most of the time Jeff and his crew worked to remove my belongings from the office, Lib sat at her desk and said next to nothing. As Jeff retrieved my various awards from a trophy case in her office, Lib shook her head and snidely said, "Conway would sure be proud of you today."

It took nine hours to get everything out, and it was not an amicable departure. At one point Charlene Quire, Lib's personal assistant, grew irritated and defensive for her boss. "Since we can't go out to lunch because of what you are doing, you are going to have to pay to bring lunch to us," she groused. "And your guys are drinking our sodas. So I'm going to keep track of every one and give you a bill." It was nitpicking, and Charlene laughed about it later, but everyone's emotions were raw that day and nerves were tight.

I was scheduled to play in Verona, New York, that week, so I traveled to Nashville early on Wednesday, August 10, to meet the crew that was loading the trucks. I wanted to look them in the eyes and tell them that even though Lib was no longer part of our team, I still wanted them to work for me. Almost all of them stayed on board. Richard Logsdon, Doug Griffin, and Charlene Quire, all of whom had been originally hired by Lib, decided to stay on and work with her. It would be several years before I could ever explain to them what had actually caused the split.

I met with the band and stage crew before the show in New York and explained to them the new arrangement. Most of the guys had been with me for more than twenty years, so they were accustomed to seeing Lib at the shows. More than anything, I wanted to assure them that we'd all be okay. None expressed any concerns, and nobody decided to quit because our longtime manager was gone.

Gary Haber continued to work with me as my business manager, as well as Lib's, for a while. Even after the divorce, he often showed up, urgently asking me to sign some new document. Once, Mary and I were in Nashville, about to head back to Texas, when Gary called, saying, "I have to get this document signed before you leave. Time is of the essence." We met at a restaurant, and just as he had done so many times before when he had worked for both Lib and me, Gary laid a sheet of paper on the table. He told me the document had something to do with my latest recording venture, *The Man I Am*—that it would be two albums instead of one. He handed me the last page of the document, and as I had done for years, I simply signed it without reading anything that came before it.

It wasn't until later that I discovered that the document stated that the two volumes of *The Man I Am* would *not* be considered a fulfillment of my contract with Warner Bros. at all since it was a "special project." Consequently, by signing the document, I was in effect re-signing with Warner Bros. to record two *additional* albums. Ironically, those two albums would never be recorded, although I would have more music released by Warner Bros.

♪ ♫

On September 25, 2011, we were scheduled to play a private fund-raiser show for a hospital. The event was known as the Crystal Heart Gala. Held at the Worthington Renaissance Hotel in Fort Worth, Texas, it was a rather exclusive event, allowing for only about four hundred people to attend.

As was our practice, we arrived early in the day, and while the crew set up for the show, Mary and I decided to walk down the street to a Mexican restaurant for lunch. I love all sorts of Mexican foods, so it is hard for me to pass by any opportunity to enjoy some. Later that day, I had two or three cups of coffee, and because I had a cold I took some antihistamine medications. Apparently I took too much. Although I didn't yet know it, I was dehydrated. I felt weak and wobbly.

Just prior to the show, Jeff Davis looked at me oddly. "Are you okay?" he asked.

"Yeah, I'm okay," I said curtly, almost offended that he asked me.

The lights came up and I walked onstage, but I could feel that something wasn't right. We were only a couple of songs into the show, and I had just started "Three Wooden Crosses," when suddenly I collapsed to the floor of the stage, smashing my head on the floorboards and sending my guitar flying one way, the microphone and stand careening in another direction. The small crowd, sitting in close proximity to the stage, seemed to gasp collectively.

I had no idea what had just happened, but I knew I couldn't stay on the floor. I staggered to my feet and into the arms of Jeff Davis and a crew member, who helped me off the stage and straight to the bus. Jeff handed me a bottle of water. "Drink this," he said.

The room had been filled with high-profile doctors, and by that time several of them had hurried after me to the bus to offer their assistance. Once onboard, they examined me, making sure that my breathing was okay, that my blood pressure was all right, and that I was showing no visible signs of a stroke or a heart attack. Everything checked out. By then my body was returning to normal, and the doctors could find nothing wrong with me. They didn't even urge me to go to the hospital's emergency room to be examined. The doctors concluded that I had been dehydrated and that the caffeine and antihistamine had exacerbated matters. They assured me that with some rest and plenty of liquids, I'd be fine.

I felt confident that the doctors' opinion was correct. Something similar had happened to me in 1988, much earlier in my career, when we were traveling through Wytheville, Virginia. I hadn't even been playing a show in that city, but I'd had to be rushed to the hospital due to dehydration. With some rest and water, I soon felt good again.

In Fort Worth, the doctors stayed with me for a while to make sure I was okay before leaving, and then we pointed our bus toward home. I felt fine and just wanted to sleep. Jeff rode along with Mary and me in the bus. "Send the money back," I instructed Jeff before going to bed. The gala had already paid half of our normal fee, but I wanted Jeff to return it. I felt embarrassed and didn't want my actions to reap negative repercussions for the benefit. I also returned to Fort Worth a few months later to do a free show for the same group.

Not long after that, I told a story during one of my shows about visiting a dear friend named Sidney at an assisted-living retirement center. After my visit, one of the staff there suggested, "Randy, it would be really nice if you would walk down the hall and just say hello to some of the other residents."

"Okay, I'll be glad to do that."

We walked to the activities room, where a number of the residents were passing the time. Some of them were sitting at tables, and some were slumped in wheelchairs. I was surprised when the staff member pointed to me and asked the residents, "Does anybody here know who this is?"

Nobody responded. It was total silence.

Finally an elderly gentleman sitting in a wheelchair looked up at me and said, "No, but don't you worry about it none. You just go down to the front desk. They'll tell ya."

It was a humorous story at the time and I told it often onstage to the delight of fans. I had no idea how it felt to be incapacitated, confined to a wheelchair, and dependent upon other people. And, of course, like most folks, I could not even imagine how I would handle such a situation.

♪ ♫

Although we were still working with Creative Artists Agency to book dates and Jeff Davis to handle the touring details, I felt I was missing the management aspect in my career. Within weeks after moving out of our office at 1610 Sixteenth Avenue South, Gary Haber suggested that Jeff move our operations into another Music Row location along with Ken Levitan of Vector Management. Ken had worked with numerous top-caliber artists in the entertainment business, including Hank Williams Jr., Emmylou Harris,

Michael McDonald, Trisha Yearwood, and Trace Adkins. In January 2012, I entered into a management agreement with Ken in which Jeff would handle the day-to-day details of my career and Ken would focus on the big picture, developing longer-term plans. Unfortunately, before Ken even had a chance to present any visions for the future, I created a situation where he had to spend most of his energy putting out public-relations fires.

On February 5, 2012, Mary and I gathered with friends at my house to watch the Super Bowl. I'd never been much of a sports fan, but Mary enjoyed football, and any opportunity to get together with six or eight friends was refreshing to me. For so many years, all my personal relationships revolved around business, so I loved just getting together with people who could not possibly advance my career or who had no connection to our business—people who simply wanted our friendship.

The game itself was a nail-biter between the New England Patriots and the New York Giants. Eli Manning led his team on an eighty-yard drive in the fourth quarter to put the Giants ahead with only fifty-seven seconds left on the clock. The Patriots desperately tried to use those last seconds to score, but the Giants defense held, defeating the Patriots 21–17.

During the game, I had a few glasses of red wine. Then I had a few more. A while later, for some reason, I felt compelled to drive, so after everyone left the house, I grabbed a bottle of wine, jumped in the car, and eventually found myself passing the Baptist church in the town of Sanger, not far from our home. I still didn't know my way around my new hometown area real well. I usually was in a bus when I left home. The church seemed like a safe place, so I pulled off the road and into the parking lot. I shifted the car into park and took a few more drinks straight from the bottle, then placed it on the seat beside me. The bottle was still half-full.

I was sitting behind the steering wheel of my car, thinking about some of the recent twists and turns in my life, when one of the local police officers pulled up beside me. "Are you okay?" he asked. "What are you doing out here?" he asked.

I didn't do a very good job of answering the officer's questions. Then, he noticed the half-empty wine bottle in my car, and he arrested me for public intoxication.

The following day I issued a public apology for my foolish actions. "I apologize for what resulted following an evening of celebrating the Super Bowl," I said. "I'm committed to being responsible and accountable. I apologize for my actions."

Most folks in our area seemed to respond compassionately and empathetically. "Hey, I understand. It could have happened to anyone," one of our friends said. *Yes*, I thought to myself, *to anyone who was as emotionally stretched as I was at the time.* But no one knew what was going on behind the scenes for Mary or me.

Though I appreciated the support, something inside of me was crying out that I was out of control. If someone had tried to caution me, however, I doubt I would have accepted the warning.

I was an accident waiting to happen.

25 —— A DARK AND LONELY ROAD

As if the breakup of Lib's and my marriage wasn't bad enough, on April 5, 2012, my former wife and manager filed suit against me in Nashville for breaking our management deal without written notice. That was silly since we had entered into management arrangements years ago without any written agreement, and although we had formed several companies that related to our business over the years, we had never clearly defined her role. But firing her as my manager cut off a primary source of her income.

When Lib filed a lawsuit, my attorney advised that I countersue her, which I did about a month later. It was becoming obvious to me that the main dispute had little to do with our relationship. It was all about the money.

Worse yet, under the postdivorce management agreement with Lib, I had not earned as much profit from touring, since all the expenses were offset against my net tour revenues, but Lib continued to make her 25 percent off the top of every dime the business earned. Because of that arrangement, I had actually been losing significant amounts of money every time I went out on the road.

I tried to go about my business and continued to perform shows without ever mentioning anything about Lib's departure or her legal actions, but it still bugged me every time I thought about the situation and the events that had brought us to this contentious place. I grew especially agitated over the issues when I thought about them too much late at night.

The summer Olympics were taking place in London during the first two weeks of August that year, and Europe was pulsating with visitors, so our band made a whirlwind three-day trip to Norway, where we performed at a huge festival show. We then turned around and flew back home—stopping in Frankfurt, traveling on to Houston and then to Dallas, with Mary and me finally driving another ninety minutes north to Tioga.

That same week—on Monday evening, August 6, 2012—Mary and I entertained dinner guests at my home. It was a pleasant evening with good food and good conversation. I had two glasses of wine with dinner, but other than being fatigued from a busy international and domestic travel schedule that had taken me through several time zones from Europe to Texas to Canada to California and back, I felt fine. Our dinner conversation was lighthearted and didn't include anything about Lib's recent legal actions and accusations, and I wasn't angry or upset about anything.

Our guests left around nine thirty that night, and rather than help Mary clean up the kitchen, as I usually did, I said, "I'm really tired. I'm going upstairs and gonna try to get some sleep."

In the bedroom I noticed my travel satchel and remembered that I had a sleeping pill in one of the compartments. For years, on the road, Lib had relied on over-the-counter medications as well as powerful prescription sleeping aids such as Ambien to help her sleep, and she had given me some as well. I kept it in my travel satchel, but prior to the divorce and business controversy, I had rarely had problems sleeping.

Nevertheless, since sleep had been elusive lately, I took an Ambien sleeping pill, peeled off my clothes, and crawled into bed.

Somewhere in the middle of the night, I guess I got up, went downstairs, and poured myself a drink . . . and then perhaps another. Mixing alcohol with the sleeping medication was certainly not wise. But at the time I wasn't considering the effects of Ambien on my body. Then, at some point, I decided I wanted some cigarettes. That was odd. I hadn't smoked in years, but for some reason my foggy brain and body felt a craving for nicotine.

I went out to the garage and climbed in my restored 1998 Pontiac Trans Am, one of my favorite cars to drive. Unfortunately I was so loopy from the sleeping medication and the alcohol that I neglected to put on clothes before I got in the car.

I pulled out of our garage, traveled down the lane to our gate, eased out onto the highway, and tramped down on the accelerator. Since learning to drive as a teenager, I've always enjoyed the thrill of driving fast, so a slow ride to the store was not an option. The Trans Am roared into high gear, and in a matter of seconds I was flying over the dark road, headed toward the Pilot Point convenience store on Highway 377, about ten miles from our home. In a matter of minutes, I arrived at the store and parked on the north side of the building. I walked around to the front and stepped inside totally nude.

I told the shocked store clerk that I wanted some cigarettes, but I had no money. I obviously had no pockets where it might be hiding! I didn't know or care if the clerk recognized me. He made no indication that he did, and he certainly wasn't going to give me any free cigarettes. After a few minutes, I left in frustration.

I walked out to the Trans Am, revved up the motor and peeled out of the parking lot. I was almost back home, speeding down the two-lane Highway 922, when I came to a construction area near a bridge. Swerving to miss some traffic cones, I hit some construction barricades and lost control of my car. I veered off the road, plunged down a ravine, and flipped the Trans Am. My body catapulted forward, and my head smashed through the windshield, the impact of the crash pitching me completely out of the car.

Once again, the Lord was with me—and had His angels watching over me. At the speed I was driving, had I hit the bridge head-on, someone else would be telling you this story. But by the grace and mercy of God, I survived.

Dazed and bleeding from my head, I crawled away from the crumpled car, scratched and clawed my way up out of the ravine, and rolled myself onto the road, but that's as far as I got. I lost consciousness, lying there stark naked in the middle of the road.

I don't know how long I remained there, but when a driver approached from the Tioga side of the bridge, apparently he saw me sprawled motionless on the road. Shaken at the sight, he dialed 911 and said, "I just found a guy laying in the road!"

The operator immediately asked the caller a series of questions, trying to determine his location. After a minute or so, she asked, "Is he responsive?"

"I haven't gotten out of my vehicle yet," the man replied.

"Which side of the bridge are you on?" The 911 operator tried to ping where the driver was calling from.

"Has he moved at all since you've been there?" she asked.

"Not that I see."

"Are you okay?"

"I'm spooked out."

"Because you sound like you are a little out of breath." She continued asking questions to the caller, trying to pinpoint his position. "And he's just lying there? There's no vehicles around him?"

"I don't see a vehicle. There are a couple of cones scattered. But I don't know."

"There's a couple of what?"

"There's the road construction cones moved."

"Okay. Do you think possibly he could have had a wreck?"

"Um, maybe. I don't see any vehicles anywhere."

After nearly three and a half minutes, the Grayson County 911 operator called in the report to the police dispatch officer, "I have a male on 911; he's right outside Tioga on 922. He's come up on a male subject lying in the roadway. He does appear to be nonresponsive."

A short time later, the Tioga Volunteer Fire Department rescue team arrived and found me just as the caller had described. Apparently, they determined that I was DOS—"Dead on scene"—so they were in no particular hurry to scoop me off the pavement. Since they assumed I was dead, they just sat in their vehicle, waiting for the police and the coroner.

It must have scared them out of their wits when the naked dead man suddenly struggled to his feet and started walking up the road. Talk about night of the living dead!

About that time two officers pulled up in a police car, red lights flashing. They immediately turned on their dashboard video cameras and let them roll nonstop for the next three hours.

When the paramedics realized that I was bleeding from my head but alive, they asked me if I wanted to go to the hospital to be examined. I told them that I didn't. Why they complied with my wishes when I was obviously bleeding, dazed, and incoherent remains a mystery. But rather than loading me in an ambulance and whisking me off to the hospital, the officers handcuffed me and walked me toward their car, the dash cameras continuing to record.

Once they had me secured in the police cruiser, a paramedic leaned in the window. "Hey, Randy," he said. "It's Jonathan, the paramedic." Apparently, by then they had recognized me.

"All right," I said.

"I just want to make sure you don't want to go to the hospital and have your head scanned, to make sure you don't have a bleed or nothin'."

"No, I don't," I answered, refusing medical treatment again. Even the officer in whose car I was sitting questioned my decision. "Mr. Travis, it looks as though you hit pretty hard," he said. "Are you sure you don't want treatment?"

I emphatically refused again. But it was obvious that I was delirious and not functioning normally. I had already been out there on that dark road for a couple of hours.

Looking back, I guess I appreciate that the officers respected my wishes, but it was easily observable that I had suffered head trauma. I could barely see out of my swollen right eye, and I was still bleeding. They had no idea of my physical condition. They didn't know whether I had sustained internal injuries. All they knew was that I smelled of alcohol, was talking out of my head, and was being belligerent toward them. So they had handcuffed me and led me still naked to the police cruiser. They made no attempt to cover my nakedness, so I made my first—and only—nude video, although I was totally unaware of it.

In the car I continued talking nonsense, one moment telling a police officer that I would have prayed for him if he hadn't cuffed me, and the next making vile threats.

The police took me, still in handcuffs, to the hospital in nearby Sherman to check my blood-alcohol levels. But for some reason, the medical staff didn't admit me, even though my right eye was swollen almost shut, I was clearly bleeding from my head, and I might well have suffered a concussion.

Since the medical analysis found that I had a blood alcohol level of .21, more than twice the .08 legal limit for driving, the police transferred me from the hospital to jail in Sherman. They took me inside the police station, booked me, and took a mug shot, a photo that was soon seen around the world, showing me with a bruised right eye and various cuts and abrasions on my face. I was charged with driving under the influence, threatening the troopers, and retaliating against a police officer. The felony charges carried a potential sentence of ten years in prison and a ten-thousand-dollar fine.

Around four thirty in the morning, the officers called Mary, who was sound asleep and unaware that I had even left the house. They informed her that I was in jail and that they planned to keep me there overnight. In the morning, a judge would decide my bail.

Mary and our friend Al Weir arrived at the police station a few hours later and found me still spattered with my own blood, with broken glass fragments still in my scalp. After they paid the $21,500 bail set by the judge, we walked out of the jail and were met by a bevy of photographers and reporters. I was barefoot, wearing blue hospital scrubs and a Texas Longhorns hat given to me in jail. Al and Mary hurried me to the car.

On the way home, I was hungry, so they stopped at a fast-food restaurant to get me something to eat. I hadn't eaten since dinner the previous night, and the officers in the jail hadn't offered anything, so even fast food seemed like a feast. By the time we got to our ranch about forty-five minutes away, helicopters loaded with media cameras were already circling the property and media vehicles lined the road.

Once inside the house, Mary helped me change clothes, then went to work trying to clean me up and get the glass fragments out of my head, but the broken glass was in too deep, and she couldn't get it out. Since I was still bleeding, Mary waited for the cover of night and then took me straight to Baylor Emergency Medical Center in nearby Aubrey, Texas, where the doctor and nurses extracted the glass from my scalp. "Why didn't they clean him up last night?" one of the nurses asked.

"I have no idea," Mary replied. "Especially since they already had Randy in the hospital to do the blood test."

The doctors at Baylor Emergency X-rayed me and confirmed that I had indeed suffered a concussion, in addition to a number of cuts and bruises. They sent me home with a few bandages and instructions for Mary to keep an eye on me.

We knew that "the less said, best said," so I didn't make any public state-ments about the incident. Our publicity representative expressed my remorse and made apologies on my behalf. In truth, I remembered few details from that night, and most of what I have just shared with you has been recreated with the help of a number of sources. To this day I still don't recall what happened between the time I went upstairs to bed and the time Mary and Al brought me home the following day.

Most people in Tioga were incredibly kind to me in the aftermath. Those who saw me after my arrest were quick to say, "I'm prayin' for you, man." Then when word of the incident hit the news, I received numerous cards and letters saying, "We hope you're okay. We're praying for you." My fans were so gracious and forgiving, and I was deeply grateful but regretful for my actions.

Unfortunately, some concert promoters weren't so gracious. A make-up benefit concert for the State Theatre and St. Joseph's Catholic Academy in State College, Pennsylvania, was canceled as soon as the incident went viral. I was also dropped from an event associated with the Republican National Convention in Tampa, Florida. Eleven other shows canceled as well, but after the initial flurry of negative publicity, most of our concerts went on as scheduled.

A few days after the incident, Jeff Davis, Gary Haber, and my brother Dennis flew to Texas to visit with me, with Mary's consent and my knowl-edge that they were coming. They didn't say why they wanted to see me, but I could guess.

When they arrived at our ranch in Tioga, I met them in our kitchen, my eye still swollen and still walking with a limp. We sat down in the living room, and I beat them to the punch. "What's this intervention all about?" The guys could tell that I was not completely comfortable with this sort of confrontation.

Gary, Dennis, and Jeff looked at each other. They didn't seem to know where to start. Finally Jeff said, "Hoss, this is no intervention. This is a family meeting. We're just here because we love you and are concerned about you. Some of these things we're hearing don't seem like you."

We talked for a long while, then Gary had to head back to Los Angeles. Jeff and Dennis stayed overnight, so we shot some pool, and Mary went out and got us some great barbecue for dinner. Jeff and Dennis flew back to Nashville the following day. I appreciated their concern, but I really had no answers for them, especially since so many of the details of the Tioga incident were so foggy to me.

I didn't try to hide my embarrassment, but nor did I grovel in it. At my first show back, the band brought me onstage to the tune of Ray Stevens's humorous hit song "The Streak." The fans loved it.

26 —————————— AMBUSHED

On August 24, a few weeks after the incident on the road outside Tioga—just as the media frenzy was calming down—Mary and I drove to Prestonwood Baptist Church, a large church in Plano that Mary had formerly attended. Earlier that day, about three thirty in the afternoon, Mary had received a phone call from her teenage son, Raleigh, asking her if she could pick him up there when he returned from a church youth group trip that evening.

It was an innocuous request made much more complicated because Mary and her husband, Ritchie, were still in the midst of contentious divorce proceedings. According to predivorce custody and visitation policies determined by the court, it was "Mary's weekend" to have the kids, but it was only Thursday, and her weekend did not technically begin until Friday. So we planned to meet Raleigh, take him to get something to eat, and then take him to Ritchie's house.

We were sitting in our vehicle waiting for the bus to arrive, when Mary's daughter, Cavanaugh, pulled in behind us, ready to welcome her brother home. About the same time, I saw another car approach in the parking lot and stop right in front of us. Mary's husband, Ritchie got out. Mary's older brother Barnes pulled in behind Ritchie. Barnes had been working on some construction projects for Ritchie and the two men had become friends. Both were unhappy that Mary and I were together as a couple.

"I better go talk to him," Mary said. "I'll be right back." Mary got out of our car and went to speak to Ritchie. For a few moments, I watched from our vehicle, but I quickly realized that their conversation was turning ugly. Both Ritchie and Mary were yelling at each other in the church parking lot.

I understood that discussing divorce details could be difficult, so I wasn't too concerned at first, but then Mary's husband crossed a line. He suddenly grabbed Mary's head and slammed her against the hood of his car.

I jumped out of our car, ran over to the couple, and tried to intervene, but Ritchie was not about to back off. Technically he and Mary were still married, although separated, but what mattered to me was that she was hurt and distressed. I waded right into the middle of the domestic dispute between Mary and her estranged husband.

Ritchie spat out some unkind words to me, and that triggered my temper even more. I shoved Ritchie away from Mary, and the fight was on.

About that time I heard another car door slam and saw Cavanaugh running toward her mom. Barnes bounded out of his car and ran toward us.

Cavanaugh began kicking her dad. "Leave Mom alone," she screamed.

Barnes grabbed Cavanaugh and pulled her away from Ritchie, and with her arms still flailing at him, he threw her to the ground.

A big, strong man, Barnes jumped into the fracas between Ritchie and me. I tried my best to defend myself, but they landed more devastating blows to my head and face. I stumbled to the ground, and Barnes jumped on top of me, smashing my head against the pavement, while Ritchie ran behind his car, cursing and yelling at me in the vilest of terms.

The Plano police showed up almost instantly. I later learned that Ritchie had called them on his cell phone. By then my face was bleeding, my clothing was torn, and my right eye was swollen—the same eye that had suffered severe contusions just a few weeks earlier. Within minutes two more police cruisers showed up, along with the fire department and an EMS team. The paramedics quickly checked me over and determined that I was okay. "Because of his previous injuries," they told Mary, "you may want to take him by the emergency room and have him checked out again."

"I'm fine," I said, brushing myself off and glaring at Ritchie and Barnes. "They didn't hurt me."

As the police filled out a report, both Ritchie and Barnes claimed that

I was the aggressor, so the police charged me with simple assault. They also charged Cavanaugh with assault for attacking her dad and Barnes. Ritchie, who had slammed Mary's head on the hood, and Barnes, who was still pummeling me when the Plano police officer showed up, were not charged at all.

When the episode hit the news, some people immediately assumed the worst—that I had been drinking and had gotten into a scuffle. That was not the case, and despite the salacious accounts on less than reputable media outlets, a police spokesperson confirmed that there was no mention of alcohol in the arrest report regarding the incident.

Ironically, we later learned through sworn affidavits that the lead police officer—who was not even scheduled to be on duty that evening—was a patient in Ritchie's dental office. Around ten thirty that morning, Ritchie had contacted him, and, apparently the two men had made their plans. Around six thirty that evening, about the time Mary and I had arrived, the same officer had parked his police cruiser in the southeast section of the church parking lot, so when the call from Ritchie came in, the officer had been able to be on the scene in a flash. That may explain why the conflict was diffused so quickly.

Contrary to many media reports that included a mug shot of me drawn from the car wreck incident near Tioga a few weeks earlier, I was not even taken to the police station. Although the officer refused to permit us to take Raleigh with us, he allowed Cavanaugh, Mary, and me to drive away from the scene of the incident without being further detained.

Nevertheless, I now faced two court cases.

27 ———————————— THE MAN I AM

As the summer of 2012 turned to fall, my mind turned away from pending court proceedings to more creative projects. I wanted to get back into the recording studio and do something positive. Rather than simply singing some new songs, I wanted to pay tribute to some of the great artists and songs that had helped shape my life—artists such as Merle Haggard, Lefty Frizzell, Ernest Tubb, and even Louis Armstrong. I wanted to sing songs that I'd loved all my life, songs that had influenced me as a person and as an artist. I was planning for some recording sessions in Nashville when I received an unusual offer.

A year or so earlier, a man named Pierre de Wet had contacted Eleanor Davis, Mary's sister-in-law, saying, "I love Randy Travis, and I heard that you know him." Eleanor had passed the message on to us, so we'd called Pierre and discovered that he had a fascinating story.

Years earlier, Pierre's wife had died of cancer, and he had emigrated to the United States from South Africa with his two young daughters, aged two and four. He'd arrived in New York, a daughter under each arm, with nothing but a duffle bag and eighteen hundred dollars, and he could barely speak English. Starting from scratch, Pierre had worked his way across America, and in 1998 he developed a fabulous vineyard known as Kiepersol, located in Bullard, just south of Tyler, Texas. Along with an exquisite restaurant, Pierre's property included a lovely bed-and-breakfast, a conference center known as Bushman Celebration Center, and a retail store where his famous wines were sold.

In his broken English, Pierre told us over the phone that he wanted us to visit. "I cook you the best steak you've ever had," he said. "And we play music."

So we traveled to Kiepersol. True to his word, Pierre provided great food, and then we played music in his living room 'til four o'clock the next morning. Although Pierre was not a professional musician, some of his family members were talented, and he sure enjoyed hearing all of us singing and playing.

A large, direct sort of man, Pierre had become a naturalized American citizen, and he was a passionate patriot who loved America. Compassionate and generous, he especially had a heart for "wounded warriors"—injured veterans—and frequently hosted events for them at his Celebration Center, which boasted an eight-hundred-person seating area and a large stage. On several occasions, when Pierre heard of a soldier who had been killed in action, he either paid off the mortgage or built a new home for the family of the fallen soldier. Sometimes he also paid the educational expenses for the soldier's children.

Behind the conference center and gift shop, Pierre had built a beautiful state-of-the-art recording studio known as 333 Studios, replete with a grand piano, vocal booths, and an assortment of great guitars. When I told him that we were thinking of recording a new project, Pierre suggested, "Why not do it here? I want you to do it at my studio."

"I'm not sure if you have all the equipment we need," I said.

"Well, how can we find out?" Pierre wanted to know.

"I guess I could have Kyle Lehning check it out."

I called Kyle, and we arranged for him to come to our home. Then our friend Al Weir picked us up in a helicopter and flew us over to Bullard. Kyle was reluctant and skeptical, but he was impressed with Pierre's studio.

We had dinner with Pierre, and after we left, I asked Kyle, "What did you think?"

Kyle looked back impishly. "I wanted to hate it. But it is unbelievable." Two essential pieces of equipment were missing, but as soon as Kyle told Pierre what we needed, he purchased them according to Kyle's specifications.

Pierre gave us complete access to his studio, so we went to work. It was the first time I had ever recorded outside of Nashville. In another first, rather than bringing in studio musicians, Mary suggested that I have my own band members play on the album. The guys were overjoyed.

We recorded for two days and laid down thirty-two songs within twenty-four hours. I was in good voice, and the band was perfect, so everything just came together naturally. Some of the guys had been with me for more than two decades, so they knew exactly what sort of feel we wanted for the music. We did some songs in one take after we had rehearsed them.

"This is just steamrolling!" Kyle said after we recorded another song without a glitch. "I'm not sure what else we can do to make this song any better. Let's move on to the next cut."

Throughout the recording sessions, Pierre sat in the control room with Kyle, enjoying his role as honorary executive producer. He was thrilled that his studio was being used not merely to record music, but to record a *legacy* of country music. And he and his family treated our musicians and engineers like kings, feeding and lodging us at his excellent facilities on the property.

Since we had enough music for two albums, we decided to release them on Warner Bros. as *Influence: The Man I Am, Vol. 1 and Vol. 2.* The first album was scheduled to debut on September 30, 2013, with the second to follow in the middle of 2014. Unfortunately, by the time the songs hit the radio and the albums were placed in store racks, I would be unavailable to effectively promote either album.

Shortly before Thanksgiving 2012, my longtime hero, George Jones, wrote me a personal note inviting me to his final concert he had scheduled for one year later:

> Well, you may have heard that I set my last show in Nashville for November 22, 2013. I would rarely ask, but I sure would like it if you could come be with me that night. Heck, maybe do a song or two with me. Please let me know if you can celebrate my career with me . . . I might be eighty-one years old, but I'm not in the grave yet.
>
> You've been a true friend, and I love you for that. The times we've spent together have always been so special. Your friendship to Nancy and me is so appreciated. Thanks for always being there for me.
>
> George Jones

I was thrilled to get the invitation and immediately made plans to join George for his final concert. But ensuing events in both of our lives made that last show an impossibility for either of us to attend.

♪ ♫

In the meantime, I couldn't get too far removed from the pending court cases. The assault case came up first for some reason. Just a few days before Christmas on December 21, 2012, I pled not guilty to the assault charges filed against me. My defense was that I was simply breaking up a fight between my fiancée and her estranged husband. I felt fairly confident since we had solicited and received signed affidavits from eyewitnesses who had been in or near the parking area and had seen the entire fiasco unfold.

My attorney advised me that I should also file suit against the two men who had double-teamed me in the fight to defend Mary's honor and, in the process, severely injured me and purposely humiliated me in public. I did so on January 14, 2013. But then we discovered that my court appearance involving the DUI incident in Tioga was scheduled for the end of January or early February. We asked for and received deferred adjudication in the assault case, but I remained on ninety-day probation until the case could be heard.

The charges against Mary's daughter, Cavanaugh, stemming from the parking lot ambush concerned me more than those against me. Cavanaugh was young and had her whole life in front of her. An assault charge on her records could be a serious drawback. Beyond that, by kicking her dad and Barnes, she had only been trying to defend her mother and me.

Raleigh, Cavanaugh, and I have always been close. Even before Mary and I got together as a couple, I enjoyed having them around. Then as their parents' relationship deteriorated, I felt an increasing concern for the kids' well-being. I went out of my way to attend their school events, to notice their achievements, and recognize their friends. I engaged them in conversation at every opportunity. We talked about trivial things and important matters. Since I'd never had children of my own, I tended to talk to Raleigh and Cavanaugh as though they were adults. They didn't mind. In fact, rather than boring, confusing, or putting them off, our "sophisticated" conversations intrigued them.

We frequently discussed the Bible and Christianity. "It's really important that you maintain your faith in God and your relationship with Him," I told them, "no matter what adversity you face."

The kids often saw me reading the Bible, and that piqued their interest. "What's so interesting?" one of them might ask.

"Well, it's hard to hear from God if you don't know His Word," I said. "That's why I try to read a little from the Bible and talk with Him every day." Raleigh and Cavanaugh knew that I wasn't perfect, but I really wanted to be a godly example for them. They had many questions about how to live a Christian life, and I did my best to answer them. I understood that they might be confused by some of the things that had happened, including the destruction of their former family life, as well as Mary's and my relationship. "Troubles will come. People may disappoint you. Parents make mistakes, too," I told them, "and the devil will try to tempt you, but don't let him get the best of you."

Most of all, they seemed to appreciate the fact that I was interested in what was happening in their lives. At a time when their own father appeared distracted or disinterested, I became sort of a surrogate father to Raleigh and Cavanaugh. I took that role seriously. I felt that I was filling an important gap during a crucial period in their lives and they responded like metal to a magnet.

I recognized that Cavanaugh, seventeen months older than Raleigh, especially needed some stability in her life, as well as a positive, patient role model. We put that to the test, however, when I taught her how to drive a car with a stick shift. She stalled the engine dozens of times before she got the hang of it. When she finally learned how to operate the clutch and gas pedal at the same time, I rewarded her by allowing her to drive my restored Camaro. Like me, Cavanaugh enjoyed speed, so as we roared up the highway, she was in car heaven.

She and I rode horses together, played pool, watched movies, and even practiced target shooting. Cavanaugh wasn't really into guns. Nevertheless, she allowed me to teach her how to shoot a handgun and other methods of self-defense. Independent and strong-willed, she was also a beautiful, petite young woman, and I felt increasingly protective of her.

When her first high school boyfriend came to the door to pick her up for a date, I came downstairs wearing one of my six-shooters in a holster and carrying another gun in my hand. "You're gonna take good care of Cavanaugh tonight, right?" I said, spinning the bullet cylinder of the gun as I spoke. "Make sure to get her home safely and on time."

"Oh, yes sir, Mr. Travis," the young man said, his eyes glued to the gun. "I certainly will." And he did.

When Cavanaugh accepted an invitation to attend her high school prom, she asked me to go along with her to shop for her dress. It may sound crazy, but that was one of the most rewarding experiences of my life. I'm not certain that I provided any valuable couture expertise, but I was excited and honored to help Cavanaugh find just the right dress. To see the smile on her face as she modeled her new dress was worth more than any award or accolade I have achieved.

If Cavanaugh went to a party where activities took place that Mary and I did not condone, rather than getting angry with her, I tried to talk with her about how easily we can compromise our longstanding good reputations. Cavanaugh understood that I was speaking from experience. "This is why your mom and I think you can make better choices," I would say.

In all of our conversations, I attempted to encourage her and uplift her. "You can accomplish your goals," I told her. "Your mom and I believe in you. We know you are good enough, smart enough, and strong enough. You can achieve great things and have a wonderful career and life." Cavanaugh almost always responded positively.

As Mary and Ritchie's divorce case dragged on, the bond between the kids and me solidified even more. That's not to say that everything was always rosy. As anyone who has experienced a blended family knows, it is not easy to balance the awkward relationships between the biological family and the newly established family. But Raleigh and Cavanaugh made my role a pleasure.

That's why I couldn't stand by and let her take the rap for a fight that clearly was not her fault.

Eventually we struck a plea bargain in which I said, "I will plead guilty if you will keep the charges against me but not Cavanaugh." The attorneys agreed to drop the charges against Cavanaugh, and the case went away after the ninety-day probation, but the incident remained on my record.

As an odd consequence of the Prestonwood incident, a school official at Prestonwood Christian Academy, where Raleigh attended and was the starting running back on the football team, "suggested" that Mary and I sit on the Visitors side when we attended the high school football games to watch Raleigh play. Perhaps because of the simple assault charges resulting from the fracas in the church parking lot near the beginning of the season, Mary and I were regarded as troublemakers. Ritchie was welcome to sit on the Home team's side, but we were not, even though Mary had attended that church since 1982.

Rather than sitting on the opposing team's side, Mary and I simply stood behind the end zone for the entire game. But even that was considered disruptive. During one game Mary and I were standing in the north end-zone area along with Michael Irvin, former Dallas Cowboys wide receiver and member of the Pro Football Hall of Fame, and Sean Payton, the coach for the New Orleans Saints. The school official and one of the pastors of the church approached us and said to Mary and me, right in front of our friends, "You all need to go over and sit on the Visitors side."

Michael waved his large hand in the school official's direction and playfully said, "Man, just leave us alone."

But the official simply wouldn't let it go. "Well, if you all come back next week," he said, looking directly at Mary and me, "you need to sit on the Visitors side."

How embarrassing! I had done concert performances at Prestonwood and Mary had volunteered a lot of time and money over the years.

More important, when we really needed some Christian friends around us, to encourage us and to build us up, we became unwelcome "visitors." I'm not a Bible scholar, but it seemed to me that it ought to have been just the opposite.

On January 31, 2013, I pled guilty to driving while intoxicated the previous August. I was fined two thousand dollars and required to spend thirty days in an alcohol treatment center. As part of my plea bargain, I was also required to do 150 hours of community service and would remain on probation for two years.

On the plus side, the judge in Grayson County granted that if I fulfilled my requirements, the horrendously embarrassing police video of me naked would be destroyed because it revealed medical information and my mental health issues that night, which under current laws, would be a violation of my privacy. And he put his decision in writing. Besides that, I think the judge understood that the video would not serve any purpose except to titillate people looking for salacious or crude content. I appreciated the judge's wisdom and discretion.

I immediately went to work fulfilling my sentence. I did all that the judge required of me. I paid the fine, went to rehabilitation, and did more than 180 hours of community service, working with various charities, singing for free at several nonprofit fund-raisers, participating in some programs for kids at McDonald's restaurants, and that sort of thing. My probation officer, Allan, complimented me, "Randy, you always do above and beyond, far more than is required, all the time."

In the midst of all the turmoil following my arrests, on February 11, 2013, I was asked to sing at the memorial service for American hero Chris Kyle, a former Navy SEAL. Chris was known as one of the best sharpshooters in the Iraq War and for his book, *American Sniper*, the profits of which he gave to the mother of another SEAL who died in service to our country. Chris himself had been murdered at a shooting range by a fellow serviceman who had returned home from Iraq suffering with post-traumatic stress disorder.

Taya Kyle, Chris's wife, contacted Jeff Davis, and requested me to sing "Whisper My Name," the couple's favorite love song, at the memorial service. I didn't hesitate for a moment to say yes. Shortly after I had confirmed, Jeff contacted me again, informing me that the funeral organizers had called back and asked if I would also sing "Amazing Grace" during the memorial. Of course, I was honored to do so.

A crowd of nearly ten thousand, including many military troops and officers, gathered for the service conducted on the field of Cowboys Stadium in Dallas. Taya Kyle spoke movingly about her husband, and her presence, as well as that of their two young children, inspired millions of people watching on television and those in the stadium.

With Chris's casket centered on the star painted on the ground at midfield, Joe Nichols, Neal McCoy, and I sang at various points in the program. The last portion of the service was powerful. First a soldier played taps while Chris's helmet and boots were on display at the podium. Then an entire band of bagpipers led the casket, carried by a group of the military officers, out of the stadium.

Spending time with Chris's family and other American heroes at the memorial service really helped put my recent troubles in perspective for me. Granted, I'd had a tough couple of months and even years, but when I thought of the sacrifice Chris and his family had made on my behalf, I was truly humbled and inspired.

28 ——————— FEELIN' MIGHTY FINE

I had performed at a benefit concert for the Texas Wounded Warrior Foundation in October 2012. Sitting on the bus after the show, I put my hand on the shoulder of Jeff Davis and said, "Hoss, we're gonna keep doing this until we are too old to do it or we don't want to do it anymore." It was a statement that we had often made to one another after a particularly meaningful show, and we had just experienced another one. That same month on October 24, I taped a *CMT Crossroads* special with the folk-rock sounding Americana group, the Avett Brothers. Ken Levitan came up with the idea and put the program together as part of the effort to improve my tarnished image following the highly publicized negative incidents in August 2012. Although we had weathered the immediate media storm fairly well, suffering only about a dozen cancellations, concert promoters seemed reluctant to book me for new shows during the first six months of 2013. Ken felt that the *CMT Crossroads* special might help.

For my part, I was tickled to work with the Avett Brothers. The guys had grown up in Concord, North Carolina, just down the road from where I had lived in Marshville. They told me that my music had made a huge impact on them, so it was great fun combining their youthful sounds with my "more mature" music. I loved their enthusiasm, and the show came out great. The program aired on November 23 and was so well received that CMT reran it several more times before the end of the year. The special served as a major step forward in rejuvenating my tour schedule. Prior to the *CMT Crossroads* broadcasts, I had only ten concerts scheduled for the first six months of 2013. Ordinarily, I'd have ten shows booked each month. Following the airing of the special, we booked 33 shows for the second half of 2013.

I was feeling good about my life again, so I scheduled several shows at Las Vegas's Golden Nugget near the end of the year, during the rodeo finals. Things were moving in a good direction for me.

In February 2013, I worked on a new movie called *The Price*, written by a woman named Kim Hughes. I felt certain that my involvement in the project was divinely orchestrated, and we would later see that confirmed.

It all started with a phone call from Kent Hughes, Kim's husband. "I know you don't know us," Kent told Mary on the phone. "But my wife, Kim, has written a movie, and she really feels strongly that Randy is meant to play the leading role."

"Well, why don't you come visit us?" Mary suggested. "And we will talk about it."

The couple showed up at our front door, and the four of us became instant friends. Kent was listed as coproducer of the movie, along with Kim, but he made his living as a tremendously talented plastic surgeon.

The movie was developed as a direct-to-DVD film, not a big-budget blockbuster, but it looked like fun. The plotline involved a dying country music legend (guess who they wanted to play that part?) and an old flame who had given birth to a son twenty years earlier. Now the son, played by James Dupré, is also an aspiring country singer who wins a television singing competition and discovers that I am his biological father. The two singers butt heads but eventually forgive each other as my character is on his deathbed.

It was a simple movie, but a great story of redemption, and I was excited to do it. As an added incentive, the film featured my own fiancée, Mary Davis, as the onscreen woman with whom I'd had a relationship twenty years previously.

The first day on the set, I met James Dupré, who had recently appeared on season nine of the NBC-TV hit *The Voice*. I shook hands with him, and before long we were talking music. I pulled out my guitar. "I want you to hear a new song I've just written," I told him. James seemed surprised. We enjoyed sharing some music and quickly struck up a friendship. He did a great job in the movie, and I felt sure we'd work together again.

That same spring I worked with Billy Ray Cyrus on the pilot episode of his CMT comedy series *Still the King*. Billy Ray starred as Vernon, an out-of-luck Elvis impersonator just released from prison, who was posing as a preacher for a small-town church. I played a stern Southern sheriff who was on Vernon's case in more ways than one.

When Billy Ray first sent me the script for *Still the King*, I noticed that my role required someone who could drive a fast car, ride a horse, and shoot a gun. *Perfect for me*, I said. Then I read the scene where the sheriff (me) is chasing down "Burnin' Vernon" (Billy Ray) and finds him drunk, naked, and lying in a creek. *I might be a little too familiar with this story*, I thought half seriously.

But the show sounded like too much fun to pass up. I called Billy Ray that same day and said, "I'm in."

In one scene I was supposed to chase after "Elvis," roar up to the church in my squad car, do a 180-degree turn, and come to a stop right in front of Billy Ray. The stunt man who was driving the car worked for a while and couldn't quite get the car scene to work. Finally, our bus driver, George Hampton, who was watching nearby, called out, "Put Randy in the car. He can do that one-eighty."

"Really?" the producer asked, looking at me.

"Well, I'd be happy to try," I said.

In a matter of minutes, we were set up ready to film the scene again, this time with me driving the car rather than the professional stunt man. Billy Ray was standing out in front of the church waiting. "Are you sure you can do this, Randy?" he called.

I just waved at him and smiled. I stomped down on the accelerator, raced toward Billy Ray, jerked hard on the steering wheel, and then slammed hard on the brakes as the car whirled around in the opposite direction, bringing the vehicle to an abrupt stop in a cloud of dust, right in front of Billy Ray. At the end of the take, I got out of the sheriff's car and high-fived Billy Ray. "It sure feels good to be on this side of the law," I said with a laugh. Billy Ray cracked up laughing as well.

The stunt man was astounded that I had nailed the scene and just shook his head. "How did you do that?" he asked.

"I've had a lot of practice," I deadpanned, then broke into a huge grin.

We did another take just to make sure the cameras caught everything, and I made the turn again, right on the spot. Ironically, by the time the show aired, I would not be able to drive at all.

♪ ♫

In an attempt to reorganize my life and get a better handle on my business, I spent some time in early April 2013 trying to figure out where my financial resources were located and where all the money that I had earned over the previous thirty-two years was invested. I assumed that Lib and my business manager Gary Haber had diversified my portfolio, but I had never paid much attention to financial matters. I left them to Gary and Lib and trusted that all was in order.

I did know, however, that I had at least five million dollars invested with UBS Financial Services through their offices in Nashville and New York City. I called Bob Elmo, my investment accounts manager with UBS in New York, to get some information. When Bob came on the phone, he was his usual congenial self. "Hey, Randy, so good to hear from you. I haven't talked with you in a long time. How have you been?"

After some brief small talk, I got to the reason for my call. "Bob, I'm calling about my investment accounts. I know that you have handled my investments for all these years, and I'd like to know how much money I have invested with UBS. What accounts do I have with you?"

Bob's phone demeanor soured instantly. "Um, Randy, you just need to call Gary Haber."

"What? Why? You have handled my money for years?"

"You just need to talk with Gary," Bob repeated, and abruptly got off the phone.

I called Gary and asked him about my accounts. "I need to know where I am, financially speaking," I said to Gary, "and where all my money is invested." I pressed Gary to give me an overview of all the money that I had earned over the course of my thirty-two-year career through album sales, songwriting royalties, concert tickets, merchandise, properties, and other businesses, plus investments. Of course, we had also incurred lots of expenses and had lived well, but that did not answer the basic question: Where's the money?

Gary responded, "I have it under control."

About twenty minutes later, Bob Elmo called back. "I talked with Gary. You should talk with him." Again, Bob ended the conversation quickly and said a hasty good-bye.

I didn't mention to Bob that I already had talked to Gary, but Bob's call was a red flag to me indicating that something was seriously wrong.

When we finally found out what was going on, we discovered that the investment accounts were gone. Apparently the money had been moved by someone who had the passwords.

When we called Gary to object, Gary responded by sending an email containing a letter of resignation, stating basically, "Well, if you don't trust me anymore, I'm resigning." Gary had worked for me and handled our accounts for more than twenty-six years. Although he distanced himself from Mary and me after sending his resignation email, he would continue to represent Lib until he passed away in 2014.

When we started looking further into my fiduciary matters, we discovered that even my frequent-traveler accounts were empty. I knew that I had more than a million frequent traveler miles on one airline, and those points were now gone. When I confronted Lib about the missing frequent traveler points, she said, "I used those points for Eamonn and me to go to Italy for Christmas." Because she had been my manager at the time, and had been for so long, she had legal access to all my account numbers and passwords.

My lack of attention to financial matters and my misplaced trust in individuals whom I had thought had my best interests at heart were coming back to bite me—hard. I was angry both with them and myself, but I was soon reminded once more that some things are much more important than money. My hero and friend George Jones passed away on April 26, 2013, at the age of eighty-one.

I had hoped to participate in the tribute to George in November, but now my plans shifted dramatically. On May 1, along with a number of country artists such as Brad Paisley, Mel Tillis, Alan Jackson, Larry Gatlin, Barbara Mandrell, Trace Adkins, Ralph Stanley, Bill Golden, John Rich,

Dierks Bentley, and Brenda Lee, Mary and I attended a private visitation to pay our respects to George.

Then on May 2, 2013, several thousand people gathered for George Jones's funeral service, held at the Grand Ole Opry House. The service was aired in its entirety by the CMT network. I sang "Amazing Grace," and the list of participants in the service looked like a who's who of country music, including Vince Gill, Patty Loveless, Ronnie Milsap, Charlie Daniels, Travis Tritt, Kenny Chesney, and others. Everyone wanted to honor the Possum. To close, Alan Jackson sang one of George's greatest hits, "He Stopped Loving Her Today." It was a touching and deeply moving time.

Afterward, George's wife, Nancy, sent me a personal note of thanks for singing at the memorial service. She wrote:

> Randy, words cannot describe how much I appreciate and love you. Your kindness, friendship, and love have been felt by me and the entire family. I have come to realize that George is gone, but his music and memories will last forever. You're a part of many of those memories. Thanks for being there for me when I needed you the most.
>
> Your performance at the funeral was incredible. Please keep in touch with me, as the days and nights are quite lonely. Please stay happy. Life is too short.
>
> Nancy Jones

Nancy wasn't the only person moved by George's funeral. Shortly afterward I received a fascinating and most compelling letter from Elvin Fisk, a Tioga fireman.

> Randy,
>
> You may not remember me, but you and I had a two-hour conversation out on Highway 922 late one night. We had got a call saying that there was a man in the highway, possibly dead. When we arrived, you were lying in the road, and the EMT said you were DOS, Dead on Scene.
>
> Needless to say, we were a little surprised when the dead man rose up in the road! When I walked up and tried to help, I saw who you were and told my partner, "That's Randy."

He said, "Who?"

"You got up and started walking toward home. I was the one that yelled, "I am a fan!" as you were walking down the highway.

You just dropped your arms, turned, and walked directly to me, looked me straight in the eye, and then we both got down on one knee. You told me about your family and the problems you were going through, and even invited me out to ride horses.

Most of the ones there that night are too young to know the real Randy Travis and the heart that I knew you once had . . . and I could write a lot more.

To get to the reason I am bringing this up: I listened to you this morning on TV singing "Amazing Grace" for George Jones, which brought tears to my eyes. That was one of my mom's favorites songs, and she used to sing it in church a lot. I just lost her at the age of ninety-five last month, and your singing brought back a lot of memories.

I still get asked all the time about answering the call that night and finding you out on the road. I just tell them that you were going through some bad times and hoped that you get back on track and back to where you need to be with the Lord. Remember, He is not hard to find. Just go back to where you left Him last, and that is where He still is, just waiting. Could be a good country song.

I remember telling you that I did not want you to become one of those wooden crosses on the side of the highway. And I really meant that.

I am no saint myself. Just a fifty-seven-year-old fireman and still a fan. I just wanted you to know that your song touched me and tells me that you still have what it takes. Keep singing.

A fan,

Elvin Fisk,

Tioga Fire

Mr. Fisk's letter touched my heart and brought tears to my eyes—not only because I knew he was right, but because he had cared enough to encourage me in my faith.

Unfortunately, the Tioga incident resurfaced in a negative context around that same time.

On May 14, 2013, I filed suit against the Texas Department of Public Safety and the Texas Office of the Attorney General to prevent the three-hour police video from my late-night arrest in August 2012 from being released to the public. A tabloid TV show and other media outlets had requested the video when someone discovered that for some reason the video had not been destroyed as the Grayson County judge had ordered. We were shocked to learn that it still existed. Apparently someone had kept a copy and was willing to release it.

The DPS said it could release the police video because it came under the classification of "open records." The Attorney General's office ruled that the Grayson County judge had made a mistake by ruling the video to be destroyed and sequestered from public view. In other words, the powers-that-were in Austin said that decision was wrong.

I was outraged. I had already "served my time" and done everything the judge had requested that I do, and now the state said the county judge should never have made that ruling. But the judge in Grayson County *had* passed sentence, and according to his orders, the video should have been destroyed. When the state government allowed it to be released five years later, after I had already completed the judge's requirements, it was almost like double jeopardy, not to mention a violation of my privacy—in effect, the unlawful release of my medical information and mental health condition when I was under extreme duress.

My attorney, Larry Friedman, a high-profile and high-dollar Texas law-yer, had urged me to accept the Grayson County judge's deal—fine, rehab, probation, and community service. I had accepted my responsibility and felt the judge ruled fairly. But part of that ruling had involved the destruc-tion of the embarrassing video, and that hadn't been kept. The state hadn't held up their end of the deal. When the police video strangely resurfaced, Larry Friedman simply threw up his hands as if the release of the video was inevitable.

The only thing left to do was to file suit in federal court, in an attempt to keep the full three-hour video from being released to the public. We filed the suit but had little hope that we could prevent the video from getting out.

Since the embarrassing incident, I had made a conscious effort to elimi-nate alcohol abuse from my life. I got back in the habit of working out for

three to four hours every day. I stuck to a high-protein diet and started
working on some new music. Most important, I got back into my routine
of getting up early and reading my Bible each morning. Despite my ongoing
legal issues, I felt as though life was coming together well. To top everything
off, Mary and I were making plans to be married after her long, drawn-out
divorce was final.

A day or so after George Jones had passed away, I received a request
from Cris Lacy at Warner Bros. to record a new song, "Tonight I'm Playin'
Possum," as a tribute to George. I hadn't yet heard the song, but the first
time I listened to it, I quickly realized how well Keith Gattis had written it.
The writer included a number of song titles of George's greatest hits right
in the lyrics. Within forty-eight hours of first hearing the song, I went into
the studio in Nashville and was excited to record it. Keith Gattis joined me,
and Joe Nichols came in and helped sing on the project too.

I purposely didn't perform the song publicly until the 2013 CMA Fest
in Nashville. On Friday, June 7, 2013, the festival invited me to participate in a special "Remembering George Jones" panel discussion, along with
George's longtime drummer, Bobby Birkhead, and artists and songwriters,
Jamey Johnson and John Rich. Making it even more special, the panel was
hosted by George's wife of more than thirty years, Nancy Jones.

We shared some emotional, poignant memories of George, but Nancy
never allowed the event to remain too solemn for long. She provided some
hilarious moments when she told a story about how she taught George not
to impatiently blow the car horn while waiting for her: one time he honked
his horn, and she came out of their house dressed only in her underwear!

As part of my presentation, I performed the new song "Tonight I'm
Playin' Possum" and it was an especially emotional time for me. The hundreds of fans and music industry folks in attendance responded with a
rousing standing ovation. I think George would have been pleased.

The most moving part of the event, however, came near the close, when
Nancy told the audience about some of the last moments she shared with
George before he went to heaven.

He'd been in the hospital for several days, suffering from complications
due to a respiratory infection, and he seemed unable to speak. But then,
Nancy told the audience, "We were standing at the foot of the bed, and

George just hadn't said nothing. All of a sudden, he opened his eyes, and I was fixin' to go toward him, and the doctor kind of held me back.

"And George said, 'Well, hello there.' He said, 'I've been looking for you. I'm George Jones.'"

In a hushed voice, Nancy told the crowd, "I believe he was introducing himself to God. A few moments later, George was gone."

Nancy's words spoke to me deeply. Besides being good friends, both George and I had fought our demons, the devil, and the bottle, and had found a renewed relationship with God in the process. I was sure going to miss him, but I believed with all my heart that I'd see him again—in heaven.

That night I debuted "Tonight I'm Playin' Possum" for the enthusiastic CMA Fest crowd at a packed LP Field (now known as Nissan Stadium), and thousands of country music fans cheered all the way through the song. Then on Wednesday, June 12, we released the song to the general public as a single for my upcoming album, *Influence: The Man I Am, Vol.1*, which was due out in late September.

♪ ♫

During the first week of June 2013, Mary and I went to St. Martinsville and Lafayette, Louisiana, so I could work on a made-for-television movie, *Christmas on the Bayou*. Ed Asner played "Papa Noel," a pretty convincing Cajun version of Santa Claus. Also starring in the movie were Hilarie Burton, Markie Post, Tyler Hilton, and two adorable kids, Brody Rose and Ariana Neal. I played the owner of Greenhall & Sons Mercantile, a small general store. Most of my scenes were shot during sweltering days in an old, deserted feed and hardware store, located along the street of what was once a bustling town square. The store had been closed for about fifty years.

During the filming, I noticed what appeared to be a lot of dust particles, dormant mold spores, or something floating in the air. Between takes, the crew turned on fans that stirred up the particles even more. Rather than wanting to clear the air, the film crew thought the particles added a cool dimension to a lot of the shots. Someone quipped, "It makes Louisiana look like Bethlehem." Maybe so, but breathing that stuff was not good for me. At the time, I had no idea it might kill me.

Shortly after the filming wrapped, I traveled with part of my band to St. Peter's Island in the Caribbean. A young couple was getting married, and we were the entertainment for the reception. It had been a long time since I'd performed at a wedding, but this high-paying, private acoustic show in a gorgeous location was truly a special event.

I especially enjoyed having Robb on the road with us because he was almost as much of a health and fitness nut as I was. Regardless of where we were in the country, he and I got up earlier than most of the other guys in the band so we could spend some time working out. If the hotel had a decent exercise room, we'd go there, but if not, Jeff Davis would find us some local gym or fitness center. Sometimes, Jeff worked out with us, too, and I always made sure I rewarded him with a protein shake afterward.

Occasionally, when we were taking a break from exercising, someone might come up to me in the gym and say, "Excuse me. Aren't you Randy Travis?" I guess they were surprised to see us, but I enjoyed meeting folks and always tried to spend some time talking with them.

Road life can be tough on a body, so most of the guys in the band and crew did some sort of physical exercise—walking, lifting a few weights, or something. But Robb and I really kept up an intense physical routine, doing our best to stay toned. The workouts helped relieve stress, as well. In fact, I was feelin' mighty fine.

In early summer of 2013, we did some concerts in the northeast and then one at an outdoor venue in Sterling Heights, Michigan, near Detroit. On June 29, we performed another outdoor concert with Loretta Lynn at RiverEdge Park, an amphitheater in Aurora, Illinois. Mary and I went over to Loretta's bus to visit with her before the show. She and I had been buddies ever since I first arrived in Nashville in the early '80s, and I knew that she loved me.

This was the first time that Mary and Loretta had met. When I introduced the two women, Loretta stood up and held Mary, looking her right in the eyes. "You better take good care of him," she said sternly, then broke into a broad smile. We all laughed and enjoyed some special time together. Everything seemed so normal, and I felt fine. I'd always loved Loretta, and I could not have imagined that I would never speak clearly to her again.

After those shows, I was planning to take a week off because we were getting ready to do a long run—a more prolonged tour of Canada in July. We were scheduled to head out toward Deadwood, South Dakota, doing four shows in a row, then skipping a day or two to let everyone catch some rest after crossing the border.

That night in Aurora, just as we'd done for twenty-five years, with the band already in place, the stage lights went dark moments prior to my introduction. Jeff Davis placed his hand on my shoulder in the dimly lit backstage area and said, "I just want to let you know, Hoss, that we're all countin' on you." I looked toward Jeff, and we both chuckled at our old joke that had become a ritual. I walked out while the lights were still down, and L.D. leaned over and said, "Wish me luck, Hoss."

I laughed as I usually did. L.D. needed no luck. He was one of the most professional musicians alive, and he knew our show in his sleep. But that was another tradition we maintained before kicking off each show.

That night we did a great show, and everything was clicking. To close, we sang "Forever and Ever, Amen," just as we had done for twenty-five years, and the moment the guitar kicked off the song, the fans responded enthusiastically. That song never lost its luster to us.

I paused on the last line, near the end of the song, "Forever and ever . . ." just as I had done in almost every performance since 1988, and the crowd roared in anticipation. When I sang that last "A . . . men," curling my voice around the word as I liked to do, the audience rose in applause and cheers.

The song was as special that night as it was the first time I ever sang it. None of us had any idea that we would never perform it together quite like that, ever again.

29 ——————————— FLATLINE

The first week of July, we were getting ready to head out on our three-week tour throughout the northwestern US and Canada. On Thursday we celebrated the Fourth of July around the swimming pool on our ranch with lots of family members and friends and plenty of food. The kids were all swimming and the adults were shooting off fireworks and having a good time. As I had done every morning for years, I started the day by reading my Bible as I ate some fruit and drank a protein shake. Then I spent three to four hours working out in our home gym before everyone arrived. I probably needed that, especially since I gobbled down several burgers later that day, but it was a fun time and I felt fine. I remained the picture of good health: no weight, heart, or cholesterol problems and consistently good blood pressure.

The following day, July 5, I woke up early, as I usually do. Everything seemed normal except that I didn't get to work out. We spent the early part of the day packing the tour bus, a major chore for any trip, but especially when we'd be traveling across international borders. We had to pack in such a way that everything could be easily removed from the bus for inspection when we went through Customs and Immigration. Some border agents do a thorough but relatively quick inspection and wave us on through with just a nod; others want to see everything inside, under, and around our tour bus.

We had discovered from previous trips into Canada that it helped to have an accurate inventory, even of personal items.

The preparation was time-consuming and tedious, and at some point during the process, I noticed I was having trouble breathing. My heart seemed sluggish, and I felt as though a cold or flu was settling in. That's a singer's worst nightmare—or at least, so I thought. I wiped the sweat off my forehead and told our bus driver, George Hampton, who was working on the bus, "I'm gonna take a break. I'm not feeling real good."

I went inside the house, drank some water, and sat down for a while, but I really felt no better.

Beginning at lunchtime a group of us—Mary and I; Jeff Davis, who had flown in; our attorney friend Bubba Tomlinson; and our public relations and business advisors—gathered around our dining-room table for what turned out to be an eight-hour meeting. Although it was an inspiring day, it left me exhausted. I assumed my sluggishness stemmed from missing my workout. But I still felt awful, and the difficulty in breathing was getting worse.

"I'm not feeling well," I told Mary. "I'm going to bed early."

I barely slept at all that night, and by morning the congestion was making me miserable. "Do you want to go to the emergency room?" Mary asked. "We need to get you feelin' better."

I've never been one to complain or run to the hospital for every bump, scratch, or sniffle. But by that point I felt so uncomfortable that I didn't resist the idea. "Let's go," I barely whispered.

We went to the hospital ER, where the doctor diagnosed me with walking pneumonia, prescribed some medications, and released me. We drove to Denton to purchase a nebulizer and to fill the prescriptions for antibiotics and an inhaler. I went home, took my medicine, and dutifully used the nebulizer and inhaler, trying to open my bronchial passages.

At that point I felt okay but was still having trouble breathing. Nothing else in my body ached or hurt in any way, other than simply feeling a deep congestion in my chest. I had no other symptoms, yet I was breathing like someone with a heavy chest cold.

Again, early that evening, I said to Mary, "I just don't feel good. I'm going on to bed."

Sunday morning, July 7, I woke up tired, which was unusual for me. I've always been a morning person. Ordinarily I wake up early, energized and ready to get busy. But on this day, I felt terribly lethargic and weak.

"How are you doing today?" Mary asked.

"Not so good. I'm tired, and I can't hardly breathe at all. It's much worse."

"Well, let's go back over to Baylor Emergency," Mary suggested.

We did. On the way Mary called our dear friend, Al Weir, who lived nearby, and Al met us at the med center. We walked into the center, where Mary quickly filled out the paperwork. Soon a friendly nurse took me back to an examining room. Mary and Al followed.

"Oh Mr. Travis," the nurse said. "I've always enjoyed your music. I know you aren't feeling real well, but could I ask you for your autograph?"

"Sure." I smiled at the nurse as I signed the paper on her clipboard. I didn't know it, of course, but that was the last right-handed signature I would sign.

By then, although I didn't know how or what was happening, both of my lungs had filled with fluid. At Baylor Emergency a doctor examined me and said, "You have full-blown pneumonia now."

It was shortly after lunchtime on Sunday afternoon, and I was scheduled to leave on Tuesday, but I could barely breathe. Mary had them call an ambulance to take me to Baylor Scott & White Medical Center–McKinney, about ten miles from where we were and a step up from our smaller local facility. She watched nervously while the paramedics placed me on a gurney and wheeled me to the back of the ambulance. "I'll be right behind you, honey," she said, kissing my hand before the paramedics closed the doors.

Mary and Al got in their own vehicles and followed the ambulance, which led the way with its lights flashing. On the way Mary called Jeff Davis, who was back at his home in Nashville. "Jeff, I'm following an ambulance taking Randy to the hospital. I just want to alert you to the situation." Mary was aware that we had buses scheduled to roll toward South Dakota Monday evening. We planned to meet the band and crew in Deadwood on Wednesday evening.

At Baylor McKinney, they rushed me right to the ICU, a glassed-in room near the emergency room where the nurses hurriedly poked a needle into my arm and hooked me up to an IV. Mary left her car out in front of the emergency room and ran in behind me, with Al following close behind.

I was really starting to worry now. I couldn't get air enough to breathe. The doctors tried to force air into my lungs to no avail. "Guys, I can't breathe," I kept imploring the doctors. I looked at Mary and Al, who were in the room with me, looking on helplessly. Frustrated, I pushed the oxygen away from my face.

Mary picked up on my irritation that I couldn't get any air. "Help me understand," she implored the doctor, "how he can get any air if both lungs are full? There's nowhere for the air to go."

The doctors seemed baffled as well.

My heart was straining, which complicated further my inability to breathe. As the best life-saving option, the doctors hoped to perform a fifteen-minute surgical procedure to run an Impella 2.5 heart-pump device up through my left groin area to assist my heart, so they asked Mary to step out. She kissed me before she left the room. "Baby, I love you. It's gonna be okay," she said.

I smiled openly back at her. "Don't worry," I said, my voice barely a whisper. "I'll be fine."

Mary and Al stepped out of the ICU briefly, and Mary went to move our car while the doctors went to work on me. She was gone for only about five minutes, but that was the last normal conversation Mary and I shared.

Al returned and stayed with me, right inside my room, along with the ICU nurse. "I'm not feeling so good, Al," I told him.

Al asked me again, "Randy, are you sure you want to do this?"

"I hope it'll work," I sighed.

Suddenly, without warning, the monitors starting screaming, and immediately I was gone. Instantly. I felt no pain, nothing. I couldn't speak, feel, hear, or see a thing.

Al was still in the room, however, and he saw and heard the monitor beeping faster and faster, screaming incessantly . . . and then . . . nothing. *Nothing!*

I had flatlined. My heart had stopped, and I was not breathing.

"We're losing him!" the doctor said as he went to work on me. Al was still standing there, transfixed by the horror unfolding in front of him.

Weirdly, the nurse looked up at him, nodded toward the doctor, and said, "He'll get him back."

Seconds passed . . . then a minute . . . and I was still gone. The doctor shot me full of drugs and slapped the defibrillator shock paddles onto my sides. *"Clear!"* he yelled as the voltage shot through my system, attempting to shock my heart back into beating.

Another minute passed, with the ICU personnel working as hard and fast as they could. Al later told Mary that to him this looked like a frenetic scene from a hospital show on television. But it was the real deal.

Finally, after more than two and a half minutes, my heart jumped back to life. The heart monitor began to blip. I was alive—unconscious, but *alive!*

About that time Mary returned from parking the car. Al met her in the hallway as she approached my room. She immediately saw that the room was crowded with nurses and doctors. "What's going on?" she asked.

Al said to her, "I'm glad you left."

"Well, that's not nice," Mary quipped. But then she noticed that Al wasn't smiling and his face was pale.

"Mary, Randy died," he told her quietly, his eyes moistening. "He flatlined, and they brought him back."

"He what?" Mary was shocked. Tears filled her eyes. I had been okay except for my breathing just a few minutes earlier, and now Al was telling her that I had died and come back to life.

Mary burst into the ICU, demanding answers. She got few that made any sense. And I couldn't help her because the doctors had put me into an induced coma so my heart would not have to work as hard to keep me alive.

Al stayed with us throughout the day as the doctors monitored my condition. I could not speak or move. Al called Jeff Davis and Bubba Tomlinson to inform them of the situation. Somewhere during the evening, Bubba drove in from Dallas and stayed with Mary and Al for a while.

Around eleven o'clock that night, Mary told Al, "Please go home and get some rest. I'll call you if there is any change." Al left and, shortly after, Bubba did too. Then it was just Mary and me.

By the wee hours of the morning, the Impella 2.5 wasn't helping, and my condition had worsened. At five o'clock the morning of July 8, Mary insisted that the doctors transfer me to the Heart Hospital at Baylor in Plano. The doctors at McKinney agreed. They had hoped to insert an Impella 5.0 but concurred that, in my current condition, such a procedure could be more safely performed where more sophisticated life-support was available. So I was rushed to the Heart Hospital. I was totally out of it by now, so Mary was having to make life-or-death decisions about my situation all on her own, trusting God to guide her.

Dr. Michael Mack, one of the founders of the Heart Hospital, met us there about five thirty in the morning. A kind man, and one of the premier cardiologists in America—he had actually invented certain artificial heart valves—Dr. Mack had seen almost every heart-related situation over his storied career. He was now doing more teaching about heart surgery than actually practicing.

The doctors at McKinney had called ahead to Dr. Mack and suggested the Impella 5.0. But when Dr. Mack assessed my condition, he said, "It might help, but we don't have time to try it and merely hope that it is going to work."

Through a series of highly specialized tests, Dr. Mack detected that I had developed a virus in my heart. He diagnosed me with viral cardiomyopathy, a virus that attacks the heart. The virus had caused my heart to weaken, which in turn had caused my lungs to fill with fluid. That's why I hadn't been able to breathe.

Dr. Mack explained to Mary why my symptoms had seemed so similar to full-blown pneumonia and why the virus had shut down my lungs so quickly. "Viral cardiomyopathy sits dormant for four to six weeks before attacking," Dr. Mack said. "Then it does its damage in twenty-four to forty-eight hours, filling the lungs like pneumonia does. Then it disappears, leaving us to deal with the aftermath."

The doctors had connected me to a form of life support called extracorporeal membrane oxygenation (ECMO), which involved a long incision in my right groin area and tubes connecting me to a complicated series of machines that took over my heart and lung function. They kept me in the induced coma so my heart would not have to struggle so hard and then went to work, trying to deal with the virus affecting my heart.

Prior to Dr. Mack's analysis, we had been to four doctors who declared emphatically that I had pneumonia. All four were fine doctors, but they had been wrong.

"Where have you been within the past four to six weeks?" Dr. Mack asked Mary. "Any exotic trips or locations?"

"I can tell you exactly where we were five weeks ago," she told Dr. Mack. "We were in Louisiana shooting a movie." She told Dr. Mack about the hot, humid conditions in the old deserted feed store where most of my scenes were shot.

Dr. Mack nodded knowingly. "That may be where all this started."

Of course, I knew none of this at the time. I was in a coma with machines keeping my heart beating, my lungs breathing, and my blood flowing.

My brother Dennis and Jeff Davis flew in from Nashville early Tuesday morning and came straight to the hospital. My condition was not looking good. Jeff had spent Monday trying to slow down or reroute our trucks and buses, which were already packed, loaded, and moving toward South Dakota. He'd contacted the band members, informing them that the tour was on hold. He then had the daunting task of informing all the concert promoters, who in turn had to decide how to inform ticket holders. Because he had no idea what was going to happen, Jeff canceled only the shows scheduled for that week and one week later. The number of cancellations would increase with time.

Kyle Lehning arrived on Tuesday, and that evening Dennis, Mary, Jeff, and Kyle, and our good friend Pastor Jeff Perry, who had flown in from St. Louis to be with us, met with a room full of doctors in the hospital conference room to discuss my condition and possible treatment.

At the conclusion of the meeting, one of the lead doctors mentioned that the hospital was being inundated with calls from the media, requesting information. The streets were lined with media trucks and personnel, their cameras and microphones ready to broadcast or record any tidbit of news about my condition. One overzealous television crew had hoisted a camera high in the air on a truck-mounted crane. When Mary looked out the window of my fourth-floor hospital room, she was shocked to find a television camera staring back at her.

The doctors suggested they hold a press conference. So at ten o'clock on

Wednesday morning, Mary sat with the doctors as they gave a cautiously optimistic report that I was in critical but stable condition.

The doctors had scheduled some further tests before they brought me out of the coma. That process would require several hours to bring me back to full consciousness.

Around two o'clock that afternoon, Dr. Mack called a meeting, asking Mary, Dennis, and Jeff to join him in his office.

That didn't sound good.

It wasn't.

When they had all gathered, Dr. Mack spoke straightforwardly. "Randy has suffered a massive stroke."

Dr. Mack theorized that it had happened somewhere between my dying and being revived, but they hadn't realized it until they slowly brought me out of the coma, more than seventy-two hours since I had flatlined. Because I had been in the coma for so long, it was far too late to treat me with any blood-clot-busting medications. My eyes were not moving, my right side was paralyzed, I had no feeling in my feet, and I couldn't speak a word. Worse yet, my brain was swelling. "We've got to do surgery to relieve the pressure on his brain by six o'clock tonight or we'll lose him," Dr. Mack told Mary.

He explained that the swelling in my brain had caused the midline of two cranial sections to already shift a distance of eight centimeters. If the midline moved twelve centimeters, I would die. "We have a three- or four-hour window here," Dr. Mack said somberly, "so you have to decide what you want to do."

The doctors showed my family and friends the X-rays of my brain. Then they outlined their planned approach regarding what they hoped to do, punctuating each step with the ominous comment, "Or he might die." Dr. Mack paused momentarily and then added, "You should also know that even with the surgery, we have only a 1 to 2 percent chance that Randy will survive."

Dr. Mack explained that at least seven segments of the procedure had to work, beginning most crucially with the way my body responded when the doctors disconnected me from the ECMO life-support machines. If my heart didn't start beating and I didn't immediately begin breathing on my own, it was over. My system had to rally and kick into gear, since they couldn't do the surgery with me still on life support.

It was also imperative, the doctor said, that my system did not throw another blood clot, causing another stroke or worse. He then briefly outlined five other medical issues that had to turn out positively for me to survive the surgery.

Mary gulped hard at that information but didn't blink. She looked back at the doctor and said, "Well, at this point, the 1 to 2 percent chance is a 100 percent chance over zero. Let's do it." She then prayed like she'd never prayed before. "God, please let me have him back—any way, shape, or form."

Although Mary and I were not yet officially married, she and I had signed power-of-attorney documents more than a year earlier, so she had a legal right to sign for the surgery. But as my next of kin, my brother Dennis went ahead and signed all the paperwork. Soon I was having emergency brain surgery in which the doctors removed half of my skull and literally "stored" it in my abdomen to keep the skin tissue alive until the skull could be replaced at a much later date.

For the next forty-eight hours or so, I was touch and go. The doctors continued to give Mary little hope that I would survive. "If he does survive, he will probably never be able to speak or walk again," they told her.

Mary listened to their dire predictions, but she refused to accept them. Instead, she prayed, "Lord, please give him back to me."

My brother Ricky and sister Rose came in from North Carolina the following day. Friends in the music business stopped to visit, though of course I didn't know it. Nancy Jones, still grieving the loss of her husband George, came to sit with Mary and me in the hospital room. She brought along with her some gospel songs George had recorded and gave them to Mary so she could play them for me. My good buddy John Anderson was performing in Dallas and came to the hospital around one o'clock in the morning, along with Rocky Thacker and Tommy Rivelli, my original bass player and drummer, who were now playing with John. They, too, just wanted to sit quietly with me.

Josh Turner was playing in Texas, too, and when John Anderson told him what had happened, Josh contacted Mary and asked if it would be okay to stop by to see me. Mary told him, "Yes, by all means."

Josh and Jennifer, their two boys, and Jennifer's mom came to the hospital to visit me. The boys had drawn some special, handmade get-well cards for me, and we still have them in our home.

Jennifer and her mama pried Mary away from my bedside for a while. She had been at the hospital around the clock, since I'd been admitted, so Jennifer said, "You need some time away from here. Come on, we're going to take you out to eat. Josh can stay here with Randy."

The women and boys left for a while, and Josh stayed with me. My head was bandaged like a mummy, I couldn't see, I had a tube down my throat, and I couldn't talk to him, so Josh simply picked up my Gibson Dove guitar, which Mary had brought into the room. He began playing songs and singing to me, one song after another. He sang some of my songs, some of his, and some others that he knew would be meaningful to me.

For more than an hour, it was just Josh and the guitar and me—with the occasional nurse or doctor coming into the room to check on something. Josh sang "Cold Shoulder," "Everything is Fine," "Firecracker," "Beyond the Reef," "That's Where I Wanna Take Our Love," and "Set 'Em Up Joe." I heard them all, although all I could do to respond was to smile crookedly and tap my left foot a little. The songs took my mind off everything that was going on in my body.

I thought he was done, but he wasn't. Josh launched into "Is It Raining at Your House." "Diggin' up Bones," "Storms of Life," "Why Don't We Just Dance," and even "Long Black Train." I thought for sure he was all sung out, but Josh kept going. He sang "Time Is Love," "I'm a One Woman Man," "Folsom Prison Blues," "Hawaiian Girl," and Josh's favorite classic gospel song, written by Mylon LeFevre, "Without Him."

I knew that Josh Turner had sung hundreds of concerts by that point in his career, but none were any more meaningful than that private concert Josh performed just for me.

My current band members back in Nashville contacted John W. Hill, who drove our band tour bus, leased from Nitetrain Coach. The company donated a bus, and John volunteered to drive it from Tennessee to Texas for free, just so the band guys could come to Dallas for the day to see me.

Mary had some of my music playing quietly in the room when they came in two by two. I was so glad to see the guys, but I could barely respond to them. I could sense the sadness in their spirits, and I felt bad for them. They looked as though their hearts had gone through a shredder. The guys awkwardly tried to express their encouragement and their love, and I was deeply grateful.

Few people thought that I would leave the hospital alive. But although I remained in critical condition following the brain surgery, once the surgeons relieved the life-threatening pressure by removing a large portion of my skull, I started to improve. Over the next few days, the swelling in my brain incrementally subsided. Mary continued to pray. And God continued to answer her prayers and those of the millions of other people we felt praying for us.

Two days after the emergency brain surgery, Mary was standing at the nurses' station out in the hall when a man in a suit approached her. He didn't look like one of the doctors on the hall, so she was surprised when the man said, "Mary, I need to talk with you." He led Mary back into my hospital room.

To Mary's surprise, the man said, "Randy has been approved for a heart transplant. I need to talk to you about the details."

"What?"

"Yes, the ejection fraction, the percentage of blood being pumped out of Randy's left ventricle with each heart contraction, is down to about five. There's no way he can recover from that and live a healthy life—*if* he lives through all this."

Mary was furious. "First of all, let's go back outside in the hall," she said. "I don't want Randy to hear any negative conversations in this room."

Mary and the man went back out in the hall. She listened but made no commitment to the transplant man. Instead, she went to find Dr. Mack.

"Are we not even going to give the heart a chance to heal?" she asked. "We're just going to go directly to a transplant?"

Dr. Mack kindly attempted to explain my condition to Mary. "Well, if he's down to a five, that's serious. A perfect heart is a sixty. That's like a marathon runner. And there are many people who live productive lives with only a thirty ejection rate. That's acceptable. But Randy is at a five because of the damage the virus did. So the transplant might make sense if his heart muscle does not improve quickly."

With all the other things going on in my body, however, Mary was unwilling to take the chance on the transplant, especially with the many possibilities for rejection, plus all the immunosuppressant medications that would be necessary for the rest of my life.

Mary prayed, and I'm convinced that God heard that prayer. Within a short time, my ejection rate began to improve and, although it took many months, it eventually topped out right at fifty! So the man in the suit didn't get to sell a heart transplant to us.

♪ ♫

At some point early during my hospitalization, it became clear to everyone involved that I was not going back out on the road any time soon. That triggered an important question for Mary, Jeff Davis, and others trying to cope with the business fallout caused by me being incapacitated and still in critical condition at Baylor Heart Hospital. Did we have insurance that covered canceled concerts and disability insurance that would kick in should my ability to sing or perform be impaired? For most of my career, I had understood that we carried a policy with Lloyd's of London, insuring my voice against any such calamity, but no one seemed to know the details of that policy or where the paperwork was located.

Mary, Dennis, and those close to me in the hospital were more concerned about whether I would make it through another night. Nevertheless, somebody needed to check on the insurance, so Mary called her sister-in-law Eleanor Davis, who had been taking care of our home in Tioga for us, answering calls, and handling basic household concerns while Mary stayed with me at the hospital. "Eleanor, please call Gary Haber's office and find out what we need to do to activate our disability insurance," Mary requested. Gary had abruptly resigned as our business manager in April of that year, so we were still in the dark on many of our financial issues.

Eleanor contacted Patt Delaney, Gary's assistant, regarding our coverage. The answer she received was shocking. "Randy doesn't have any disability insurance," Patt said. "Nor does he have any concert no-show insurance."

This was huge. Lib and Gary Haber had been managing my career for more than thirty years, and we had paid between $225,000 and $250,000 a year for insurance on everything from Lib's jewelry and furs to our office and bus, but we had no insurance on my voice or anything to cover canceled concerts at which I could no longer appear. That was absurd—and terrifying.

This financial oversight—or perhaps willful disregard or mishandling of my fiduciary affairs—was the first indication that my health issues were not going to be the only problems we faced.

30 —— THE TEAR THAT CHANGED EVERYTHING

On July 31 I was discharged from the Heart Hospital at Baylor in Plano, where I had been in critical condition since I had been admitted early on July 8 suffering viral cardiomyopathy and a massive stroke. But even though I had been released from the hospital, we didn't get to go home yet. The doctors said I needed a stringent rehabilitation program, so Mary decided that it might be better for me to do the rehab in Nashville at Stallworth Rehabilitation Hospital, part of the Vanderbilt University Medical Center system. Her thinking was that my band members and so many friends were there, plus there was so much support in the music community, and she assumed that Stallworth would have an excellent music therapy program that might be helpful to me. Also, I owned a condominium a few miles away from the Vanderbilt area, so we would have a ten-minute commute compared to more than an hour's drive from our home in Texas to a rehab center.

The transfer from Texas to Tennessee was a nightmare. I was placed on a stretcher and loaded onto the plane along with the pilot, an air medic, and Mary. The small air ambulance craft had no air-conditioning, so within minutes, I was soaking wet with perspiration. My vitals started skyrocketing again, and I was miserable. The two-hour flight through turbulent weather seemed to last forever.

When we finally arrived and got settled in at Stallworth, Mary was disappointed to discover that one of the premier rehab centers in Nashville did not have a music therapy program. The facility did not even have a piano in the building.

When she mentioned the lack of music to one of the nurses, he nodded. "If you'd like, I'll be happy to come in after work and play guitar for Randy in his room."

Mary took him up on it, and the entire time I was there, he brought his guitar into my room after his work shift and played for me. He urged me to sing along, and I tried as best I could. To me, he was an angel with a guitar.

For a while at Stallworth, I was doing great, sitting up in bed and acknowledging the many friends who stopped by to visit. Nancy Jones made several visits, as did my band and crew members and Jeff Davis. Our friends Jeff and Patsy Perry stopped by often to pray for me. Even though they lived in St. Louis, their children attended Belmont University in Nashville, so our pastor friend and his wife took advantage of campus visits to spend time with Mary and me, bolstering our faith and urging us to keep trusting God.

I even heard from actor Kirk Douglas, who sent me his book, *My Stroke of Luck*, which he had written after having a stroke of his own. Kirk included a handwritten note on his letterhead, encouraging me. At the close of his note, Kirk asked me to write back to him whenever I was able. Although I still had little strength and no control of my right hand, I looked forward to the day I could respond to him.

But then, just as I seemed to be getting better, I got much, much worse. My vitals started going wacky again, my blood pressure dropping. I developed a severe staph infection, and the breathing problems resurfaced. Once again, the doctors blamed pneumonia. Some other medical personnel at Stallworth told Mary that I had suffered food inhalation—where food went into my lungs instead of my stomach. But when I was tested, they discovered I was swallowing perfectly. Apparently nobody wanted to admit that a lesion had caused a collapsed lung as a result of pseudomonas and serratia, bacteria I had picked up in the hospital.

Because my condition was deteriorating rapidly, doctors transferred me to Vanderbilt University Medical Center's ICU. My body was completely septic, and once again I was intubated, trached, and hooked up to a machine to help me breathe. I was weak and emaciated—my weight had dropped from around one hundred fifty pounds to barely one hundred pounds. I looked like a sack of skin and bones. I felt like a skeleton. My skin looked sallow.

One week stretched to two with no improvement, with the doctors basically telling Mary to pull the plug. "He can't survive this," they told her repeatedly.

At one of my lowest points, John A. Hobbs, my first employer in Nashville, now in his eighties, came to Vanderbilt to visit me, accompanied by two of his adult sons. I felt horrible and could barely function, with a tracheostomy in my throat and a baseball cap on my head to protect the surgical field where part of my skull had been removed and not yet replaced. I couldn't talk and couldn't see clearly, but then I heard John A's unmistakable voice. In a gravel-toned growl that sounded like an angel in a metal drum, he called my name, and I knew immediately who it was. I was too weak to raise my head off the pillow, but I cracked a trace of a smile in response.

John A. walked right over to my bedside and said, "You can beat this, son. I know you can. You're a fighter. You are gonna get up out of this bed."

Mary was standing nearby, and although I couldn't see her, I knew her eyes were filled with tears. I appreciated John A.'s encouragement, but at that moment I wasn't sure I'd ever get up again.

Josh Turner stopped by the hospital to visit me, and the moment he walked in, I could tell by the expression on his face that I was in dire condition. Our bus driver, George Hampton, was there, too, as were Mary, L.D., and Jeff Davis. One look at me in my emaciated condition, and Josh seemed emotionally overcome and almost lost his composure right there in the room.

Josh later told me that he'd thought it was over, that one of his heroes was soon to be gone. He didn't see me pulling out of it. *This is it*, Josh thought. *This is the last time I'm going to see Randy.*

Josh spied a guitar that L.D. and some of the other band guys had been playing for me. Josh nodded toward the guitar. "Do you mind if I play you a song?"

I weakly nodded my head for him to play.

Once again, Josh played the song "Without Him" for me. The theme of the song is that without Jesus we can do nothing. Afterward he prayed over me and hugged me. "I love ya, Randy," Josh told me. He quickly said his good-byes and exited the room with George, both of them with tears flooding their eyes. They didn't expect to ever see me again—at least, not alive on this side of heaven.

Mary knew that I was fading fast, so she rarely left my bedside. Emotionally exhausted from the long, stressful hours in the hospital with me, her nerves frayed and frazzled from the medical roller-coaster ride we had endured now for more than two months. Mary was running on empty too. The medical community's lack of faith didn't help her. The doctors kept reiterating that there was little hope that I could survive. Still, Mary refused to give up on me. She knew that I was a fighter, and she continued to pray and believe that God could raise me up.

With my systems failing, I slipped back into a comatose condition. The doctors told Mary that it was only a matter of time before my heart would stop beating and my lungs would cease to breathe—and that it would be easier on me and less draining on her if we simply stopped. "It's time to let him go," they said.

Mary didn't believe that for a second. She leaned in close to me and pressed her hand into mine. "Honey, you have to let me know if you want to keep fighting," Mary said through her tears.

I couldn't speak. I was lying flat on my back, hooked up to machines that were keeping me alive. I wanted to shout, "Yes! Yes, we can beat this thing!" but no words came out of my mouth.

Finally, a single tear trickled from my eye and down my face.

Mary saw it.

With my last bit of remaining strength, I squeezed Mary's hand. She felt my grip and understood what it meant. She knew that I would battle back. Even if other people had given up on me, I had not given up on myself. I still wanted to fight.

In that moment Mary decided that nobody but God was going to take me out, and if I wanted to live, the doctors needed to do everything possible to help me. It was time to start thinking about life rather than death. And that's what she told them. She met with the doctors in a conference room, and said, "There's a fighter in there," nodding in my direction. "I suggest that everybody get on board and do everything you can to save him," she urged the doctors.

It was just one tear. But that tear was a turning point in my recovery, and nobody again dared to suggest pulling any plugs. Everyone understood that I wanted to live!

During my third week at Vanderbilt, a new doctor entered the rotation—Dr. James Tolle, who had treated our good friend George Jones a few months earlier. He met with Mary to discuss my condition, treatment, and prognosis. Mary poured out her heart to the doctor as she reviewed what had been happening during the previous weeks. She told Dr. Tolle about the treatment I had received and about some of the negative attitudes expressed to her regarding the possibility of my recovery. For instance, when Mary had asked some members of the hospital staff if I could be moved to a room with a window, a hospital official had said, "Well, we put the people who are terminal in the inside, windowless rooms."

Dr. Tolle seemed visibly upset to hear that. With tears in his eyes, he said, "Mary, I'm going to do everything I can for Randy. I just lost George not too long ago. I can't lose Randy too."

He adjusted the antibiotics I was receiving to fight the staph infection, but he was gravely concerned about doing so. He told Mary, "We have only a few days. These antibiotics are really strong, so we can only administer them for a short time before they will start doing more harm than good."

That's all Mary needed to hear. For the next few days, she prayed constantly with me. And three days later, Dr. Tolle reported that I had stabilized. "The numbers are dropping on the staph infection. I think we've turned a corner. Now we just have to be able to reinflate the lungs."

"Okay," Mary said. "But as soon as we're released here, I want to get Randy back to Texas."

"I understand," Dr. Tolle said.

At Vanderbilt they gave me a nickname, Mr. Strawberry Bowfin. I had no idea why. Perhaps it was a security procedure, but after a while I grew accustomed to hearing the nurses say something such as, "Mr. Bowfin, we need to draw some more blood." They drew so much blood, my veins felt like pincushions. I simply smiled and watched as they poked me again.

Although I didn't know it at the time, all the while I was enduring the pokes, probes, and prods, Mary had been dealing with the final stages of her divorce from Ritchie. Indeed, when I was at my lowest point, struggling to survive another hour, the judge in Texas had designated the week for Ritchie and Mary's divorce trial proceedings.

Mary refused to leave my side, even to attend the hearing for her hard-fought divorce. She appealed to the court for a continuance, asking to postpone the trial for a couple of weeks. "After five years of legal wrangling, what's the rush, now?" she asked. To help influence the judge's decision, Mary's attorney, Larry Friedman, instructed her to get written opinions from two of my doctors stating that I was in critical condition, fighting for my life moment by moment. The doctors willingly complied with Mary's request. Under those circumstances, everyone thought, surely any compassionate judge would see the logic of a few weeks' delay.

The judge in Texas, however, mysteriously refused to grant the continuance. Mary and Ritchie's divorce trial proceeded, the financially devastating details of her divorce were decided, and she was declared divorced without her even being present in the courtroom.

Over several more weeks in the hospital, my condition continued to stabilize. When it came time to return to Texas, Al Weir contacted Ray Davis, the owner of the Texas Rangers Major League Baseball team. Ray graciously offered to fly to Nashville in his private jet to bring me back to the Dallas area, and we gladly took him up on his offer. With me snugly strapped down on a hospital gurney and attended by two nurses, Mary, Ray, Al Weir, our friend Bill Blythe, and I made the trip in comfort—a tremendous improvement over the nightmare flight that had initially brought me to Stallworth.

We returned to the Heart Hospital in Plano for ten days because I was still septic and had to remain in isolation. There Dr. Mack removed the tubes in my lungs that had been inserted at Vanderbilt. Within two days my lungs had reinflated and I was breathing well again.

Once I was no longer toxic, we moved to Baylor Institute of Rehabilitation in Dallas. The next step was to replace the chunk of my skull that had been removed and carefully secured in my abdomen. In late October, that procedure was done by Dr. David Barnett, chief of neurosurgery at Baylor Dallas, and our friend, Dr. Kent Hughes, one of the best plastic surgeons in America. It had been Kent and his wife, Kim, who had solicited my services for their movie *The Price*. At the time I'd thought that our coming together was a providential gift. Now I was sure of it.

A number of good friends went out of their way to visit me in the hospital in Dallas, and even though I had difficulty communicating with them, I was thrilled to see them. One of those was Bill Blythe, who had once worked with Conway Twitty and had become a good friend after I moved to north Texas. Now he took on a new task for himself—fattening me up. Because I had dropped so much weight over the past months, one of the issues for me in the hospital was trying to get some more meat on my bones. Bill knew that I loved milkshakes, so he drove from Plano to Dallas every day, bringing along with him a milkshake for Mary and one for me.

Al Weir came to see me almost every day, too, and he and Bill had an ongoing competition to see who could bring us better food from the "outside" so Mary and I didn't have to live on hospital food. We'd been in one hospital or another for nearly six months and knew the hospital menu by memory, so we really appreciated Al and Bill bringing us treats.

The Oak Ridge Boys stopped by to visit me and pray for me. Jamey Johnson came by often and sang to me. Actor Jon Voight and our good friends Hank and Dorothy Paul, who owned Crystal Sky, a movie production company in California, made a special trip to come visit me while I was in the hospital in Plano. Country artist Tanya Tucker and her two kids came by to see us as well. And songwriter, Mike Curtis, who had written a number of the songs I'd recorded on my gospel albums, came to visit with Reverend James Robison. Other than Jeff Perry from St. Louis, James Robison was the only pastor who visited me in the hospital, and Mary and I were sure glad that he did.

I can't stress enough how much such visits meant to Mary and me. Although I couldn't communicate well with any of our friends, their presence and encouragement inspired me to keep going.

31 ——————————— HOME AT LAST!

A few days before Thanksgiving 2013, I was finally discharged from Baylor Institute of Rehabilitation, where I had gone after being released from the Heart Hospital in Plano. Mary and I left early in the morning, and amazingly there was hardly anyone around as we went out through the main lobby. My vision remained severely blurred, I still could hardly speak, and couldn't walk, so a nurse and Mary transported me in a wheelchair.

"Honey, we're going home," Mary said, as she wheeled me out the door.

My first response was, "Wheeee!" With a small sack of laundry in my lap, I raised my left arm above my head and said, "Bye!"

I had been hospitalized for nearly six months. Six weeks of that time I had been in a coma. I had endured ECMO life support, two brain surgeries, five tracheostomies—not the ideal situation for a singer, especially when I pulled the tubing out of my throat and had to be restrained—collapsed lungs, numerous intubations, ports, and thirty-eight IVs—so many that my veins collapsed. I suffered through several chest tubes and pneumothorax fluid-removing procedures. I'd been fed through a tube and dropped to less than one hundred pounds—losing more than a third of my normal body weight. On top of that, I'd suffered several serious infections while in the hospitals, including staph, pseudomonas, serratia, and three bouts of pneumonia.

For those six long months, it had been one thing after another. But now we were going home.

Kurt and Dolores Hessinger, my two loyal employees in Santa Fe, now worked for us on our ranch in Tioga. Mary had asked Kurt to get our house in Tioga wheelchair accessible and ready for me. He also had the legs on our bed cut down so I could slide into the bed easier. Mary had been doing a lot of the basic care for me even in the hospital, so she wasn't worried about taking care of me at home, even though our ranch was out in the country, far away from quick access to a major hospital.

Both of us were so glad to be home, although I still had a lot of recovery to do. At first I couldn't understand many things that had been normal, everyday functions before my hospitalization. For instance, when I first came home, I couldn't recall what a television remote control was, much less how to use it. I didn't remember how to flush a commode. Things I had taken for granted for years I now had to relearn, almost like a child.

Thankfully many things came back relatively soon, but others took much more time, and some I'm still working on. At times, I became frustrated that I was progressing so slowly. Sometimes even Mary would get discouraged because it seemed that I had plateaued at certain levels. Then something good would happen—I could pick up an item by myself or I could say a new word—and we'd take that as a sign that God wasn't done with me yet. We always called those "giant baby steps."

Speaking remained especially challenging for me. Putting together a sentence was even more difficult due to apraxia and aphasia, the loss of ability to express or understand speech because of a brain injury. In my case my brain was functioning, and I could understand what Mary said to me, but I could not respond in anything close to a sentence. When we first returned home, I could barely speak at all. We spent three months in speech therapy before I learned to say the letter *a*. Eventually, after about a year and a half, I could say *yup*, *nope*, and *bathroom*. I could also say "I love you" and a few other phrases, but not much more. All this was extremely frustrating for me; I felt like I was trapped inside the shell of my body.

While in the hospitals, Mary had surrounded me with as much music as possible, and she increased my listening when we got home, playing all the great country music artists that I loved so much. I attempted to sing along, and sometimes did pretty well, since I knew so many of the songs by memory. That part of my brain, it seemed, remained intact and was working. But I struggled to sing a new lyric that I'd not already known prior to the stroke.

At times I became exasperated with my slow progress, but Mary was always right there to encourage me. She refused to allow me to quit, and I had no intention of giving up.

The doctors prescribed a vigorous physical rehabilitation regimen, and I attacked it with a vengeance. I had to learn to walk and do a lot of activities all over again, getting my body to respond to what my brain was telling it. In some instances, I was actually using *new* parts of my brain, circumventing some functions that had been normal for a lifetime. Select rehabilitation center was located in Denton, about forty-five minutes away from our ranch. We were there four hours a day, every day, for two and a half years.

The owners, Ricky and Darla Powell, and the staff and therapists at the rehab became like family to us. My lead physical therapist, Tim Massengill, was about my size and body type, and he worked with me far more hours than he was paid. Tim even came to our home to help me during his days off work. We laughed a lot together, and thanks to Tim, I actually looked forward to my therapy. Tim was good medicine for me.

A woman named Tracy worked in the rehab's marketing office. She'd been a music major in college and played keyboard, so she often took her lunch break to come in and play music with me. With untiring patience, Tracy helped me to begin singing, first a few notes at a time, then eventually a tune.

"Does Randy have a song he really likes," Tracy asked Mary one day. "Something slow that might be easier for him to sing?"

"He's always loved 'Amazing Grace,'" Mary told her.

So the next day Tracy suggested, "Let's try 'Amazing Grace,' Randy." She began playing the song, and I perked up. Prior to the stroke, that song had been one of my favorites, and I usually sang all four verses of it. So when Tracy suggested it, I wanted to sing, and I tried, but the words and melody would not come together in my mind.

Tracy refused to give up, however. She and Mary patiently worked with me on each syllable of every word. It was a long, slow, arduous process. We worked on that one song for months. Finally the day came when I could sing a full verse of "Amazing Grace" along with Tracy and Mary—the first time I'd sung it by memory since the stroke. With their help I would also eventually learn parts of "How Great Thou Art" and one of my early hits "No Place Like Home."

Encouraged by my ability to sing, we looked for other ways to stimulate my rehabilitation. We were told that hyperbaric oxygen treatments—giving high dosages of oxygen under pressure in a special chamber—might help rejuvenate the damaged areas of my brain more quickly. We felt that anything was worth a shot, so we tried the hyperbaric chamber and for three months did all the sessions that the doctors recommended. The treatments weren't uncomfortable and didn't hurt in any way, but I couldn't detect any measurable improvements. We were discovering that there were no quick fixes for my condition. This was going to take time, a lot of patience, and a lot of prayer.

Knowing how much music is part of my soul, Mary had surrounded me from the beginning of our ordeal with music she hoped I might recognize. I think this was helpful and healing for me. But when we first came home from the hospital, I found it difficult to listen to my own music. The first time she put on one of my CDs for me to hear, I sat and cried.

"Okay, honey," she said. "Maybe we're not ready for that yet." She turned off the music.

Slowly but surely, though, I found it easier to hear my former self singing. I began listening to some of my gospel albums and even some of my early hits such as "Diggin' Up Bones," "He Walked on Water," and others. Each song stirred something in me, evoking memories as I mouthed the words. I couldn't yet sing the songs, but the lyrics were somehow on my tongue.

One of the most frustrating aspects of my recovery was that I had lost most of my vision in both eyes. I could see dimly, but everything was blurry, and I couldn't make out details. It was difficult enough getting around with my lack of mobility due to my stroke-impaired right side, but not being able to see clearly made everything tougher. Slowly, very slowly, my sight began to come back in stages—blurry at first, then increasingly better, so I could see the outlines of shapes and people. When it finally did return after about nine months, I could see as well as I ever could. I had used reading glasses even before the stroke, and I still do. But otherwise my eyesight returned completely.

Mary soon discovered that too much time alone was not good for me, so she employed herculean efforts to get me out of the house. She showered me, shaved me, and dressed me—none of which I could do on my own yet—and we went to see Tanya Tucker in concert when she played nearby. When we learned that Josh Turner would be in concert at Mesquite, Texas, just east of Dallas, Mary called him and said, "We want to come see you."

"What?" Josh could barely conceal his surprise. The last time he had seen me was at the hospital in Nashville, when I looked like a skeleton. When we arrived at Josh's show, we parked by Josh's bus. I had gained weight, my hair had returned, and I was grinning from ear to ear.

"This is amazing!" Josh said as he bounded out of his bus. His eyes welled with tears and he leaned over and hugged me in my wheelchair. He kept expressing his astonishment at my recovery.

Mary and I sat offstage and watched Josh's entire show, loving every minute of it. At one point Josh informed the crowd that I was in the building, and Mary pushed the wheelchair out onto the stage a few feet. The crowd erupted in a long, standing ovation as I waved and smiled, and Mary brushed away tears on both of our faces.

I received a tremendously heartwarming surprise just before Christmas 2013, my first celebration of Christ's birth since the incapacitating stroke. Mary and I were having a quiet evening at home, watching the movie *Forrest Gump* on television, when she noticed some people coming up the driveway. My vision was still blurred from the stroke, so Mary rolled my wheelchair to the front porch so I could hear what was happening. What I heard brought tears to my eyes. Several firetrucks, with lights whirling and sirens whistling, were headed up the driveway.

About twenty of our Tioga neighbors, including several local firefighter friends and their kids, enthusiastically sang Christmas carols to us. They weren't professional singers, and they didn't all hit the notes just right, but I sure didn't care. I bobbed my head and tried to sing along with them. The words simply wouldn't come out, but I was so blessed hearing them.

A number of the adults and the kids gathered around my wheelchair as they sang, and I hugged everyone I could reach. When they concluded with "Jingle Bells" and "We Wish You a Merry Christmas," I felt overwhelmed. As they were saying good-bye and starting to walk to their vehicles, I struggled out of the wheelchair and stood to my feet to wave farewell.

When the carolers realized I was standing for them, they all turned around and applauded. That moment was tremendously emotional, I think, for all of us.

We continued going to the rehab center daily, but I finally got to the place where I shut down. I wasn't progressing the way I wanted, and all that work seemed like a hopeless waste of time. At one point, when the technicians tried to get me to do something, I said, "Nope" and just sat motionless. We needed a new approach.

One of the best things Mary did to help with my rehabilitation was taking me to attend concerts by some of our friends. That sounds simple if you are merely going out for the evening, but since I could still do very little for myself, it was a major effort on Mary's part to get me showered, dressed, and ready, then to transport me to our SUV by wheelchair, wrestle me inside, and get me into the venue.

But when we heard that my buddy Neal McCoy would be playing a benefit concert for the charity Smiles for Life at the Majestic Theatre in Dallas on February 7, 2014, we decided to give it a try. Mary worked hard to keep everything low-key, but many folks were still surprised to see me at the show. Because it was one of my first public appearances since my hospitalization, we sat side-stage in the wing and tried to remain inconspicuous.

After the show, Neal invited us to join him for a meet and greet. Many people who saw us there realized for the first time how debilitating the stroke had been and how slowly my recovery was going. Some of them looked shocked when they saw me. More than a few had tears in their eyes. Others offered prayers and get-well wishes. It was great to be greeted by fans, and I was glad to support Neal's efforts.

The following month we traveled to Thackerville, Oklahoma, to surprise Dolly Parton. Dolly had surprised me onstage several times, so it was fun to catch her off guard by being there for her show. Then in July we attended Willie Nelson's Fourth of July Picnic show at the Fort Worth Stockyards. The show featured Dierks Bentley, Charley Pride, David Allan

Coe, Jamey Johnson, the Josh Abbott Band, and numerous other artists. We stayed for the whole thing, and I bobbed my head to the music all day long.

In September Mary and I attended the Four Rivers Outreach fundraiser in Sherman, an event that helps raise funds for underprivileged people who have hit hard times with the law, experienced broken homes, or faced other life tragedies. I used a walking stick to help me keep my balance as I stepped into the North Texas Regional Airport, where the fund-raiser was held. It was a strange feeling. I had performed at the event along with Larry Gatlin the year before; now I needed a cane simply to walk into the room. But I made it, so I felt that was a victory.

♪ ♫

In addition to becoming more physically mobile, we entered a positive season of spiritual reconciliation and redemption about that time, prompted by a surprising source. Mary's brother Barnes—who had participated in the church parking lot ambush—confessed that he had been fooled by Mary's former husband, Ritchie. Barnes acknowledged that his opinions had been greatly influenced by Ritchie's money. When he discovered glaring inconsistencies between Ritchie's words and actions, Barnes realized that he had made a terrible mistake. He had parted ways with Ritchie and now wanted to be reconciled with his younger sister—and with me.

Mary met alone with Barnes initially and he confessed and apologized to her. Mary possesses an amazing forgiving spirit, so she willingly forgave her brother.

Later that summer, Barnes met with Mary and me at a restaurant. The last time I'd seen Barnes, he had been pummeling my face against the pavement. Now, he sat across the table from us and poured out his heart to me. "Please forgive me, Randy," he said. "I had no idea what was going on and I was wrong in what I did." With tears welling in his eyes, Barnes said, "I'm sorry for hurting you, and for the pain I've caused you and Mary and the kids."

Barnes wasn't the only one with tears in his eyes. Tears trickled down Mary's and my faces too. I accepted his apology and expressed my forgiveness to Barnes as best I could in my limited ability to speak. With my voice thick with emotion, I hoarsely said, "Thank you." I knew that God had forgiven me. How could I not forgive someone else, even someone who had hurt me so deeply?

Our ranch managers, Kurt and Delores, returned to New Mexico in July 2014 to be closer to their kids, so we needed someone to help us with the ranch work, caring for the animals and the property. When Mary and I considered our options, Barnes was a natural choice. He had the skill set, having been raised around horses and farm animals, and, since ending his business with Ritchie, he had the time. He volunteered to come out to the ranch and give us a hand. Before long, he was there every day, and by October 2014 Barnes moved onto our property full time. Realistically, it took a while to get past the awkwardness and rebuild trust in our family relationships, but our reconciliation, based on God's love and forgiveness, was real.

By November 2014 I was walking short distances with minimal assistance, and I was learning to write with my left hand. I even signed a few autographs! Mary says I have a new style to my autograph. I was also working on playing the guitar again. I could form chords with my left hand, but I was struggling to get my right hand to cooperate when it came to strumming the guitar or picking out notes on the strings.

Jamey Johnson visited with us and stayed several times at our home. He spent long hours with me, sitting in our kitchen, playing some of his songs for me as well as Haggard stuff and even some of mine. I was glad for Jamey's company and enjoyed every song he played.

A few days before Thanksgiving, Mary and I attended a Joe Nichols concert at Billy Bob's Texas in Fort Worth. Joe sang a beautiful rendition of my 1989 hit single, "Promises," in my honor. I couldn't speak, but I waved my thanks to him.

I was still doing therapy every day and trying hard to recognize words and to talk. Mary thought that a trip to Nashville might spur my progress. Flying with all my medical paraphernalia, including a portable wheelchair, was more difficult than driving. Always willing to go the extra mile, Mary packed everything we needed into the car, and we headed to Music City.

I accomplished a major milestone on the road trip from Texas to Tennessee. We were leaving Memphis, heading east, when I recognized a word on one of the overhead highway signs. Sitting in the front passenger seat as Mary drove, I slowly said the word aloud: "Naaashville."

Mary hadn't mentioned seeing the sign, so she knew that I had recognized it on my own. "Yes!" she cried. "Yes, Randy! Nashville. You saw it. You *said* it!"

That was a huge turning point for us and gave us hope that more and more cognitive parts of my brain would soon kick into gear. We knew we had to be patient—and that was hard for both of us—but we celebrated every little victory.

A number of neurologists had cautioned us not to expect much from my long-term memory. So during that first trip back to Nashville, Mary drove me around some of my old stomping grounds to see if the sights triggered responses. Besides driving around Music Row and some of the other locations close to our condo, we traveled a couple of hours out of Nashville to Flynns Lick, a rural town close to communities with names such as Difficult, Defeated, and Algood. We were definitely in Tennessee!

Back in 1985, we had shot the cover photos for my first album, *Storms of Life*, in Flynns Lick. I had posed leaning against an old pickup truck in front of a general store. Now, as Mary drove down a narrow road and we went around a bend, I looked up and pointed.

"What, Randy?" Mary asked. "What is it?"

There in front of us was what remained of the general store. Although it had been through some storms itself, I recognized the location.

Mary was beside herself with joy that I knew the place. We stopped long enough to take a photograph with me posed in front of our SUV in front of the dilapidated old store.

The following day we drove to Ashland City. Mary had never previously been in that area, so she had no idea what I might recognize there. At one point, however, we made a right-hand turn, and I pointed vigorously with my left hand. There was the Church of Christ where I had been baptized.

Traveling out of town, we drove near a small stream. I couldn't speak, but I pointed repeatedly, trying to say, "There! There!" I had seen a dirt road off to the left.

"What?" Mary asked.

"There! There!" I stretched my left arm and pointed again.

"Did you live somewhere on that road?" Mary asked.

"Yeah, yeah," I struggled to say, pointing again toward the dirt road.

Mary turned the car around, and we drove down the road with me pointing along the way. We drove and drove as I continued pointing vigorously all the way to the house where I had lived more than twenty years earlier. I knew exactly where it was located. Tears trickled down Mary's face as she realized that my long-term memory had not been erased by the stroke as the doctors had warned but was still intact.

We spent nearly a week driving around Nashville, passing by the Grand Ole Opry House, the Nashville Palace, and a host of other places. Almost all of them triggered enthusiastic responses from me. More than just sight-seeing tours, those drives evoked hope: "We can get better!"

Mary played music for me constantly now, not merely my songs, but all my favorites—George Jones, Merle Haggard, and so many others. I still couldn't get my voice to cooperate, but I mouthed the lyrics to almost every song, rarely missing a word. Those songs were down somewhere in my long-term memory. My enunciation wasn't great, but the songs were still in me. Doctors told Mary and me that things like memorized lyrics are stored in the right side of the brain, while sentences that haven't been memorized are formed out of the left side, so I'm still working on that.

♪ ♫

On January 16, 2015, Mary and I accepted an invitation from Taya Kyle to attend a screening of the movie, *American Sniper*, produced and directed by Clint Eastwood and based on the life of her husband, Chris Kyle. I still hadn't been out in public a great deal, so we were a bit hesitant about going to a crowded theater, but the sponsors assured us that we could go in the back way and move directly to our seats. Security at the theater was high, so we parked behind the theater, and the police came out to escort us inside.

This was my first navigation of steps in public. To help me maintain my balance, I leaned on a beautiful, ornate cane given to me by Zac Brown when we went to one of his shows. In presenting the cane to me, Zac showed me its most unusual feature. He pressed a button on the side of the cane, and a long, sharp sword popped out!

I loved the look of the fancy cane and was proud of it, so I didn't consider that I was taking a hidden weapon into a packed theater showing a movie about a sniper. At the conclusion of the movie, as two police officers once again kindly escorted Mary and me out to our car, I couldn't resist showing the officers the cane's interesting feature. Sitting in the passenger side of the car with the door still open, I pressed the button on the side of the cane, just the way Zac had shown me. The sword zipped out of the end of the cane. "Look!" I called to the officers who had been so kind to me. "Look!"

The officers jumped back, startled at first, and then they both started laughing. "Whoa! Oh, man, we sure didn't know that," one of them said.

"Randy!" Mary said, aghast that I had pulled a sword in front of the police officers. "Honey, you can't pull that out in public and show police officers that you have a weapon like that."

"Okay," I said sheepishly. But I was so proud of Zac's gift to me, and once they got over their shock and laughter, the officers seemed to enjoy seeing it.

A few weeks later, Mary and I traveled with Bubba Tomlinson to Nashville for a meeting with Cris Lacy, now a vice president of A&R at Warner Bros., hoping to determine the amount of royalties I had earned from the albums I had recorded at Warner. Cris invited Peter Strickland, Warner's chief operating officer and key financial guy, and a number of the department heads to join us. None of the Warner execs had seen me since I had suffered the stroke, and they were all so sympathetic and gracious to me.

After bringing everyone up to speed on my physical condition, Mary got down to business. "Why have we not been receiving any royalty payments from Warner Bros.?" she asked straightforwardly.

The Warner execs cast knowing glances at each other, as though they all knew something we didn't, but nobody wanted to speak up. Finally, Cris broached the uncomfortable subject. "There are many reasons why you have not received a check from Warner Bros.," Cris hedged, "but the main one is that you have not yet recouped your advances against royalties."

"What?" Mary asked. "How could Randy have sold more than twenty-five million records and not recouped the initial money you gave him up front?"

"Well, over the years, there have been a lot of draws against those royalties," Peter offered.

Mary and I both were fuming. She asked numerous questions, and the Warner executives tried to explain where all the money had gone. The conversation grew more complicated, and finally Mary said, "We probably just need to have a full-scale audit of Randy's account with Warner Bros."

"Yes, you are always welcome to do that," Peter said, "although the audit would be at your expense."

That was standard procedure for audits within the music business, but this was uncharted territory for Mary—and for me too. We both recognized that although Mary was learning fast about managing our business, we needed help. The folks at Warner felt the same way. They were uncomfortable discussing financial matters so starkly with one of their artists. Those kinds of discussions usually involved a manager.

We took a break from the meeting, and Cris had an idea. She called Tony Conway, one of the most respected managers in Nashville. Tony had worked for more than three decades with Buddy Lee Attractions, a top management and booking agency, and had even become president and part owner, before launching his own company in 2010.

Cris quickly explained our conundrum to Tony. "I have Randy and Mary Travis here," she said, "and Espo (John Esposito, Warner's CEO), and I feel they might need a person who is well-established in Nashville to deal with us. Can you come over and meet them?"

"Well, I've known Randy for years," Tony said. "Sure, I'll come over." Tony's office at the Orbison building was in walking distance of Warner's, so he arrived within minutes. "Oh, no!" I teased when I saw him. Tony and I hugged and Mary introduced herself to him.

Tony had that "what-am-I-doing-here" look on his face, but he seemed glad to help. We resumed the discussions, and one by one, everyone answered questions about my account within their areas of expertise and then left the room, leaving only Cris, Peter, Mary, Tony, Bubba, and me. After the meeting, Mary said to Tony, "We need a manager to help us navigate this mess. Would you be interested?"

It was an odd request since we all knew that I would not be making new studio albums any time soon. Nor would I be going out on the road performing shows or making movies. So what was there to manage?

Tony looked at me and said, "Well, yeah, I'd be interested, but let me think about what I can do to help you."

A few days later, we got together with Tony again, and he had some brilliant ideas, one of which was a series of arena concerts in which my former band members would play live and my part would be included by playing videos of me performing live, videos drawn from our recorded archives of my concerts. Tony had seen something similar done with Elvis Presley's performances, in which the music was played live, with Elvis performing the vocals "along with the band," simultaneously on a video wall. It was a technological wonder that created an illusion of actually being in a live Elvis concert. Tony felt he could recreate something similar, with the added advantage that I could be there and greet the fans personally, and possibly sing "Amazing Grace."

We signed a management agreement with Conway Entertainment Group on March 2, 2015. Soon after, Tony went to Warner Bros. to discuss my contract. Out of a long appreciation for my contributions to the company, Warner was willing to continue our relationship. Tony went straight to my friend and producer, Kyle Lehning. "What can we do?" Tony asked.

Kyle thought about it for a few moments. "Well, there's never been a Randy Travis album backed by a full symphony orchestra," he suggested. "What if I took some recordings of Randy's voice and rerecorded the tracks with the orchestra?"

"Can you do that?" Tony asked.

"Sure," Kyle said. "Warner already owns the tracks with Randy's vocals on them. I'll pay to record the orchestra myself, and if we can't get Warner to buy it, we can figure out what to do with it."

Kyle went to work and did an incredible job matching my original vocal tracks with Bergen White's symphony arrangements to twelve of my greatest hits, along with my band playing the songs as we performed them live. The "recreated" album sounded fantastic! To maintain our artistic credibility—since I hadn't really gone into the studio to re-sing the songs— Kyle whimsically titled the album *This Never Happened*. Warner loved it and purchased it from Kyle, so he was reimbursed, I was charged recoupment, and Tony had an album we could release. Before long, Kyle found a dozen or so other new songs that we had recorded but had never included on an album, so we now had two "new" albums of Randy Travis music ready.

♫ ♪

After rehab each week on Wednesday, our pastor at Denton Bible Church, Tommy Nelson came over to the facility with his assistant, Penny Wootten, and we had a Bible study—just the four of us, Mary, Penny, Pastor Tommy, and me. These were special times, and I was growing stronger spiritually, even though my physical body was still damaged and weak.

Mary and I had planned to get married in the fall of 2013, but our plans had been disrupted by my prolonged hospitalization and then extensive periods of rehab. When we finally got into a less intensive rehabilitation routine, we decided the time had come. Early in March Mary called Penny at Denton Bible Church and asked, "When does Pastor Tommy have time to perform a wedding?"

"We'll figure out something!" Penny responded. She found an opening in Pastor Tommy's schedule, and we set the date.

We didn't have a big, meticulously planned wedding extravaganza. Just the opposite. On March 21, 2015, we called our friend Bill Blythe and asked him to come over to Denton Bible Church that same morning. We didn't even tell him why we were asking him to come. But he showed up quickly, dressed in his khakis and a white golf shirt, and we asked him to be part of our wedding. Pastor Tommy then conducted a full, traditional wedding ceremony for us with Bill and Penny as our witnesses. It felt good to finally formalize Mary's and my relationship, legally in the eyes of the public, but especially in the eyes of God.

For our honeymoon, we stopped to get a bite to eat and went back home.

Mary's commitment to me has been truly astounding. I was healthy, in fantastic physical condition, and a highly successful country star when we fell in love. But she married me *after* I had been incapacitated by a stroke, knowing full well what she was getting herself into. That was a major commitment—a commitment of love.

I would not have blamed her if she had walked away. The doctors had told her that my future was extremely unpredictable and that I would most certainly require long-term care. Mary could have bolted. But she didn't. Instead, she has been a loving warrior when it comes to my care, and we still have loads of fun together. We get up every morning with smiles on our faces, and we laugh every day.

Mary has allowed me to live and to enjoy my life. Even though I am more limited physically than before, she doesn't smother me. She doesn't control me. She wants me to do things for myself, and she encourages me to take risks. She doesn't shut out my friends; quite the contrary, she invites them to our home or takes me to theirs. She doesn't try to protect me from other artists, writers, or people who simply want to love on me. She loves country music; she loves my fans and always goes out of her way to make time for them; and she loves me. Most of all, she loves the Lord and helps me with my spiritual walk. Waking up with my best friend through thick and thin is such a blessing, and simply enjoying time together makes every day special.

A few weeks after our wedding, Mary and I decided to take another step of faith and to attend the Academy of Country Music Awards show on April 19. Diverging from its usual West Coast location, the 2015 show was airing live from AT&T Stadium in Arlington, Texas, about an hour-and-a-half drive from our home. We hadn't mentioned anything in the media about our marriage, but that night millions of people found out at once. Lee Brice, known for his emotionally moving hit song, "I Drive Your Truck," saw us in the audience, sang a verse of "Forever and Ever, Amen," and then introduced me to the crowd. I was still a bit shaky, but I stood to my feet and waved as they showed my new look on the Jumbotron. The audience erupted in a prolonged round of applause. It felt so good to receive those expressions of love. I was still a long way from performing onstage, but I was home.

Mary and I continued visiting various artists any time they performed in our area. We went out to see Josh Turner when he played Billy Bob's Texas in Fort Worth. It was great to see Josh and his wife, Jennifer, who homeschooled their children so they could travel together as a family. They seemed so appreciative of me coming to see them, but they were the ones who were blessings to me.

We enjoyed a special occasion on September 25, 2015, when we visited the Grand Ole Opry House in Nashville for the first time since the stroke. Jeannie Sealy was celebrating her forty-eighth year of performing on the Opry, and Tanya Tucker was one of the headliners. It was a fabulous night, and once again, the crowd made me feel incredibly welcome.

I was looking forward to the day when I could stand on the stage again and sing, but my first public performance came at a sad time. During the

last week of January 2016, we received a call from Kelly Doherty, Pierre de
Wet's girlfriend and an executive at the Kiepersol winery and estate. Pierre
had unexpectedly passed away due to a heart attack at only sixty-one years
of age.

Pierre had often said to me, "When I die, I want you to sing at my
funeral." Of course, that had been well before I had suffered a stroke. But in
typical Pierre fashion, he had preplanned his funeral as a celebration of life
including great food and wine, and music. I knew I had to make the effort
to fulfill Pierre's wishes.

The celebration of Pierre's life was held on February 3, 2016, at Pierre's
Bushman Celebration Center in Bullard, with more than a thousand people
attending. Randy Owen, a great friend and the lead singer from Alabama,
sang several songs to honor Pierre during the ceremony, and then it was my
turn. For the occasion, Mary had helped me put on a dark suit and a white
open-collared dress shirt with a black T-shirt beneath it. She wheeled me
onto the stage and helped me as I struggled to stand up to honor our friend.
She stayed close by as I stood between two representatives from Kiepersol,
one of whom held my hand to steady me.

I stood behind the microphone and started singing the first verse of
"Amazing Grace," for the first time in public since suffering the stroke. My
voice was a bit shaky and garbled, but nobody seemed to care. I had barely
started singing when Kelly, Pierre's daughters, and the many friends and
Kiepersol employees began singing along with me.

My voice wasn't perfect, and I was still pretty wobbly, but I knew it
would not be my last public singing performance.

32 —————— BITTERSWEET REUNIONS

Early in 2016 Jeff Davis called Mary and me and informed us that Bill Mayne had contacted him and wanted to get together. Since departing from Warner Bros., Bill had gone on to become chairman of the ACM Awards and more recently CEO of the Country Radio Seminar. We hadn't had a real conversation in a number of years. He didn't need to reach out to me, but I was so glad that he had.

Jeff, Bill, Mary, and I got together for dinner at a popular Nashville restaurant, and Bill poured out his heart to us. "It is so good to see you, Randy," Bill said. "My heart has been broken for years because I couldn't understand why you hated me so much." We all had tears in our eyes as Bill described his side of the story regarding the circumstances that led to my leaving Warner Bros. "I just want you to know that those things you were told by the people around you were bald-faced lies."

Bill went on to tell me things that I had never previously heard about the situation. Before the conversation was over, both he and I started crying. Bill got up from his side of the table, came around to my side, and hugged me. "I love you, Randy Travis," he said. "This is one of the greatest days of my life." I could feel Bill's tears brushing against my face. It didn't matter what had been said or done all those years ago or who was right or wrong. What mattered to Bill and me was that we had cleared the air and extended forgiveness to each other.

Later that year, when the old Warner Bros. building in Nashville was demolished, Bill plucked some bricks from the rubble. He had one of those bricks inscribed for me: "In remembrance of all the fun we had and the magic we made at 1814 Division Street." That brick is one of my most cherished mementos.

The get-together with Bill was the first of a number of reconciliations with friends and business associates from my past—relationships that had been severely damaged because of the actions or attitudes of some controlling people around me. The restoration of those relationships was particularly meaningful to me because the people involved had nothing to gain by reaching out. Some were already retired, and I could do little to help the others in their careers. What mattered to them—and to me—was that our friendships were renewed and forgiveness worked on both sides, leaving us smiling again.

I was surprised when our longtime friend and newly acquired agent, Tony Conway, asked Mary and me to join him at the offices of the Country Music Association on March 20, 2016, for a special interview with Sarah Trahern, the association's CEO. "It will be all yes or no questions," Tony promised, "about some exciting upcoming CMA events." Although it meant a long trip by auto from Tioga to Nashville, Mary and I gladly complied with the request.

When we showed up at the CMA offices, Sarah came out and greeted us in the lobby. We were ushered into the brightly lit foyer of the CMA offices, with a couple of interview chairs at the front. A large number of photographers had already gathered.

"Have a seat, Randy," Sarah said. She nodded toward the chairs, and Mary and I sat down for the interview.

Sarah took the seat opposite me and broke into a broad smile. "We're not really going to do an interview, Randy," she said. "We just wanted to know if you would be our next member of the Country Music Hall of Fame?"

True to Tony's word, it was a yes or no question, and I answered, "Yes!"

The cameras flashed, I smiled, and Mary bawled.

It was some of the most marvelous news I'd ever received in my entire life. Sarah informed us that I would be inducted into the Hall of Fame in October of that year, along with superstar Charlie Daniels and Fred Foster, the founder of Monument Records. At the time, only 127 individuals in the history of country music had been so honored.

The CMA officially announced the 2016 inductees at a press conference held in the Country Music Hall of Fame's rotunda on March 29, 2016. Charlie, Fred, and I were all there for the announcement. When my time came, Brenda Lee read the official Hall of Fame career summary and then said, "Please welcome our modern-era inductee with his adoring wife, Mary Davis-Travis!" Kyle Lehning accompanied Mary and me to the podium.

The audience stood to their feet and applauded . . . and applauded . . . and applauded. I was completely overwhelmed, although my only response at the podium was a brief, "Thank you." At least I was able to get out the words! I tried to say a few more but couldn't, so finally, I simply said, "Okay, yeah. Thank you."

Recognizing that I was struggling, Mary spoke up for me.

"I've been asked to take on the daunting task of being the voice for this man who so eloquently put words to melodies and made beautiful music for the world to enjoy," Mary began. "He lived and he loved the songs that he wrote and the songs that he sang.

"He's a man of great courage, as you all know. He's kind, he's gentle, and he has God-given talents. He went to take lessons from Miss Kate Mangum when he was nine years old and his brother Ricky, who was ten—it was a story he told me several times, and I'm glad I listened—but Ricky decided he didn't want to sing. They both played guitar, and their daddy had told them that one of them had to sing. Ricky was the oldest, so he got to choose, and he chose not to sing. So that's how Randy Travis started singin' at nine years old. It was under duress—and thank God for that.

"In 1969 he entered into a fiddlers' convention and he won 'Most Improved.' I don't think that when he did either one of those in rural North Carolina, he had his sights set on the Country Music Hall of Fame.

"I know he chose a career that he hoped to make a difference in . . . and that career made a difference in him. He often spoke of the people he got to meet and the places he got to go, the artists he got to work with, the band and crew he got to live with on the road.

"The five USO Tours that he was able to take—he spoke of those fondly.

"We were with Larry Gatlin the other day at a benefit we did in Texas.

Larry Gatlin said about the Gatlin Brothers, 'We were hot and doing every-thing just right in the mid-1980s, and we were selling out forty-five thousand seats at the Houston Livestock Show every year. And then along came this kid named Randy Travis. He had forty-*nine* thousand people there. We knew we were done.'"

"Randy Travis has had some storms in life," said Mary. "But he believes that God Almighty has carried him through each and every one, and they have made him the man that he is.

"He is honored, beyond words"—Mary paused momentarily on that phrase, so poignant to us since the stroke, then continued—"To join those before him that are members of the Hall of Fame and the ones that no doubt will follow. He thanks God for the privilege of being able to do what he's loved to do. He told me it doesn't seem right that he gets to sing the songs that he loves to the people that he loves and to be honored in such a way.

"Thank you to the CMA, to all the people who are members of the CMA, and to those who gave him a chance, who helped him along the way and believed in him. And who now have allowed him to hang his hat on the walls of fame with the greats who have gone before him."

I stood next to Mary as she conveyed the message that I wanted to express to so many friends, fans, and fellow artists. She thanked Kyle Lehning, Martha Sharp, and Jeff Davis, and she thanked Lib as well. She especially thanked our friends "who stood by us these last three years . . . when they told us in the hospital to go ahead and pull the plug because there was no hope." Mary continued with deep emotion. "I went to his bedside and said, 'Baby, you gotta give me some more fight.' I knew that he had had a little talk with Jesus because he squeezed my hand and a little tear fell down. And I knew that he wasn't through yet."

We said thank you one more time, and the Hall of Fame rotunda echoed with loud applause again.

The actual induction ceremonies for Charlie, Fred, and me were sched-uled to take place in October that year. In the meantime, throughout the summer, Mary and I continued going out to concerts whenever we could. Few things energized me as much as being around country music artists and country music fans. And every time we encountered them, people were incredibly gracious to me.

In April we attended the Off the Rails Country Music Festival in Frisco, Texas. Blake Shelton surprised the crowd by bringing me out onstage. Then in an extremely kind gesture, Blake dedicated his last song of the night—his megahit, "God Gave Me You"—to me.

In June Mary and I were onstage again, this time at AT&T Stadium in Arlington, as Kenny Chesney sang "Diggin' Up Bones." Then in July we went to Billy Bob's in Fort Worth, where T.G. Sheppard was hosting a benefit for the families of five police officers who had been gunned down in a senseless attack in downtown Dallas during a protest. (Seven other officers and two civilians had also been wounded.) On the show that night were the Oak Ridge Boys, Mickey Gilley, Johnny Lee, John Conlee, and the Bellamy Brothers. I was honored to stand with them to honor the fallen police officers.

As autumn approached I grew excited about making the trip to Nashville to attend the Country Music Hall of Fame inductions. This trip would be especially meaningful to me, even historic in some ways. Mary helped the CMA with the invitation lists, planned out our wardrobes, and consulted with me about what we might say and whom we should plan on thanking. We had everything as organized as possible, and then the unexpected happened.

On October 8, 2016, Mary and I were leaving from Texas for the trip to Nashville when my brother Dennis called. "I don't know how to tell you this," he said somberly, "but Daddy died."

The news hit me hard. Daddy had planned to attend my induction into the Country Music Hall of Fame, but he hadn't quite made it. He suffered from diabetes near the end of his life, and the doctors had warned him to stay away from sweets, but he refused to change his eating habits. He'd had a box of candy with him the last time I saw him alive. He was eighty-one when he died.

We went straight from Texas to Marshville and held the funeral service that same week. It was an emotional time. Daddy had been a tough man, and he and I had butted heads many times over the years. Daddy didn't know how to love me, and I sure had trouble at times loving him. But he was still my dad.

A few weeks after we buried Daddy, my brother Dennis and his wife, Mary, went back to North Carolina to clean out Daddy's house and to bring back any personal items we might want to keep. While rummaging through

Daddy's things, Dennis discovered several large file boxes with more than a dozen dusty and well-worn scrapbooks. In the scrapbooks Dennis found every *Billboard* and *Radio & Records* chart that contained my name, starting from the beginning of my career with the first less-than-stellar release of "On the Other Hand." Daddy had meticulously pasted each chart into a scrapbook for each of my albums throughout my career. He also had kept numerous magazine articles and other items of memorabilia. There were even a few birthday cards that I had sent to him.

I was shocked. It was a real-life version of "The Box," the song that I had written with Buck Moore back in 1994. Back then it had just been an intriguing story built into a song. Now I found that Daddy had saved everything about my career, yet had never told me—similar to the dad in the song. I realized after he was dead that despite his gruff exterior, and his inability to express feelings other than anger, Daddy really did love me and was truly proud of me. How I wish he could have told me that years earlier. It might have saved both of us a lot of suffering and heartache.

Following Daddy's funeral, Mary and I traveled back to Nashville, arriving a couple of days prior to the Hall of Fame induction. Mary happened to notice that songwriter extraordinaire Don Schlitz was playing a "songwriters in the round" show, a concept he had helped pioneer, at the Bluebird Cafe, a small music venue near our condo that was now one of Nashville's best-known venues for hearing songwriters. "Would you like to go see Don play?" Mary asked.

"Yup," I replied.

I hadn't seen my old buddy Don Schlitz in ages. Although we had been pals for more than thirty years and had spent hundreds of hours playing and writing songs together, I had never heard Don perform a live show. We were friends, but we never went out to have fun or just hang out together. Lib had never encouraged us to get together unless we were working.

Mary and I drove over to the Bluebird, where Stacey Schlitz and Mary introduced themselves to each other. I'd known Stacey for a long time, but this was the first time that Stacey and Mary had met.

Stacey immediately went out back to tell Don that we were there. "Don! Randy and Mary are here," she gushed to her husband.

"Really? Randy and Mary who?" Don asked.

"Randy and Mary *Travis*!" Stacey said.

Don came inside the Bluebird, and we embraced for the first time in years. It was a special reunion. The Bluebird gave Mary and me front row seats not much more than ten feet away from Don. He put on a sensational show, telling funny stories about so many of the hit songs he wrote or co-wrote. Mary and I were laughing and having a great time. It was a real treat for me to hear Don perform, especially some of the songs he had written for me.

At one point in the show, Don asked his wife, Stacey, to sing a few songs with him. One of the songs he asked her to perform was a female version of "On the Other Hand." Stacey sang it great, and I loved her voice. More importantly, I was thrilled with the love that Don and Stacey obviously shared. It wasn't a business deal. It was a genuine love, the sort of love that Mary and I now know.

Don later told me that on the way home that night he'd asked his wife, "Okay, Stace, what's it like to sing 'On the Other Hand' in front of Randy Travis?"

Stacey is an attorney with a creative mind and a quick wit. She responded, "I didn't look at him the whole time I was singing. It was like saying, 'Sit down, Elvis. I'll take "Hound Dog" this time!'"

Actually, however, I was the one who'd been honored. Don had helped write some of the signature songs of my music career, including "On the Other Hand," "Forever and Ever, Amen," "Deeper than the Holler," and "Heroes and Friends." In a real way, he was a hero to me. The lyric we wrote for "Heroes and Friends" expressed our love for each other:

> Your heroes will help you find good in yourself;
> Your friends won't forsake you for somebody else.
> They'll both stand beside you through thick and through thin
> And that's how it goes with heroes and friends.

Don later told a mutual friend, "If I've ever been party to writing lines with someone from whom I continue to learn, it was those lyrics with Randy Travis: 'Your friends won't forsake you for somebody else.' That's Randy Travis. For a songwriter, that's rewarding, but as a human being, for a friend, even more so."

33 ——— OLD FRIENDS AND NEW

The official medallion ceremony for my Country Music Hall of Fame induction took place on Sunday evening, October 16, 2016. I sat in a wheelchair and waved as Mary, Cavanaugh, Raleigh, and I passed by rows of country music fans lining the red carpet that led into the Hall of Fame. We stopped frequently to pose for pictures with fans as we made our way to the Ford Theater. Also being inducted into the prestigious group that night were Charlie Daniels, the sensational artist, and Monument Records founder and producer, Fred Foster. It was sure to be a fabulous evening of stories and songs.

Kyle Young, the CEO of the Country Music Hall of Fame and Museum, was the master of ceremonies, introducing each inductee.

Dolly Parton honored Fred Foster by singing, "Dumb Blonde," a song from her debut album that Fred had produced. Brandy Clark sang Roy Orbison's hit, "Blue Bayou," also to honor Fred. Kris Kristofferson and Charlie McCoy also performed in honor of Fred Foster. Then Vince Gill officially announced Fred as a new member.

Next came the ceremony for Charlie Daniels. Tricia Yearwood, Jamey Johnson, and Trace Adkins honored Charlie, singing "Long Haired Country Boy" and "The Devil Went Down to Georgia."

Then it was my turn. Mary and I sat on the front row as Kyle Young summarized my career. He closed with, "Merle Haggard said, 'Down the road, somebody is going to idolize Randy Travis.' We're a long way down that road now, and time has proven Merle Haggard right."

The audience burst into applause.

Before performing on my behalf, Alan Jackson spoke directly to me from the stage. "You opened the door to a lot of guys and girls who wanted to sing real country music," Alan said. He then looked at the audience and nodded toward me. "He was like Elvis," Alan said with a twinkle in his eye. "When he sang, the women were screaming and fainting. And he was singing *real* country music." Alan then sang "On the Other Hand."

Before Brad Paisley sang "Forever and Ever, Amen," he said to me, "You were a beacon of light on the radio when you first started, and you are still one of the greatest singers we've ever had." I appreciated Brad's kind words, and he did a fabulous job on the song with only a guitar as accompaniment.

After Brad sang, Kyle Young waxed downright poetic. "You may have heard that Randy Travis lost his voice," Kyle said, "due to a devastating stroke in 2013. You may have heard that he's struggling to get that voice back. But Randy Travis's voice is indelible, and what is indelible cannot be lost. Randy Travis speaks to us at our will, in a voice that's 'Deeper than the Holler' and stronger than the river. His voice carries with it the lessons of 'Honky Tonk Heroes,' who helped him find good in himself. His voice sings through the ages, rich and warm, dipped in molasses and shaded by Carolina pines, 'Forever and Ever, Amen.'"

Just before Garth Brooks placed the medallion around my neck and pronounced me as the newest member of the Country Music Hall of Fame, he sang "Three Wooden Crosses" and honored me in his comments to the crowd. "Name me any artist from any genre in the history of all music," Garth said, "who took a format and turned it one hundred eighty degrees back to where it came from and made it bigger than it has ever been before."

Again, the audience burst out in applause.

With Garth on my right side and Mary on my left, I listened carefully and gratefully as Mary thanked everyone for me. "Randy stared death in the face," Mary said, "but death blinked. Today God's proof of a miracle stands before you . . ." She paused, momentarily overcome with emotion. "Okay," she said, trying to regain her composure. From beside her I said, "Okay," as well, and the crowd laughed, breaking the tension.

As I stood by her side, Mary said, "We smile every morning, and there are some nights that we cry, when we go to bed in frustration. We pray differently now, and we trust faithfully, and we fight on."

She continued, "Every day we sing. It's a special thing to hear Randy Travis sing, wouldn't you agree?"

The audience responded enthusiastically.

"Sometimes we sing the greatest redemption song of all time," Mary said. "And it fills us with thankfulness. That song is 'Amazing Grace.'"

Then in a heartfelt moment for all of us, Mary did something totally unexpected by everyone in the Hall—everyone but me, that is. Mary paused momentarily and then said, "Ladies and gentlemen, heroes and friends, tonight I want to give back to you the voice of Randy Travis." Mary choked up a bit as she said, "If you would all join in with Randy singing 'Amazing Grace.'"

I took the microphone and said, "Okay," again with a nervous laugh.

Standing onstage behind me, Garth slipped up to my side. "Garth will help you," Mary reassured me.

I was grateful for Garth's presence, but I started the song strong all by myself. Meanwhile, Garth stood to my right, facing me. He teared up, tilted his head back, and closed his eyes. He joined me in singing but let me take the lead, "Amazing grace! How sweet the sound, that saved a wretch like me. . . ."

No one at the ceremony other than Mary had known that I was going to sing—or that I *could* sing. Although I couldn't pronounce all the words perfectly, the audience didn't seem to mind. They spontaneously joined right in with me, and tears filled many eyes, Mary's included. Charlie Daniels pulled out a handkerchief about the size of a tablecloth and started wiping his eyes and blowing his nose! Not far from him, the Oak Ridge Boys were all crying as well. Tears streamed down the faces of Raleigh and Cavanaugh too.

I made it through *all four verses* without prompting. Mary and I had been practicing for weeks so I could sing the entire song—a first since suffering the stroke more than three years earlier. At the close of the song, the crowd erupted in applause again, the entire audience appearing to rise to its feet in one motion. I was so blessed and honored.

The ceremony concluded with the Oak Ridge Boys leading all the participants and attending members, including Charley Pride and Ralph Emery, in a rousing rendition of "Will the Circle Be Unbroken." I sat onstage in my wheelchair between the Oaks and sang along as best I could.

The words of that classic song are inscribed in the rotunda of the Country Music Hall of Fame above the more than one hundred thirty bronze plaques depicting the members who have shaped the history of country music. One of those plaques now depicts my image. Looking at it, Charlie Daniels quipped, "Yours is one of the best looking in here!" And Mary agreed.

After the ceremony, one of the first people to hug my neck was Bill Mayne, who had been a longtime supporter of my being inducted into the Hall of Fame. He had talked with members of the election committee when my name was brought up previously, but because of some of my actions and some of my former wife's actions, nobody gave me a prayer of ever being voted in. But Bill brought my name up again anyhow.

"I love you, Randy, and it's about time!" Bill said.

Following the induction ceremony, Brad Paisley posted a message on social media: "Sunday, at the Country Music Hall of Fame, Randy Travis gave country music an inspiring moment. He very simply took the mic and led the room in 'Amazing Grace.' It was nothing short of miraculous. Randy has endured so much, battling back from viral cardiomyopathy and a stroke, and it speaks volumes about his spirit and faith."

For me, the celebration continued on October 18, when Mary and I stopped by for a surprise visit at the Grand Ole Opry House. A week or so later, we were at a radio station in Nashville where Kane Brown was doing an interview. Born in 1993, Kane was among a new breed of young country artists who appreciated traditional country music. We had become fans of Kane after our daughter, Cavanaugh, said, "You need to listen to this guy on YouTube. He's singing one of Randy's songs." We pulled it up and were so impressed with Kane's voice.

Bailey Dombroski, a young friend of ours who worked at a Nashville radio station, informed us that Kane was scheduled to do an interview and sing a few songs live on the air. We had never met Kane in person, so while we were in Nashville, Mary and I decided to surprise him. Kane didn't know that we were in the radio station studio, and he was singing one of my songs, "Three Wooden Crosses," when we slipped up behind him. When he saw us, he abruptly stopped singing and blurted, "Dude!" Kane walked across the studio to greet us. "I don't think I can finish this with Mr. Travis in the room," he only half joked. "Can I give you a hug?" Kane asked.

"Yeah," I responded.

"It's so nice to meet you, man," Kane said with a huge smile. He turned to the radio engineer and said, "This is crazy!"

We encouraged Kane to continue, and I moved up and sat on a stool next to him. "This is awesome," Kane said before continuing with the last verse of "Three Wooden Crosses."

I am so thrilled to see young artists such as Kane perpetuating a love for traditional country music. Mary and I have become big fans, and we try to see him in concert any time he is in our area.

Then, at the November 2016 CMA Awards show, the opening number was a showstopper with the theme: "Then. Now. Forever Country." Carrie Underwood and Brad Paisley led a group of artists in a medley of some of country's greatest hits, including Vince Gill singing "Mama Tried," joined by Merle Haggard's son Ben; Roy Clark and Brad performing "I've Got a Tiger by the Tail"; Carrie Underwood doing "Stand by Your Man"; and Charley Pride thrilling the audience with "Kiss an Angel Good Morning." Then Alabama lit up the stage with "Mountain Music," and Charlie Daniels kept it going with "The Devil Went Down to Georgia." Reba McEntire, decked out in a gorgeous red dress, sang "Fancy," and Dwight Yoakam brought back "Guitars, Cadillacs, and Hillbilly Music." Clint Black sang "Killin' Time," Ricky Skaggs wowed everyone with "Country Boy," and Alan Jackson reminded everyone, "Don't Rock the Jukebox." All these songs and artists were part of the opening medley. With each hit song, the audience grew more enthusiastic with their applause.

Then it was my turn. Dressed in a black Manuel tux, I took my place center stage as Brad kicked off "Forever and Ever, Amen," joined by Carrie Underwood. The other artists who had stayed onstage all joined in, as did many in the crowd. I stood on the stage with the performers, even though I didn't sing all the lyrics. Brad and Carrie brought the song to the close and then paused as Carrie said, "Ladies and gentlemen, the newest member of the Country Music Hall of Fame, Randy Travis!" The artists onstage allowed me to sing my signature "amen" at the end of the song, and the audience roared its approval. It was a special moment for me, and others have told me since that they thought that opening to the CMAs was one of the most moving and inspiring performances in country music history.

In late January 2017, Mary and I made a surprise visit to Billy Bob's in Fort Worth to see Scotty McCreery. We caught him about an hour or so before he was scheduled to take the stage. We had a great visit and then took a seat to enjoy the show. At some point Scotty deviated from his normal set list and told the audience that I was on the side of the stage. He introduced Mary and me and then sang "Forever and Ever, Amen."

I was honored and so appreciative that the young artists such as Scotty and Kane Brown hadn't forgotten me.

My attendance at the show sometimes evokes some interesting responses. After Dwight Yoakam's stellar performance at WinStar World Casino and Resort in Thackerville, Oklahoma, three of Dwight's band members came over to the side of the stage where Mary and I were watching. "Can you come to more of our shows?" they joked. "We haven't heard a concert like that out of Dwight in years. He really came to life because you were here. You pulled the music out of him, Randy." Of course, Dwight doesn't need me to draw out his best; he is a quintessential artist who always gives his fans a fabulous show. But I thanked the band members for their kind comments.

I still enjoy going out to hear my friends in the business. It is always a treat for me to hear live shows, and the artists often honor me simply for showing up. I appreciate that, and the music feeds my soul. Of course, the hard part about going out to shows is that I want to be back up on that stage performing. Maybe someday I will be.

34 — MUTUAL LOVE AND GRATITUDE

Still ruminating on ways he could volunteer his wealth of music industry wisdom to help me, Tony Conway came up with another great idea in early 2017. "If we can get a number of artists who have been influenced by you and your music," Tony said to Mary and me, "each of them could perform one of your songs, and we could do a tribute show. I think we could sell out the arena."

Tony contacted more than seventy acts. Every one of them consented to volunteer their time and talent to perform at the tribute show, if they could clear their schedules on the date. After booking twenty-eight acts, Tony had to turn artists down. Even those performers who couldn't do the show said, "If you ever do another tribute to Randy, count us in." I was truly honored and humbled by their willingness to help.

Tony enlisted the assistance of my friend Jeff Davis, who was now working as tour manager for the band Alabama, to handle the show's staging and logistics. Bonnie Garner, Marty Stewart's former manager and a highly respected music industry veteran known for her excellent work on high-profile awards shows involving performances by various artists, coordinated the set list and sequencing of the songs. Outback Concerts agreed to sponsor the entire event.

The multi-artist concert held in Nashville's Bridgestone Arena on

February 8, 2017, was billed as "One Night, One Place, One Time: A Heroes and Friends Tribute to Randy Travis." More than thirty acts committed to participate in the event, with proceeds going to medical research.

It was an amazing show as one incredible artist after another graced the stage and sang songs that I had recorded. Each artist was backed by guys from my band. L.D., Dave, Lance, Robb, and our most recent keyboard player, Joe Van Dyke, played for more than three hours straight.

It was only fitting that our band should play that night. We were like family. David Johnson had toured with me for thirty-six years. He was now playing violin with the Nashville Symphony. L.D. had played guitar for us for nearly twenty-eight years. He still played at a local venue right next door to where we started at the Nashville Palace so long ago. Herb Schucher, Lance Dary, Steve Hinson, and Bill Cook had been with us for a long time as well. Robb Houston was the youngest, but even he had been with the band for more than twelve years. That kind of loyalty is difficult to find in the music business.

We also had masterful help from Kyle Lehning, and one of Nashville's greatest studio guitar players, Steve Gibson, who had worked on so many of my albums. Bergen White lent his expertise in working out the keys for the wide variety of singers to better perform my songs. And of course, as he'd done for more than two decades, Jeff Davis pulled it all together, along with the help of Mike Smardak of Outback and Tony Conway, our manager and agent and friend.

The stage was set with a large tree backdrop that we had used as our set for years. Richard Logsdon, our longtime set designer, made sure that everything looked perfect. Jeff pulled in several guys who had worked on our stage crew over the years, doing sound and lights, and set design, and they worked masterfully, doing an excellent job all night long—no easy task with so many artists on the program. But our guys handled it.

Both Mary and I wore yellow-colored Western jackets—Mary wore one of the leather jackets that I had often worn onstage—with black shirts and black jeans, and we sat in large chairs onstage during the entire performance. I was overwhelmed by the outpouring of love that evening. It felt as though the heart of the entire music community was beating in unison—and it was a heart filled with mutual love and gratitude.

The roster of artists included Daryle Singletary, Mark Chestnutt, Alabama, and many, many others. Tanya Tucker sang "I Told You So." Alison Krauss and the Cox Family did "Deeper than the Holler." Josh Turner sang "Three Wooden Crosses." Travis Tritt took on "Better Class of Losers." Charles Esten sang "I Won't Need You Anymore (Always and Forever)." And Wynonna Judd ripped the place apart with "On the Other Hand."

I was especially touched by some of the young artists who sang my songs and told stories about how my music had affected their lives, many of them claiming that they had grown up listening to my music. Scotty McCreery sang "1982," Michael Ray did "He Walked on Water," Kane Brown did "King of the Road," Chris Janson sang "Look Heart, No Hands," and Chris Young performed "This Is Me."

Those youngsters were making me feel like an old-timer, for sure, the way they were expressing their appreciation and respect. Even comedian Jeff Foxworthy said, "I remember when I was the new kid, when I had first signed with Warner Bros., I couldn't be in the same room with him because I was like, oh, that's Randy Travis . . . and I was trying to get up the nerve to go talk to him. I said, ooh, I can't do it today. When I finally met him, Randy was so kind and complimentary, and I said, 'If I ever get to where I'm headlining, I'm going to treat people the way he treated me when I was opening for him.' So God bless you for that." Jeff pointed to me as the crowd cheered.

Then he really made my night when he said, "And this is the first time I've seen Randy since the stroke, and he looks so great!" Jeff looked at me again and said, "You look great!" as the crowd erupted again.

One of my favorite songwriters and a good friend, Paul Overstreet, sang "No Place Like Home," one of the first of four hit songs from my *Storms of Life* album.

Ben Haggard, Merle Haggard's youngest son, did "Are the Good Times Really Over (I Wish a Buck Was Still Silver)."

James Dupré and Shane Owens sang together on "Heroes and Friends"; Rodney Atkins did "Honky Tonk Moon"; Joe Nichols performed "Storms of Life"; and William Michael Morgan sang "Hard Rock Bottom of Your Heart."

Neal McCoy did a fantastic rendition of "His Eye Is on the Sparrow." Ricky Skaggs performed "Would I." Michael W. Smith sang "Walk with Me," and Jamey Johnson did my song, "Promises."

The Bellamy Brothers covered "Diggin' Up Bones," and Kenny Rogers, Montgomery Gentry, Daley and Vincent, and Phil Vassar also performed. Carrie Underwood could not attend, but she sent in a moving video tribute.

Garth Brooks came onstage with a flourish, saluting the band all across the stage. He came over and hugged Mary and me, then said, "There isn't anybody that's in country music today or in the last twenty years that doesn't owe their career to Randy Travis. I know that for sure. I'm one of those guys. I just love ya to pieces. You totally saved this music, this format, and anything you ever need from me, Hoss, It would be an honor to do." Garth then closed the show and brought down the house with "Forever and Ever, Amen."

I didn't expect him to do so, but Garth saved the last "amen" for me. He held the microphone in front of me, and I gave it my best—"Aaa-aa-amen." The audience, already on its feet, went bonkers. It was an incredible moment, not merely for me, but for all the fans and for all of country music.

After that, Mary escorted me to the center stage microphone. I wanted to let the audience know that my sense of humor was still intact, so I did a quick "one, two" microphone check, and the audience cheered in delight. As a hush fell over the arena, I began singing the first verse of "Amazing Grace," and as I did, each of the performers on the show stepped out onto the stage, tapping me on the shoulder and joining Mary and me for a group rendition of the hymn. I sang the lead on all four verses—my voice was a little rough, but all the other artists covered for me, and the entire crowd in the arena joined in, as well.

We finished the show fittingly with "Will the Circle Be Unbroken?" There was no way I could say thank you to everybody who had participated and all the fans who had come. I was a mess, overwhelmed with emotion. It was a night I will never forget!

♪ ♫

In March 2017 it was my turn to help someone else as I sang "Amazing Grace" again at AT&T Stadium in a benefit show that raised more than two million dollars for the American Heart Association.

In June Mary, Cavanaugh, Raleigh, and I attended the 2017 CMA Music Fest in Nashville, and during his Thursday afternoon performance at Riverfront Park, Michael Ray welcomed me to the stage. The crowd had no idea that I was there, and they gave me a rousing ovation as Mary helped me walk out to join Michael. I waved at fans, and Michael put a microphone in front of me. Then, with his band sitting idle on the stage and thousands of people in the audience, Michael graciously took time out of his show for me. I stood next to him as he began strumming the chords to "Forever and Ever, Amen" on his acoustic guitar and singing the song, encouraging the audience to sing along, which they did. I tried to sing along with them. They sang all the way to the end, but then Michael motioned the crowd quiet. Once again, he had saved the last "Amen" for me.

I pressed in close to the microphone and sang "Aaa-aaa-aaa-men." The crowd went wild, and Michael was ecstatic. He threw himself backward and pumped his fists in the air, before coming over to hug me and call out to the audience, "Ladies and Gentlemen: Country Music Hall of Famer Mr. Randy Travis!"

On Friday afternoon during the festival, I sat in the rotunda of the Country Music Hall of Fame and greeted fans for hours. I couldn't sign the thousands of autographs as I'd done over the years at Fan Fair and CMA Fest, but I smiled, said "Thanks" a lot, and shook hands—left hands, since my right hand was still not functioning fully.

So many fans came through the lines, and I was amazed at how many said things such as, "We're praying for you, Randy!" I wish I could have said more in return, but with every "Thanks," I was expressing a lifetime of gratitude.

One of my favorite people in the world was unable to attend the festival that June. Loretta Lynn had suffered a devastating stroke in early May of that year, but she'd mustered her strength in October to attend the Hall of Fame induction ceremony for our friends Alan Jackson, Jerry Reed, and Don Schlitz. As we gathered in the Hall of Fame rotunda for a group photograph, Loretta entered the room in her wheelchair, and her daughter parked her next to me. Her vision was blurred from the stroke, and she couldn't see me, but as soon as I said "Hi" to Loretta, her countenance lit up. "It's my Randy!" she said. Tears welled in Loretta's eyes.

Loretta's daughter had tears in her eyes, too, and so did Mary as Loretta reached over and took my hand and held on to it. Neither of us could articulate with words what we were feeling, but our love for each other and our love for country music were obvious.

35 —————————— FREE INDEED!

Occasionally, when I couldn't get out to see my friends, my friends made extra efforts to come see me. On November 18, 2017, the band Alabama was doing a show in Thackerville, Oklahoma, just across the Texas border. Mary and I had attended their show the previous year, and I was looking forward to hearing them again. But the date conflicted with a beautiful musical tribute show held in my honor that was hosted and directed by Dave Alexander at a college in Gainesville, on the Texas side of the border.

Following the tribute show, Mary and I boarded a tour bus owned by our friends Sherry and Dave Alexander. Instead of heading toward Tioga, however, the bus headed out of town and pulled off at a pizza shop at Valley View that appeared to be open. The shop had a sign on the window: Private Party.

I assumed that Mary may have called ahead to let the manager know we were coming, to defray any expectations on the part of the pizza shop employees that they were about to be invaded by a bus-load of passengers. I started toward the steps leading out of the bus, but hesitated because I needed help to negotiate the narrow staircase. "Why don't you ask Jeff to help you?" Mary said, smiling.

I looked at Mary quizzically. Just then the driver opened the bus door, and there stood Jeff Davis, now the tour manager for Alabama. I had no idea that he was coming, and I'm sure the expression on my face showed my surprise.

But Jeff wasn't alone. After he helped me out of the bus, I saw that Mary had set me up. There were three other tour buses parked in the lot. "Hey, Randy," I heard the familiar voice of Alabama's lead singer, Randy Owen. "Let's have some pizza!" Mary, Kelly Owen, Tony Conway, and Jeff Davis had arranged for the entire Alabama tour group to stop by for a late-night pizza party. The pizza tasted great, but to have friends like that reminded me again just how sweet life can be.

♪ ♫

After a long battle with the courts, on December 4, 2017, the three-hour-long, humiliating and degrading police video of me under arrest for driving while intoxicated was released to the public—to the benefit of nobody. There was little I could do about it, especially after suffering the stroke that had robbed me of my ability to speak. I had not previously seen the police video, nor had Mary. Even after portions of it hit national news shows, Mary was scrupulous about helping me to avoid viewing it. But that video simply wouldn't go away. Still, I may never have seen it had it not been for Lib.

Because I was no longer able to go out and earn income through new recordings or concerts, Mary and I kept digging to find where all the money I'd earned over my career had gone. It obviously was not in any account with my name on it. In March 2018 our attorneys requested a deposition from John Mason, the attorney who had worked with Lib and me for more than twenty-five years, from the very early stages of my career. Lib had fired John when divorce proceedings seemed imminent. Lib attended the deposition as well.

The reason for the fact-finding deposition was to discover why there was no insurance on my voice or ability to perform. Everyone was aware that huge insurance policies had been carried on *Entertainment Tonight*'s host, Mary Hart's legs, and disablement policies existed for almost everything imaginable nowadays. How much more would it have made sense to insure something as fragile as my voice. Worse yet, for years I had been led to believe by my managers that we carried similar insurance with Lloyd's of London, or a comparable insurer, should anything impair my ability to perform. I was under the impression that such an insurance policy existed at some point in my career, but where was it now? And who was the beneficiary of the policy? We were trying to find answers to those questions and more.

It was a relatively friendly deposition environment until near the close of the session, when Lib's lawyers had the opportunity to ask questions. "Okay, you've asked Mr. Mason these questions. Now we'd like to show a video." With Mary and Lib and the attorneys sitting in the room, the opposing legal representative pressed PLAY on the Texas Department of Public Safety police video from the night I was arrested outside Tioga. As my naked image covered the screen, my heart sank.

Why are they even bringing this up? I wondered. *Why is this relevant?*

As I mentioned, prior to that moment, Mary and I had still not seen the Tioga video. Now, five years after the incident and more than seven years after Lib's and my divorce, her attorney was showing it in a deposition regarding financial issues. It made no sense. The whole incident made me so sad. There was no real, productive reason for showing the video in the deposition, apart from a blatant attempt to humiliate me.

I was mad at Lib for playing that sort of game with me, but even more than that, I was upset with myself. It was even more frustrating because I was unable to respond. Due to the stroke, I could not competently speak to the issues involved, which made watching that video even more devastating.

Seeing that awful video reminded me, however, of an important spiritual truth—that none of us can ever completely erase our past sins. Only Jesus can do that for us. So while I must live with the reminders of the sinful things I have done in my life, I don't have to live with the guilt, shame, or humiliation of those things anymore. I can step into the future with confidence because Jesus paid the price for my forgiveness, and He has set me free.

When Satan, the "accuser of our brethren" (Revelation 12:10 KJV) tries to bring things up from the past and hurl them in my face or to tie me up in guilt and shame, I simply recall that I have overcome by the blood of the Lamb, the word of my testimony, and my willingness to lay down my life for Christ. And I say, "In the name of Jesus, Satan, take your hands off me. I don't belong to you anymore. Jesus bought and paid for my soul, and I belong to Him."

♪ ♪

In June 2018, at the CMA Music Fest in Nashville, I was presented the inaugural Cracker Barrel Country Legend Award during the Warner Bros. show at Ascend Amphitheater. The award will be given each year to a "top influencer" who has had at least thirty years of service in country music. It meant a lot to me to be the initial recipient of such an honor because it gave me hope that my life has helped to make a difference for the better in other people's lives.

I was especially tickled to stand on the stage to receive the award because it was the first time since having a stroke in 2013 that I was able to wear a pair of cowboy boots. The Lucchese Boot Company had made me a special pair of double-zipped boots that could support my legs and ankles without metal braces. Lucchese representatives Randy and Trey came to our house three times for fittings to make sure I was comfortable in them. "We just want you back in boots," they told me.

When I put them on, Mary cried. It was the first time in nearly five years that I had stood without the leg braces.

The week I received the award, I had been listening to a song I recorded in 1998 with Patrick Swayze: "I Did My Part." The song really hits home with me, because I would like to think that I did something significant not just in the history of country music, but that I did some things that will have value in eternity.

Nowadays, Mary and I are still living in Tioga, home of Gene Autry and me, two singing cowboys and two Country Music Hall of Famers. I'm still doing therapy, but mostly at home, where I can enjoy my days at the ranch with our two dogs, Luke and Bach (as in Waylon's song, "Luckenbach, Texas"), our eleven horses, some Texas longhorns, and even a few buffalo, just outside our windows.

We spend a lot of time and effort trying to help others. One of the best ways we've found to do that is by raising awareness and money for stroke prevention and research. In addition I try to "pass out hope" to other people who have experienced the debilitating effects of a stroke and to show that it is still possible to enjoy life. I want stroke patients to know that they don't have to be stroke *victims*. They can be stroke *survivors* and live victoriously despite the physical setbacks they have experienced.

I especially enjoy participating in events involving children. Shortly after I first started getting out of the house during my rehabilitation period, Mary and I went with Al Weir and his brother Lee to the Oklahoma School for the Blind. I was unable to get out of the wheelchair yet, so the kids flocked around me in the chair. Ironically, they couldn't see me, and I could barely speak to them, yet we communicated pretty well with each other.

Amazing, isn't it, how hearts can connect when nothing else can? The kids all wanted their pictures with me. I reached out and hugged every one of them, and they hugged me back. It was a tremendous, emotionally moving time.

Less than two weeks before Christmas 2016, Mary and I were watching our local news when we saw that a police officer's home in Gainesville, Texas, about a half hour from our ranch, had burned to the ground. Officer Keith Bartlett and his wife and five children had escaped with their lives, but their home and nearly all their possessions were completely destroyed, including Keith's prized possession, a Gibson guitar. Keith, the report said, was an avid guitar player and often played during church services where he and his family worshipped. While we watched, we realized that we knew the officer. He had responded to a robbery call on our property several years earlier.

The people of Gainesville rallied around Keith and his family, and his fellow law enforcement officers helped them find temporary housing. Mary and I and a lot of other people donated furniture to replace theirs. But Keith still didn't have a guitar. I have played and been sponsored by Gibson guitars all my stage life and have a lot of friends with the Gibson guitar company, so Mary and I decided to ask a favor and do something special for Keith and his family. We called our longtime friend at Gibson, Dave Berryman, and told him the situation. He worked out the details, and the folks at Gibson overnighted us a guitar for Keith. On Christmas Day we surprised him by showing up at the police station briefing room with a brand-new Gibson guitar, just like the one he had lost in the fire.

The entire Bartlett family was there with us. As Keith and I hugged, I pointed to his son, who presented his dad with the Gibson guitar. The officer's eyes welled with tears as he held the guitar in his hands. I signed the guitar with my left-handed signature, and Keith even strummed some songs for us. It was a special way to celebrate Christmas, definitely ending the year on a high note.

Besides working with various charities and benevolent groups, Mary and I continue going out to hear other artists, both to hear the music we love and also to encourage our fellow artists. I especially enjoy encouraging some of the new stars of country music, such as Cody Jinks and others. I know a little about the tough road in front of them as well as the fantastic opportunities. I want them to know that their music matters and so do they.

More than ever, I know my life is a gift—a gift that I will never again take for granted. In July 2013 I was given no hope and no chance of survival, but thanks to God, I'm still here. I'm getting stronger every day, and I've adapted to my new lifestyle. There are some things I can't do—yet. Maybe someday I will be able to do those things again. I hope so.

Sure, I'd love to get back on the stage and sing the way I did for so many years, and if God allows that to happen, I will. But if not, I'll keep singing. It may be a slightly different song, but the message will be the same:

> Amazing grace! How sweet the sound,
> that saved a wretch like me.
> I once was lost, but now I'm found;
> was blind, but now I see.

My future plans are simple. I'm going to love God forever. I'm going to love my family and friends forever. I'm going to love my fans forever. And I'm going to love you "Forever and Ever, Amen."

ACKNOWLEDGMENTS

Over the course of my career, I've written songs, performed in front of millions of people in concerts and on television, and have done untold numbers of interviews, yet nothing compares to the emotional roller coaster I've experienced in producing my autobiography. While reliving so many memories, I've laughed, cried, gotten angry, been blessed, and most of all, felt a fresh sense of God's direction as I've looked back to see His hand on my life, often when I didn't even realize it.

This book is not merely my story. It is meant to honor all the people who have helped shape my life and career, especially my family and friends, musicians and crew members, who have lived it with me. Thank you for being such a significant part of my story!

Because of suffering a stroke in 2013, recreating my life events has required a cumulative effort on the part of many marvelous people. Words on paper aren't sufficient to thank Ken Abraham for his dedication and tireless hours spent to create this unique project. You know everything about me and you still love me!

Special thanks to my precious wife, Mary, who gave so much time and energy to this project. We couldn't have done it without you!

Thanks to Tony Conway of Conway Entertainment for directing my poststroke career and to Kathy Olen of Atticus Branding, who guided me to the great editorial team at HarperCollins Publishing and Nelson Books: Webster Younce, Matt Baugher, and Janene MacIvor; and to Zach Farnum of 117 Entertainment Group; to all of you, your belief in the importance of this project has been an encouragement to me.

Heartfelt thanks to the following people who granted long, in-depth interviews with my collaborator, Ken Abraham: My wife, Mary Davis Travis; my brother, Dennis Traywick; Cavanaugh and Raleigh Beougher all provided family dynamics; music producer extraordinaire, Kyle Lehning, has been a wellspring of inspiration and wisdom; and special thanks to my tour manager for more than twenty-seven years, Jeff Davis, who has also been a valuable source for accurate information. Thanks to Martha Sharp, the person who first signed me to Warner Bros. records; and to Jim Ed Norman, who was Martha's boss at Warner, and who believed in me enough not to fire Martha for signing me!

To L.D. Ricky Wayne Money, one of my first guitar players who was with me at the beginning of my career and was still on stage with me at my last concert nearly three decades later; Charlie Monk, my first music publisher, who recommended me to Martha; Keith Stegall, who produced my first full album, done live at Nashville Palace; and to John A. Hobbs, who owned the venue, gave me my first job in Nashville (as a cook!), and paid for the recording. Their stories are reflected in these pages.

Thanks, too, to country music radio and television icon Ralph Emery, who not only had me as a guest on his programs many times but also took such a personal interest in helping me to tell this story. And to the "new guys," Bill Cody and Charlie Mattos on "Coffee, Country, and Cody" at WSM-AM radio in Nashville. Their "voices" are here as well.

To Bill Mayne and Neal Spielberg, former Warner Bros. execs; Bill got my music on the air and Neal got my albums into the stores and into the hands of fans. I appreciate them sharing their heartfelt stories for this project.

Special thanks, too, to Don Schlitz and Paul Overstreet, two guys who don't grant many interviews. Yet they graciously gave of their time for this book. Thanks, guys. I think you might make it as songwriters someday!

To Josh Turner and Nancy Jones (wife of George Jones), who are not only dear friends, but the stories they contributed to this book brighten my spirits.

Thanks to Pastor Skip Armistead, whose congregation helped us recall details about the *Forever and Ever, Amen* video, and to Pastor and Mrs. Dan

Harless, who helped me recreate the early parts of my spiritual journey, including my baptism.

Charlene Quire, Robert Harrar, Ron Avis, dedicated members in our office and on the road, contributed important information and insights for this project.

And heartfelt thanks to Al Weir, who has seen me through thick and thin. Mary and I appreciate Al's friendship and his recollections regarding those frightening hours in the hospital have helped me to recreate the story you have here.

♪ ♫

Special thanks to Andre Hari Oziol. I first met Andre and his mom, Laura, when he was a child living in Hawaii. He and I became buddies. The time has flown by as I've watched him grow into a fine young man. Now married to Rachel, the love of his life, Andre lives and studies in Jerusalem. Thank you, Andre, for always being a good friend to me. The time you spent with us on the road still makes me smile today.

And gratitude to Mary's and my godson, Luke Powell. When he was a little boy, Luke and I formed a special bond while riding horses together. He was a natural when I taught him how to quick-draw Colt six-shooters, and now at thirteen years of age, Luke is a champion golfer. Although they live in California, his family is part of ours, and we try to get together often. Thank you, Luke, for your love, for your help, and for always encouraging me, and thanks to your mom and dad, Denise and George, who share you with us. We are excited to see what God has planned for you!

♪ ♫

Dozens of other individuals have contributed stories or bits and pieces of information that have been helpful to this project, and we are indebted to you for your assistance.

Thanks also to Cathy and Ronny Robinson, Lynne Ricart, Eleanor Davis, Christina Boyd, and Lisa Abraham who read various drafts of our manuscript, offered helpful suggestions, and assisted in fact-checking.

I also sincerely appreciate all the people who took the time to offer endorsements of my book and their kind words said about me. I am so very blessed.

Others to whom we are deeply grateful include: Jennifer Larson, archivist at Opry Entertainment; and the staff of the Country Music Hall of Fame. Thanks also to Kathie Johnson and Deb Hix for their help in facilitating travel to work on this project.

Most of all, I am grateful to the Lord Jesus, who never gave up on me, and who continues to bless my life. He *is* the final "Amen!"

ABOUT THE AUTHOR

RANDY TRAVIS is a country music singer, songwriter, guitarist, and actor. Since 1985, he has recorded twenty studio albums and charted more than fifty singles on the *Billboard* Hot Country Songs charts, and sixteen of these were #1 hits. His debut album, *Storms of Life*, sold more than 4 million copies and established him as a major force in the neotraditional country movement. Travis followed up his successful debut with a string of platinum and multiplatinum albums. He has sold more than 25 million records and has earned twenty-two #1 hits, six #1 albums, six Grammy Awards, six CMA Awards, nine ACM Awards, ten AMA Awards, eight Dove Awards, and a star on the Hollywood Walk of Fame. In 2013 Randy suffered a massive, life-threatening stroke from which he continues to make a remarkable, determined recovery. In 2016 Travis was inducted into the Country Music Hall of Fame.

♪ ♫

The Randy Travis Foundation provides support for victims of stroke and cardiovascular diseases such as viral cardiomyopathy, as well as music, arts, and entertainment education for at-risk children. For more information, contact:

www.randytravisfoundation.org

♪ ♫

KEN ABRAHAM is a *New York Times* bestselling author known around the world for his collaborations with high-profile public figures. A former professional musician and pastor, he is a popular guest with both secular and religious media. His books include *One Soldier's Story* with Bob Dole, *Payne Stewart* with Tracey Stewart, *Falling in Love for All the Right Reasons* with Dr. Neil Clark Warren, and *Let's Roll!* with Lisa Beamer.